WHAT REA

WHAT READERS DO

Aesthetic and Moral Practices of a
Post-Digital Age

Beth Driscoll

BLOOMSBURY ACADEMIC
LONDON • NEW YORK • OXFORD • NEW DELHI • SYDNEY

BLOOMSBURY ACADEMIC
Bloomsbury Publishing Plc
50 Bedford Square, London, WC1B 3DP, UK
1385 Broadway, New York, NY 10018, USA
29 Earlsfort Terrace, Dublin 2, Ireland

BLOOMSBURY, BLOOMSBURY ACADEMIC and the Diana logo
are trademarks of Bloomsbury Publishing Plc

First published in Great Britain 2024

Cover design by Rebecca Heselton
Cover images: Social media screen © Baan3d/Adobe Stock Images
Books © fornStudio/ New Africa/ Shutterstock

A catalogue record for this book is available from the British Library.

A catalog record for this book is available from the Library of Congress.

ISBN: HB: 978-1-3503-7514-7
PB: 978-1-3503-7518-5
ePDF: 978-1-3503-7515-4
eBook: 978-1-3503-7516-1

Typeset by Integra Software Services Pvt. Ltd.
Printed and bound in Great Britain

To find out more about our authors and books visit www.bloomsbury.com
and sign up for our newsletters.

CONTENTS

ACKNOWLEDGMENTS

I am grateful to Lucy Brown, Aanchal Vij, and all at Bloomsbury Publishing as well as the anonymous peer reviewers of this manuscript for their thoughtful suggestions. Thank you also to Dr. Monique Rooney for the invitation to present work in progress from this monograph in a seminar for the ANU Centre for Australian Literary Culture, and to the participants for their insightful questions. The writing of this monograph was supported through the Australian Research Council Discovery Grant, *New Tastemakers and Australia's Post-Digital Literary Culture*, which provided me with some teaching relief. The Reading and Writing for Wellbeing group was funded through the Interdisciplinary Seed Funding Scheme of the Melbourne Social Equity Institute, at the University of Melbourne in a team led by Professor Victoria Palmer. The project title was "A Novel Cure – the health and wellbeing outcomes of creative practices (reading and writing)" and its research received ethics approval from the University of Melbourne, project id 1545427.2. Early versions of some ideas in Chapters 2 and 4 were published in my chapter "Readers of Popular Fiction and Emotion Online," in *New Directions in Popular Fiction* (2016) and in "How Goodreads Is Changing Book Culture," *Kill Your Darlings*, June 15, 2021. I would also like to thank Professor Claire Squires for comments on the manuscript and support, as well as Clay, Julia, and Ben.

INTRODUCTION

How do readers experience books, and what do they do with those experiences? Reading is an activity that is dynamic, meaningful, and infused with energy. It is diverse, varying across time and place and involving interactions with manifold artefacts. Readers pored over the *Dream Pool Essays* of Shen Kuo, printed with clay movable type in 1088. In Enlightenment Europe, readers debated Diderot's multivolume *Encyclopedié*. Twentieth-century readers in the Philippines passed around Tagalog romance pocketbooks and popular comics; in twenty-first-century Western Australia, children learn Noongar language through locally produced picture books.[1] Reading is a bedrock of culture, a seam that runs through the past into projections about the future. Adaptable and enduring, books have not been replaced by new media but integrated into the convergent media ecosystems and transmedia story worlds of the twenty-first century. They circulate as paperbacks, hardbacks, ebooks, web publications, and audiobooks; they provide the core intellectual property for films, TV series, and video games. As books have persisted and developed across multiple forms, so too has reading, which in contemporary culture might mean listening to an audiobook on your phone, leaving a comment on a chapter of web-published fanfiction, or leafing through a giant hardcover tome.

In this book, I present a model for understanding the manifold practices of contemporary recreational readers. *What Readers Do* shows readers as active— part of evolving networks, engaged in aesthetic practices that give shape and style to life, involved in moral issues, nurturing themselves in solitary moments and contributing to energizing social activities. Readers navigate the institutions and systems of twenty-first-century life in acts that are both culturally and commercially significant.

Because it involves the acquisition of books, one way or another, reading is the foundational practice of a sizable (though not enormous) sector within the entertainment and media industries. The value of the global book publishing industry was estimated at $114.9 billion for 2023—more than the movie and music industries, less than video games—and has remained relatively steady over the past ten years.[2] While value remains stable, the production of titles has increased, particularly with the advent of digital technologies that make self-publishing and print-on-demand books accessible and low-cost. Amid the massive disruptions of the global Covid-19 pandemic, book buying surged: in 2020, book sales rose 8.2 percent in the United States, 7.8 percent in Australia, and 5.5 percent in the UK, where over 200 million print books were sold that year.[3] Sales have slipped a little since then, returning to a baseline that confirms an overall picture of stability for books and reading.[4] The economic context of readers in the twenty-first century also includes the ever-more powerful technology companies—Google, Facebook, Amazon—that have come to exercise great influence on book publishing, marketing, discoverability, buying, and reading. These companies, as well as the multinational media conglomerates that house major publishing houses and, to a lesser extent, small book-related businesses, profit from the activities of readers.

Book reading, though, is about more than money. What Elizabeth Long terms the "social infrastructure of reading" exceeds commerce to take in numerous other forms of relations.[5] Danielle Fuller and DeNel Rehberg Sedo coin the phrase the "reading industry" to describe the mesh of agents, institutions, and organizations, including government and not-for-profit bodies, that support reading for entertainment.[6] Activity in the reading industry is vigorous. Reading-related programs and events have been burgeoning for decades as established components of the creative and cultural industries. Between 2010 and 2019, for example, Melbourne's Wheeler Centre for Books, Writing and Ideas hosted 2,389 events and reached 419,927 audience members. In Africa, the Hargeisa International Book Fair in Somaliland draws an annual audience of 10,000; newer African literary festivals include the Abantu Festival in South Africa, which centers Black reading cultures, launched in 2016, and the Feminart Art and Book Festival in Malawi launched in 2019.

Reading is also vibrantly present online. BookTok, a subset of video social media platform TikTok, has amassed over 147 billion views.[7] The website Goodreads, where readers can catalogue and review the books they read, has more than 120 million members.[8] Reese's Book Club, headed by actor and producer Reese Witherspoon, has over 2.6 million followers on Instagram; #ReadwithJenna hosted by former First Daughter and morning TV show host Jenna Bush Hager has 223,000. The digital creative writing and reading platform Wattpad is visited by over 85 million monthly users, including 7 million from the Philippines, its second largest market after the United States; 90 percent of time spent on Wattpad is from a mobile device.[9]

This dynamic activity has developed despite ongoing consternation about the negative effects of screens on book reading. Or not "despite"— the dynamism of reading activity has developed alongside and in relation to the digitization of everyday life. Like listening to vinyl records and other pre-digital cultural practices, book reading has been thrown into relief as an object of interest, a pastime associated by many with an earlier, perhaps simpler era.[10] But the effects of digital technology on books and reading have been anything but straightforward. Drilling down from the big picture to consider individual readers reveals varied, distinct practices. Digital technology distracts some readers. For others, it provides new opportunities for focused discussion of reading, as well as unprecedented access to books—especially in genres such as romance and fantasy fiction.[11] Furthermore, print and digital are not mutually exclusive but coexist. A reader may read an ebook then admire its cover at a bookshop, or purchase a print book and post a picture of it on Instagram.[12] This is what it means to inhabit a post-digital environment; print and digital technologies interact in multiple, sometimes surprising, ways.[13] Contemporary book reading flexibly incorporates digital, in-person, and print-based practices.

The different ways to engage with the newer technologies of reading are just one kind of variety that is found within the matrix of contemporary reading practices. In *Reader's Block: A History of Reading Difference* (2022), Matthew Rubery explores how neurodivergent readers, including those with synesthesia and dyslexia, make sense of print, and emphasizes the vast spectrum of reading practices that exists.[14] There are many ways to read a book—cover-to-cover or in parts, fast or slow, with intensity or casually, as a treat or with a touch of resentment. What Rita Felski calls common "motives for reading"—she identifies recognition, knowledge, shock, and enchantment—vary from reader to reader, and moment to moment.[15] Reading is individualized, can change across a person's lifetime (or week), and is inflected by factors such as a reader's gender, sexuality, and cultural identity.

Sometimes this variety is not recognized by the institutions of the book industry, with negative impacts on readers and on book culture. When it comes to cultural identity, for example, research by Anamik Saha and Sandra van Lente finds that UK publishers often assume a White readership for novels, limiting the diversity of books published and the opportunities available for authors of color. Similarly, Fuller and Rehberg Sedo note that Whiteness shapes many online spaces and reading communities, creating hostile environments for racialized readers.[16] The assumptions baked into these facets of book culture highlight the need to ask the question, who reads? Is there a demographic answer?

Who Reads?

A review of recent demographic studies of readers suggests that book reading is more widespread, and more diverse, than is sometimes credited. There is no uncomplicated picture of declining reading, ageing readers, or a narrow reading class; much depends on how data is collected, and which events or practices are considered. The varied answers to the question of who reads show just how important it is to understand reading as diverse, dynamic, and multidimensional.

Reading is one of the most accessible forms of cultural participation, because it is low-cost and because the skills required are taught in the early years of school. In the broadest sense, the group of readers includes everyone who has acquired literacy in primary or elementary school. This is the vast majority of the population in the Global North, and a significant majority worldwide. According to the World Economic Forum, the global literacy rate in 2023 was 87 percent.[17] Global inequality remains, particularly between sub-Saharan Africa, the region with the lowest literacy rate, and the rest of the world: according to 2015 data, in Niger, for example, the overall literacy rate is less than 30 percent, and even for youth—who are typically more literate than older generations in the Global South—the literacy rate is low (36.5 percent of those aged between 15 and 24).[18] To talk about readers is to talk about the large majority of the world's population, skewed toward those in developed nations.

There is a difference between literacy and recreational reading, and the focus of this book is on the smaller group of people who read for pleasure. Various studies identify and describe this cohort. In 2005, Wendy Griswold, Terry McDonnell, and Nathan Wright wrote that a quarter of people did not read books on a typical day, but more than half read for over an hour; further, most people thought they should be reading more.[19] This rate has been consistent over several decades. In Australia, a 2017 report found that 41 percent of the adult population read more than ten books in the last twelve months (approximately one book per month).[20] Another national survey conducted in 2021 described 28 percent of the general Australian population as frequent or passionate readers, reading one to two books per month.[21] A 2022 Gallup poll found that 27 percent of US respondents read at least ten books per year.[22] Across these different surveys, then, the group of frequent readers seems to be about a quarter to half of the population.

These studies ask about the quantity of books read. A 2021 report by Rachel Noorda and Kathi Inman Berens took a different approach. Their representative survey of the US population found that 53 percent of respondents were avid book "engagers," engaging with four or more books per month. Their term "engager" is a deliberate widening of the term "reader" to include "buying, borrowing, subscribing to, reading or gifting a printed book, an ebook, or audiobook in part or in whole."[23]

The demographic characteristics of recreational readers also shift somewhat according to the terms of the study. Most studies agree that frequent readers tend to be highly educated, and women. Wendy Griswold coined the term "the reading class" to describe the small, but influential, group of frequent readers, who are middle class, metropolitan, and well educated.[24] The 2017 Australia Council report found that nearly half (46 percent) of frequent readers were tertiary-educated, and that two-thirds of frequent readers were women. However, there is divergence when it comes to other demographic characteristics. The subset of "avid book engagers" in Noorda and Berens's survey was younger and more ethnically diverse than the general survey population: 67 percent of Black or African American respondents and 59 percent of Latina/Latino/Latinx respondents were avid book engagers.[25] This contrasts with some other data on readers. Griswold, McDonnell, and Wright suggest that "white women have by far the highest reading rate (61%), followed by white men and African American women (41% and 43%, respectively)."[26] They describe a 2004 National Endowment of the Arts (NEA) survey which "found that 26% of Hispanics, 37% of African Americans, and 51% of white Americans read literature."

The word "literature" is a notable qualifier here. Kinohi Nishikawa has written of the massive popularity of urban fiction—cheaply printed sensationalist pulp novels—among Black Americans, and uses the term "merely reading" to describe the pleasurable, non-educational, and non-political reading of these popular novels.[27] Surveys that ask about the reading of literature may not pick up on this significant reading practice, or indeed the multiplicity of reading practices within different communities. Nishikawa uses Janice Radway's term "variable literacies" to distinguish between educational reading, where the latest results show African Americans scoring poorly on standardized tests, and reading for pleasure, where the facts are quite different: he notes a 2014 Pew Research Centre study that found more Black readers (81 percent) had read at least one book in the past year compared to White or Hispanic readers (76 and 67 percent), and that African Americans read more ebooks, audiobooks, and books in print than any other group.[28] Decisions about what kind of reading counts (and is counted) can obscure or reveal the variety of reading practices.

There is also conflicting data about whether older people read more than young people. In 2017, the Australia Council reported that frequent readers were most likely to be over thirty: nearly half were aged between thirty and fifty-nine, while another large segment, 38 percent, were aged sixty and over. Such findings are often used to paint a picture of reading as an activity in decline, as its enthusiasts age and are not replaced. Despite noting that anxiety about reading rate always accompanies a popular reading culture, Griswold, McDonnell, and Wright participate in such discourse, writing of "alarming reports" from the NEA in 1982, 1992, and 2002 showing "a steady decline in reading, especially the reading of literature and especially among young adults." They note this finding is consistent with a Netherlands report, and conclude, "there is a generation gap—older, highly educated people hang on to the reading habit, but younger ones do not."[29] Yet Noorda and Berens's study shows that avid book engagers are younger than the general survey population, suggesting countertrends and emerging bookish practices that warrant attention.[30]

Overall, the question of who reads for pleasure cannot be answered with "everyone." Recreational readers tend to be well-educated women; the archetypal twenty-first-century reader shares some affinities with what I have elsewhere written about as the middle-class, feminized literary middlebrow.[31] But, at the same time, there is not just one kind of recreational reader or reading. It is important to remain open to the diversity of readers and reading experiences. Grim accounts of a small, shrinking reading class can mask the ways reading endures and adapts. Not all recreational reading is visible, and not all of it is captured in surveys. This book aims to explore in more detail the range of different experiences within recreational reading.

What Is Contemporary Recreational Reading?

Variations in activity raise the question of the scope of this book: what reading it includes and excludes. My focus is on contemporary practices, with a scope that encompasses the twenty-first century to date. Studying the contemporary period raises several challenges, including the difficulty of accounting for the rapid pace of change, especially digital change, and discerning patterns among noise.[32] Nonetheless, studying the contemporary has particular value. Such research has the potential to intervene in current debates and practices by highlighting the obstacles to a rich reading culture, as well as the diverse positive aspects of book reading that warrant celebration and encouragement. My focus is also on recreational reading. I understand recreational reading broadly as reading that is done for pleasure. In general, I distinguish recreational reading from academic or professional reading, but there are overlaps. Both recreational and professional readers can read quickly and slowly, with passionate investment or light detachment. Further, recreational reading is not the opposite of work; practices such as writing an online book review or making a reaction video, for example, may involve considerable effort and skill. In the contemporary media environment, such activity has been theorized as "play labor" or "playbour" where it is ostensibly done for fun, or "hope labor" where the creator has an eye to future paid opportunities.[33] In book culture specifically, voluntary labor is descended from a long history of fandom practices that bestow detailed attention on texts, such as the creation of fanzines or encyclopedic databases.[34] This labor—sometimes paid, though rarely lucrative—complicates any simple division between reading for fun and for work. Still, the focus of this book is reading that is understood as undertaken for pleasure or recreation.

That still leaves the term "reading" to be defined. Reading is more than eyes on a page. In a sense, this whole book addresses the question of what reading is, and the multiple activities I elaborate resist the idea that an answer can be provided in one sentence. To clarify my scope, though, I will make temporary use of one such sentence, from Graham Allen, who defines reading as "the process of extracting meaning from texts."[35] The word *extracting* has environmentally unfriendly connotations so I'll set it to one side, but the three other elements of *process*, *texts*, and *meaning* can be unfolded to sketch some of the parameters of this book.

Reading is a process. It is dynamic, changing from moment to moment, shifting over a person's lifetime and affected by their context. The process of reading is interactive, occurring in collaboration with settings, objects, people, and institutions that themselves change. With scholars such as Long, Fuller, and Rehberg Sedo, I argue in this book that reading is social; supported by institutional and industrial infrastructure, and a constitutive element of networks of people, organizations, and technologies. All of this is in a state of constant flux, affecting the processes of readers. For example, reading is embedded in an industry and a larger capitalist system, not only because books are consumer goods (produced and marketed by the publishing industry), but also because of the commodification of attention and user data online, and the commercial imperatives that drive the broader cultural and creative industries in which readers participate. These can dramatically affect the processes of reading. When Amazon closed its subsidiary bookselling operation Booktopia in 2022, purchasing options for readers were narrowed; when Wattpad introduced its Stars program for popular authors in 2019, readers' digital engagement was overtly linked to financial opportunities for writers, which in turn shaped the stories that were published and promoted.

In the moment of reading, as well as the moments before, between, and after reading, readers move among online and offline settings. There is no simple way to approach the online behavior of readers, which slips across platforms and is integrated into diverse commercial and social arrangements. Likewise, offline reading situations are complex; state-sponsored reading activities may espouse an enthusiasm for literacy development while also emphasizing fun, for example, and the emphasis on each element may shift from one day to the next. As a process, reading also moves between the social and the solitary. Many online and offline reading situations incorporate striking, visible interactions between people. But there is also an intimate core to reading—the time that a reader spends with a book can be private. This book proposes imaginatively following readers into their different settings and scenes, in order to build the fullest possible picture of the processes of contemporary recreational reading.

Reading occurs in relation to texts. My attention in this book is primarily on the books produced by the trade sector of the publishing industry. This is not a study of reading newspapers, magazines, textbooks, reference material, or websites. I acknowledge the fluid boundary between book reading—especially on screen—and other forms of reading, which are linked in a media ecosystem. I narrow the focus to books because there is a particular status to book reading, a position in a cultural hierarchy that I am keen to interrogate. This status endures, even though book objects themselves are formally unstable, as the rise of audiobooks has made clear in recent years. Another reason for focusing on books is the distinctive trajectory the book publishing industry has traced in the twenty-first century. Unlike the music industry, for example, the key product of the publishing industry has not fragmented. Albums have largely been atomized into songs, but books are still the dominant unit of content in publishing. Not only does this affect the economy in which readers participate, but it also affects modes of consumption. I focus most on novels, which are predominantly associated with reading for pleasure. The books that I look at in this work are principally in English, and the readers Anglophone, due to my own language limitations.

Reading produces meaning, a somewhat difficult term to define. One way of thinking about meaning is that I consider reading as a cultural activity, rather than a means of acquiring information. While my approach is broad, by focusing on culture I do exclude some areas of inquiry. For example, I do not track eyeballs or look at the neurological processes involved in reading, either on print or on screen. Nor do I engage in depth with the considerable research on children's reading and the acquisition of reading skills and literacy.

I am interested in reading as culture, and culture is an amorphous concept; in Raymond Williams's phrase, it is one of the "two or three most complicated words in the English language."[36] He offers three, sequential definitions: culture was first used to describe a process of tending, including tending one's own development and growth; it developed to also refer to a group's "whole way of life"; and then further evolved to describe "the arts and learning—the special processes of discovery and creative effort" associated with museums, art, books, and so on.[37] All three senses persist, and in this book I remain alert to them all, while acknowledging the distinctions and tensions between them. Writing in *The New Yorker*, Joshua Rothman observes that people tend toward one or other of Williams's aspects, for example "toward the 'culture' that makes you a better person or the 'culture' that just inducts you into a group." These tendencies align with shifts in the positive or negative connotations of the word "culture," but Rothman argues that at its core, the word "culture" represents a wish: "that a group of people might discover, together, a good way of life; that their good way of life might express itself in their habits, institutions, and activities; and that those, in turn, might help individuals flourish in their own ways."[38] These aspirations toward flourishing, this search for meaning, is what I focus on (and indeed advocate for) in my study of reading.

Structure of This Book: Methodology, Networks, and Conduct

This book's central argument is that recreational reading in the twenty-first century is a multidimensional cultural practice that involves social and private, aesthetic and moral behaviors. Capitalism provides the ground within which readers act—it constrains and directs reader behaviors, and these behaviors in turn reinforce or oppose capitalist logics at the same time as they strive to meet readers' needs. In the chapters of this book, I develop this argument by elaborating a methodology for studying contemporary reading practices; then identifying the networks that readers constitute through the connections they form; and then working through different dimensions of reading using examples drawn from contemporary practices. These examples come from research I have undertaken over the past two decades, synthesized with other qualitative studies of book reading. This book, then, is both an overview of current reading practices based on extant scholarship and my own research and the presentation of a model for understanding what readers do: their dynamic, networked practices of aesthetic and moral conduct.

The central epistemological question of the book is a version of the question with which I began this introduction: What can we know about contemporary readers and their reading practices? In Chapter 1, "Researching Readers," I propose a conceptual model and methodology for the study of contemporary reading. The chapter begins by outlining existing approaches from literary studies, an academic discipline closely connected to recreational reading, with particular focus on reader response theory, including key theories from Louise Rosenblatt, Judith Fetterley, and, in a more contemporary context, Felski.[39] I then turn to the social sciences, especially book history and cultural sociology. I review the methods and emphases of studies of historical readers, such as the groups of women readers studied by Barbara Sicherman, the African American literary societies researched by Elizabeth McHenry, and the Melbourne reading diaries examined by Susan K. Martin, all from the nineteenth century.[40] These are complemented by work on more contemporary readers, such as Radway's research on romance fiction readers and Megan Sweeney's study of women's reading in prison.[41] The chapter then advocates a model that combines the social sciences and the humanities, bringing together attention to texts, self-reflexivity and interest in materiality, people and social relations (including commercial and industrial relations). I use actor-network theory (and similar approaches such as pragmatic sociology) to focus on the connections readers form with books, other readers, academics, critics, publishers, and authors. This model and methodology is elaborated and exemplified in the subsequent chapters.

My book is based on the actions of readers—I'm most interested in verbs, not nouns—and Chapter 2, "Networks of Readers," considers the most foundational of these actions: how readers constitute themselves *as readers* in different settings. How do they affiliate with groups, and how do these groups affect the identity of "reader"? I consider readers as consumers, moving through bookstore environments. I then look at readers as citizens, who interact with the state and the education system. And finally I look at readers as conversationalists, discussing books in clubs, at events, and online. In each case—and including a mini case study of readers at the Melbourne Writers Festival—I consider the actions of readers in attending physical spaces, as well as how they move across online platforms. The disaggregation of the category of "readers" into these different settings and groups, and the identification of some reading networks and their distinctive qualities, grounds the subsequent chapters' analyses of the conduct of readers in these networks.

Chapter 3, "The Aesthetic Conduct of Readers," elaborates how readers treat books as models for living. In using books to express their style and shape their lives, readers may take on (and perform) a general bookishness, or they may align themselves with and take inspiration from specific genres, authors or books. The chapter uses qualitative textual and image analysis to describe readers' aesthetic conduct in three settings. First, I analyze bibliomemoirs—books about reading books—as narrativized accounts of the influence of books on a life, pitched as models for everyday readers to follow. Second, I consider social media as an arena for readers to engage in aesthetic conduct, paying particular attention to Instagram. Third, I look at how members of a reading for well-being group set up at an Australian library present their aesthetic responses to one another, considering the formation of bookish identity and taste as a dynamic, modifiable process.

Chapter 4, "The Moral Force of Readers," argues that readers use their reading to form and test views on right and wrong behavior. I propose that readers' morality works on three, overlapping levels: in relation to society, by positioning reading as a valuable activity; in relation to the content of books, by judging characters and reading for empathy; and in relation to book culture and the publishing industry, by responding to the actions and statements of authors and publishers. The specific forms of moral conduct that contemporary readers enact are illustrated through analyses of book festivals, the reading for well-being group introduced in Chapter 3, and social media campaigns against books and authors.

While I have separated aesthetic and moral conduct in these chapters, the two overlap. In a special issue of the *European Journal of Culture Studies* dedicated to the relationship between aesthetics and morality, Giselinde Kuipers, Thomas Franssen, and Sylvia Hollan argue, citing Habermas, that the intellectual separation of these two domains is a historically contingent product of modernity. Instead, they propose, aesthetic, and moral judgments frequently "operate in tandem" in everyday life, as processes of meaning-making through which individuals express their sense of self and their relations to others.[42] In Chapter 5, I look at the overlapping of aesthetic and moral conduct in relation to one, intensive site of contemporary reader practice: private reading, which I argue can involve the use of reading to nurture and nourish the self.

Reading may be embedded in social infrastructure, but it also provides quiet moments of solitude. The privacy of these moments, when reading feels like an encounter with the self, is at the core of the value many people place on reading: concentration, flow, and pleasure. Through analysis of newspaper articles, blogs, and social media posts, this chapter considers three dominant discourses used to describe personal reading experiences. The first is eroticism, where erotics is understood as sensuality, desire, and satisfaction. The second is deep reading, a science-inflected understanding of the value of uninterrupted, sustained reading and its benefits for the reader. Finally, I consider the discourse of mindful reading, which sees reading a meditative practice. All three act as distinctively modulated articulations of (the often commodified concept) self-care. Their forceful normative accounts of what reading should be—passionate, profound, healing— can diminish more casual experiences, but these media accounts are nonetheless revealing as popular attempts to frame what is special about book reading.

Together, these chapters illuminate the multiple dimensions of reading as a post-digital cultural practice, through a matrix of investigation that includes both print and digital books, and both online and offline reader behavior. The picture revealed is an exciting one. With all its diversity, book reading is a creative, generative activity, one that can prompt conversation and reflection. In my own life, reading has provided meaningful interior experiences as well as cherished personal and professional relationships, developed in person and through digital communication. If this sounds like cheerleading, I want to also acknowledge the difficulties faced by readers. To speak of my own life again, I've often felt angry at the intractable Whiteness and gender inequity of the publishing industry and its products, suspicious of the use to which my online reviews and star ratings might be put, and frustrated by the difficulty of navigating my way toward books I want to read. The fact that readers are capable of enlivening their worlds through books does not take away from the harmful structures and impediments to flourishing that characterize life in the twenty-first century. There is much work to be done. The part of the work done by this book, and my motivation for writing it, is to bring about enhanced understanding of the multifaceted value of recreational reading, so that academics, arts workers, and book industry professionals can support more people to pursue their own reading practices, in their own way, and according to their own interests, thereby enriching and diversifying book culture.

The book is an argument for the vitality, agency, and creativity of readers— not just when their reading is immersive and transformative, but also when it is limited or shaped by commerce, or when it is casual or interrupted. In putting readers at the center of inquiry, I celebrate the capacity of readers to integrate books with their lives, and by so doing alter themselves and the society in which they live. Underlying my work is a pragmatic view of books as things to be used, that circulate and interact, that change and are changed. Despite the constraints that affect us all, there is a sphere of action possible for readers. They activate that space of possibility by moving among networks and expressing aesthetic and moral judgments. Amid the noise and busyness of the twenty-first century, reading books is, and remains, a cultural force.

1 A METHODOLOGY FOR CONTEMPORARY READING STUDIES

Reading is composed of complex, variable processes that have evolved with historical and cultural specificity alongside different forms of writing, from the Sumerian cuneiform tablets used over 5,000 years ago to the reflowable pages of a twenty-first-century e-reader.[1] The categories of perception that shape how reading is understood have also developed over time and across cultures. Within academia, scholarship on reading has been pursued in numerous disciplines, providing varied theoretical resources.[2] In proposing a cross-disciplinary methodology for studying contemporary recreational reading, I turn first to consider reading as it has been conceptualized in the discipline of literary studies. I pay particular attention to how literary studies' attention to texts prioritizes professional, expert reading, leading to an unsettled relationship with recreational reading. Literary studies offers insights into reading drawn from decades of careful encounters with texts, and richly elaborated concepts and vocabulary for analyzing reading experience. The second section of the chapter considers empirical approaches to the study of reading from the social sciences, especially book history and cultural sociology, most of which are based in an interest in the practices of non-academic readers. What these disciplines offer reading studies is a focus on people, on materiality, and on social structures as well as individual experience.

The most productive methodology for studying contemporary recreational readers, I argue, reconciles these two predominant approaches to reading: from the humanities, privileging texts, and from the social sciences, privileging human subjects. To achieve a rapprochement between these disciplinary trajectories, I turn to actor-network theory, which has been taken up in literary studies, and to allied approaches in the social sciences which have characterized field-leading work on reading over the past decades. A networked, grounded approach is empirical as well as theoretical; puts texts and people in relational networks; accounts for aesthetic and moral practices; and, most importantly, is reader-centered. It is ideally placed to account for the multiple significant dimensions of contemporary reading as a cultural practice. To understand how this model works, we need to know what it builds on, including a tradition of fascination with everyday readers in literary studies that has not yet translated into an ability to fully account for them.

Fascination and Disavowal: The Everyday Reader in Literary Studies

As a discipline based on the analysis of texts, literary studies has a constant interest in the figure of the reader. The principal method of literary studies is reading, elaborated and specified into different forms. Recent high-profile discussions within literary studies, particularly in the United States, have highlighted the potential of different ways of reading, including "calibrations" that oscillate between close reading and the world beyond the text, "surface reading," "close but not deep" reading, "proximate reading," and "post-critical" reading.[3] These formulations zero in on the relative positions of the reader and the text, conceptualized as forms of distance as well as attitude. It is not surprising that a focus on reading has come to the fore as literary studies' toolkit of methods has expanded through the digital humanities to include computational methods which are themselves figured as forms of reading (or not reading), such as "distant reading" or "computational literary studies."[4] Digitization, with all of its potential and limitations, brings into relief the kinds of reading that the discipline values.

Debates about the relation between the text and the reader in literary studies are built on a shared assumption: that the reader is academic. This is the case, even though the discipline's professionalized forms of reading maintain an implicit, by no means straightforward, connection to recreational reading. This connection has been the focus of another cluster of recent work from the United States, including John Guillory's *Professing Criticism* (2022), Deidre Lynch's *Loving Literature* (2015), and Rita Felski's trilogy, *Uses of Literature* (2008), *The Limits of Critique* (2015), and *Hooked* (2020). The ongoing concern to define the role of literary studies reveals an unsettled relationship with recreational reading at the core of the discipline.

Literary studies' commitment to specialized reading, rather than recreational reading, is the ground of its disciplinary existence and sustainability. Models of how and what to read drove the development of English literary studies, which originated in the 1920s and 1930s as a push to displace classics from the center of the educational syllabus. This involved asserting the validity of studying texts in English (rather than Latin or Greek), and studying relatively recent, rather than ancient, texts. As Terry Lovell observes, English literary studies thus required the concerted construction by theorists of a Great Tradition, a legitimate lineage of English literary works.[5] Creating a canon, particularly for contemporary and recent works, meant drawing a line between texts that were legitimate objects for academic study and those that were not: poetry and modernist novels fell into the former category, and middlebrow and popular fiction into the latter.[6] In the Practical Criticism movement, developed initially by F. D. Leavis and colleagues at Cambridge University in the 1920s and influential right through the 1950s, and its US-based counterpart New Criticism, poetry was privileged, and mass-culture was derided.[7] For example, Q. D. Leavis's *Fiction and the Reading Public* (1932) decried the "middlebrow standard of value" established through books written by authors such as Rebecca West and G. B. Stern, who she described as "competent journalists."[8] The discipline's gatekeeping was both gendered and classed; Claire Squires notes that the Leavis's "act of market division … largely falls along class lines," while Lovell and Kate Flint note the exclusion of forms associated with women from the emerging canon.[9]

The debate about which texts should be studied was also a debate about which practices of reading matter. Professional readers were prized over recreational readers through a focus on correct technique. Practical Criticism and New Criticism encouraged close reading and were resolutely anti-theoretical, adopting the Arnoldian emphasis on direct response to concrete texts. In some respects, this was democratizing; Practical Criticism's pedagogical orientation toward the words on the page did not require deep theoretical or historical learning and was relatively accessible in an era which saw a huge expansion of the student population in the United States, particularly from second-generation immigrants. New Criticism similarly rejected the significance of authorial biography and studied the qualities of the text itself. Both Practical Criticism and New Criticism required training and emphasized the need for expertise—Leavis, for example, often promoted difficult texts, such as the poetry of T. S. Eliot. These models of reading thereby shored up the institutional standing of literary studies, even (and perhaps especially) when they were promoted outside the academy, such as in Workers' Institutes.[10] The dichotomy between authorized, legitimate reading practices and unauthorized, leisure-based reading practices persisted through the twentieth century. Merve Emre has written of the literary studies project in the United States after the Second World War to develop "good readers," which relied on an "oppositional relationship to a curiously undifferentiated mass of bad readers" who engaged in practices such as identification and emotional response.[11] The binary opposition between good and bad readers fostered a deep attentiveness to academic reading through appreciation of its distinctiveness, an inquiry undergirded by a deep commitment to the importance of reading and texts. Yet it also made it difficult for literary studies scholars to value everyday reading practices where they diverged from those dominant in academia.

One way in which literary studies' relationship with everyday reading was worked out was through the abstractions of reader-response criticism. This strand of literary studies made its investment in reading particularly explicit, from its origins in the 1920s through to its prominence between the 1970s and the 1990s.[12] The earliest reader-response criticism argued for the consideration of the reader as an integral component of the meaning of texts: I. A. Richards conducted experiments in reader responses to poems as part of his contribution to Practical Criticism, while Louise Rosenblatt from the 1930s focused her attention on the interactions between readers and texts, including the way readers create aesthetic experiences, which I discuss more in Chapter 3.[13] In the 1970s, Wolfgang Iser posited the figure of the "implied reader," and Stanley Fish developed the notion of the "interpretive community."[14] Also in the 1970s, Judith Fetterley wrote of "the resisting reader" as part of a feminist approach to literary studies; arguing that when women read canonical texts, they must not only adopt the perspective of the male writer and protagonist, but learn to see femaleness as powerlessness.[15] Fetterley's feminist theorization of reading establishes a crucial gap between the text and the actual reader of a work, allowing a space of action for readers.

The conceptual focus on the reader in Anglo-American literary theory resonates with the work of Roland Barthes, whose essay "Death of the Author" was published in 1967.[16] Barthes provides one of the classic power-to-the-reader moments in literary theory when he proclaims that the death of the author means the birth of the reader. He argues that texts are unstable and so rely upon the reader to make meaning out of them. The act of reading is severed, conceptually, from the text. Barthes's approach is similar to that of Michel de Certeau, who argues that readers make whatever use of texts they need to.[17] Neither of these theorists, though, considers explicitly how everyday recreational readers might work with texts, and their theories have been used to authorize critics rather than to investigate the power of readers outside the academy.

Reader-response criticism offers thoughtful conceptualizations of the reader in relation to the text, including the reader's role in creating meaning. Yet it needs to be borne in mind that reader-response criticism theorizes readers rather than studying them empirically; as Shafquat Towheed and W. R. Owens note, its "theoretical models, though compelling, are not substantively supported by a body of evidence of actual reading practice."[18] Rita Felski describes the idealized readers of some reader-response critics as "curiously bloodless and disembodied, stripped of all passions," as scholars like Iser and Roman Ingarden applied a formalist template to reader response.[19] The reason for the bloodlessness is that most reader-response concepts were developed in order to interpret texts.[20] That is, they were not oriented toward understanding a broad swathe of actual reader responses to texts, but rather used the idea of the reader to better understand texts and their effects. Writing in 1982, Mary Louise Pratt explained reader-response theory as a reaction against formalist approaches to texts—the approaches of New Criticism, for example—arguing that it arose from the problem of readers disagreeing on "the aesthetic structures and properties of texts."[21] Reader-response theory was part of a turn toward self-reflexivity, acknowledging the position and role of the researcher.[22] While opening up new angles on texts, it also enhanced literary studies scholars' capacity to pay careful attention to their own reading. But it never quite extended to paying attention to the reading of everyday recreational readers.

With this history, how is contemporary literary studies equipped to understand and interact with recreational readers in the present moment? The often unspoken agreement among literary studies academics that developed over the twentieth century has persisted: literary studies is guided by the assumption that academic readers are more careful, knowledgeable, and self-aware than everyday readers. Even as the canon has loosened to allow some popular novels to be studied at university, they are read in specialized ways that are distinguished from leisure reading.[23] The gap between academic and popular reading practices remains foundational. This is reaffirmed by Guillory, who writes, with some rhetorical overemphasis, that "there is an enormous gap between reading as it is practiced within and without the academy," and that "professional reading and lay reading have become so disconnected that it has become hard to see how they are both reading."[24] This antagonistic, antithetical relationship exists for Guillory, even though, at the same time, reading for pleasure is subsumed within professional reading as its "back-formation" and necessary point of origin.[25] The distinction between professional and recreational reading has indeed taken on ever greater (though vexed) importance in the discipline, as a means of bolstering the authority of literary studies in a time when the humanities in general are often dismissed as less useful than science, and when literature departments specifically are beleaguered by the rise of creative writing programs and the expansiveness of cultural and media studies.[26] Literary studies scholars must demonstrate their value, their reason for being an academic discipline. If literary scholars won't stand up for their own expertise, who will?

Literary specialists still invoke the specter of bad readers, and still describe them as an undifferentiated mass. Most often these days, this is done by figuring bad readers as consumers. I came across an example of this when I heard literary author Charlotte Wood give a keynote address to an Australian literary studies conference, later published by *The Sydney Review of Books* with the polemic title "Reading Isn't Shopping." The target of Wood's criticism isn't readers, per se, but "the explosion of consumer culture" that positions readers as customers. She bristles at the inclusion of book club discussion guides at the end of novels, noting that "there's something so disturbing about the incursion of these marketing tendrils into the pages of the book itself." It is these imagined reader-customers that Wood critiques, as being more interested in liking and rating books than in challenge and uncertainty; she gives examples of students and audience members at writers festivals who are looking for relatability.[27] The assumption behind this critique is that there is a better way of reading, a way of reading that is beyond the reach of marketing and is more thoughtful, more tolerant of discomfort, than the reading of the average student or audience member.

The cost of setting up one kind of reading as superior to another is that it creates a rupture between expert readers (literary authors, academics, critics) and everyday recreational readers, forcing the experts to look down on the non-experts. At one moment in her essay, Wood refers to the banality of "pink-jacketed goo from the shelf labelled *Heartwarming / Relatable.*" Playful overstatement notwithstanding, where does this leave the reader who enjoys reading mass-market romance fiction? Are we dupes of marketing?

Janice Radway has written about re-learning her reading habits and tastes on entering the university, learning to disavow the kinds of novels she used to enjoy.[28] This is part of the process of professionalization: literary studies' turn away from everyday readers is grounded precisely in fact that most scholars of literature began as enthusiastic recreational readers.[29] This is a trajectory I also experienced, and navigated a way around. As an undergraduate doing honors in literary studies, I analyzed the novels and poems that I loved and found interesting, and I wrote about what I thought they meant, or why I thought they were significant. For me, literary studies was driven by a love of reading. When it came to life after the BA, I diverged from the discipline. I extended my training with a PhD in publishing studies, researching how books were brought into the world and the mediators who promoted them to readers. This was a way for me to keep my own fiction reading recreational. But for scholars who stay in literary studies, the trajectory is to acquire greater reading expertise, more detailed knowledge of form and historical context and intertextual development, and become more and more knowledgeable readers. Academic identity becomes bound up in the capacity to make judgments and offer insights into literary works. It becomes as much about being a skilled writer as about being a reader. This kind of literary studies moves ever further from everyday readers, with the only remaining point of connection the literary studies classroom—where education about how to be a good reader takes place.

As the existence of this classroom connection reveals, though, the divide between literary studies academics and amateur readers has never been absolute. Guillory maps this overlap, not only when he recognizes lay reading as being subsumed within professional reading, but also when he points out that despite their differences (he suggests that unlike leisure reading, professional reading is labor, is paid, requires training and is done as part of a community—all, notably, features that could describe reading practices outside the academy in the 2020s) both professional and everyday reading share an ethical component.[30] There is a permeability between these modes, and overlap between these roles.

One of the prompts for consideration of everyday readers within literary studies has been the turn toward post-critique, expressed as an impulse to reconnect with vernacular modes of reading (rather than to over-rely on critique). This is the project of Felski's *Uses of Literature*, which aims to reinvigorate literary studies by bringing it closer to the forms of attachment between readers and books that are forged through everyday encounters. Engaging with such attachments, and with "ordinary motives for reading," is a way to meet the need Felski identifies in literary studies for "richer and deeper accounts of how selves interact with texts."[31] The publisher's blurb promises that "*Uses of Literature* bridges the gap between literary theory and common-sense beliefs about why we read literature." Yet the extent to which common sense is "common," who gets to be "ordinary," and who is included in "we" are all open questions.

Felski distils her thinking based on her own observations, theoretical knowledge, and analysis of the depiction of readers in literary works (such as Emma Bovary and Don Quixote). In her 2020 monograph *Hooked*, she expands this evidential basis to also consider first-person accounts of reactions to artworks—including, for example, some Goodreads reviews. This expansion accords with a softening she wants to produce in the boundary between professional and everyday readers; she is interested in the similarities, especially the affective similarities, between these readers. Crucially, the purpose of this is the rejuvenation of the academy. The center point of Felski's project is the literary studies classroom; the reader-text dyad as experienced within the university. This focus produces some limits to her work, because her investigations must remain useful for literary studies students and within the bounds of what is taught to them. For example, she writes in *The Limits of Critique* that

> What remains at the heart of the discipline—for better or for worse—is a training in advanced techniques of reading, tested out in the encounter with a corpus of significant texts. A commitment to describing the hybrid networks in which literary works are embedded must be weighed against, and balanced with, the habits, preferences, and passions that define an existing field of inquiry.[32]

This is an injunction directed at literary studies scholars that upholds disciplinary boundaries ("the habits, preferences, and passions that define an existing field of inquiry"). It pushes away, say, sociology and media studies in order to focus on—to preserve—the "heart" of literary studies. Guillory, too, frames literature as the object of the discipline of literary studies, and readers as its "clientele" rather than subject matter—this is one of the reasons he gives for why post-critique has not translated into a new program of teaching and research.[33] Yet, as Felski's *Hooked* demonstrates through its greater attention to recreational readers, and as I go on to show in the rest of this book, it is richly generative to pair literary studies techniques and interests with qualitative investigation of diverse everyday reader practices. Seeing, for example, book history (and its studies of reading) not as literary studies' other but as its sister discipline can drive forward some of the most urgent debates facing literary studies today.

Felski's work reaches out, conceptually, to everyday readers, showing that the rupture between the discipline and amateur practices is not complete. Literary studies continues to value reading for pleasure at the same time as it distinguishes itself as a scholarly discipline. Literary studies has a double personality, combining professionalism with a yearning toward the (romanticized) experience of the amateur reader. In *Loving Literature,* Deidre Lynch identifies a tension at the heart of literary studies, a tension between feeling and knowing, which means that the discipline is presented "both as a knowledge practice and as an instrument of pastoral care and character building."[34] The idealization of passionate amateur reading practices as an implied shared baseline within the professional context of literary studies creates a normative expectation that limits the kinds of reading deemed valuable, and as Lynch notes this causes tension, just as the discipline's efforts to divorce professionalized reading from amateur reading do.

Literary studies, then, has a deep entanglement with ideas about how to read, one that has been present since the inauguration of the discipline and has never settled. Literary studies academics themselves have dual, conflicting identities as professional and recreational readers, and this inner tension drives much critical work on reading. Nonprofessional, everyday readers become somewhat lost in the discipline, encompassed only as its trainees, or as vestigial remains within critics. What literary studies does have to offer to studies of everyday reading is knowledge of texts, sophisticated insights into individual reading moments, and conceptual tools and language for describing the relationships that can exist between texts and readers. The discipline's interest in reading as method also potentially opens into an interest in broader cultural reception.[35]

One of the places where the border between literary studies and reception studies is softest is in studies of digital literary culture. Work in cultural analytics, for example, brings in a host of data about readers to augment studies of literary texts, genres, and periods. Marco Caracciolo introduces his analysis of a corpus of online reviews of Cormac McCarthy's 2006 novel *The Road* by writing that the last few decades of literary studies have seen efforts to "build on the responses of flesh-and-blood readers rather than relying exclusively on the interpreter's own intuitions."[36] He sees analysis of reader reviews as both a qualitative complement to quantitative methods in literary studies (often led through digital humanities), and a way of "overcoming the limitations of reader-response theories … which were based on speculation and introspection."[37] Studying digital practices such as online reader reviews draws literary studies close to other disciplines. It introduces considerations and methods from the social sciences to sit alongside literary studies. It requires comfort with different kinds of data, and it calls for theoretical models that put readers' statements and practices alongside texts and academics. At these moments, literary studies research introduces empirical evidence to balance the weight of theory, moving toward interdisciplinary crossovers. That is to say, literary studies is a discipline with edges, some of which overlap with qualitative research on readers, including work from the disciplines of book history and sociology. Exploring and working with these edges can provide literary studies scholars with a way to advance understanding of their role in relation to recreational readers, as well as benefiting other disciplines through sharing decades of insights into texts and reading.

The Everyday Reader in Book History and Sociology

The discipline of book history has produced several influential works outlining the history (or histories) of reading.[38] In a 2018 article surveying the state of reading studies, Simone Murray identifies five shared commitments for reading historians: that reading is active; that material format influences textual interpretation; that reading is geographically and historically specific; that theoretical models of reading require empirical substantiation; and that all reading has social elements.[39] Murray's typically incisive summary is a virtual manifesto for research on reading. These commitments do, though, pose challenges, particularly for scholars working on historical periods. Robert Darnton's influential model of the communication circuit, published in 1982, traces the different stages in a book's life cycle, from author to printer to bookseller to reader, and aims to bring together the field of book history.[40] With regard to the reader, Darnton notes a wave of book historians interested in reading experiences—"rare books and fine editions had no interest for them; they concentrated instead on the most ordinary sort of books, because they wanted to discover the literary experience of ordinary readers"—but sounds a warning that has become much repeated in the field: "reading remains the most difficult stage to study in the circuit followed by books."[41]

Book historians know that reading is elusive, and are properly cautious about accessing the reception of books in the past. They build their research on the few traces that readers leave behind. This can include constructing oral histories based on interviews, or looking at reading journals, commonplace books (scrapbooks of transcribed quotes), marginalia, and borrowing or purchasing records.[42] To take just a few examples of research centered on the late nineteenth and early twentieth centuries, Lydia Wevers analyzed the records of a New Zealand sheep station's library of around 2,000 books, mostly contemporary Victorian fiction, and Susan K. Martin examined diaries kept by three middle-class women readers in Melbourne, including their visits to circulating libraries to acquire fashionable novels, as well as their reading of newspapers, travel writing and religious material.[43] Martin explains that "exploring what these diarists read, their responses and the records of responses of others ... gestures at the complexity of literary consumption and circulation in the colonial context."[44] Barbara Sicherman's work on different communities of women readers in nineteenth-century America affirms the point: even work on a small scale, that looks at just a few readers, can open up important insights into what reading is and does.[45]

In addition to the commitment to studying specific readers, the discipline of book history has a methodological emphasis on materiality. It is attentive to the situations of readers: Roger Chartier notes that reading "is not only an abstract operation of the intellect: it puts the body into play and is inscribed within a particular space, in a relation to the self or to others."[46] The focus on materiality and embodiedness is one of the strengths of book historians, since it resonates with what people outside academia find magnetic about books and reading. The back cover blurb of Alberto Manguel's 1996 trade book *A History of Reading* appeals to readers by endowing physical books with mystic effect: "At one magical instant in your early childhood, the page of a book—that string of confused, alien ciphers—shivered into meaning."[47] Gillian Silverman has written of the intense sensory engagement experienced by some autistic readers, a "tactile sensibility" of touch and smell, which bears similarities to the passion for the book-as-object described by bibliophiles.[48] Book historians' focus on materiality can also inform contemporary debates about the effects of screens and digital reading practices, as, for example, in Laura Dietz's work on readers' reactions to ebooks, or Simon Rowberry's research on "ebookness" and the different formats of Amazon's Kindle e-reader.[49]

Book historians' insistence on the social contexts of reading connects them with another discipline: sociology, including work that can be loosely described as the sociology of literature. Writing in *New Literary History*, James English notes the term "sociology of literature" as out of fashion, but argues that actual research that combines sociological and literary insights constitutes a "multifaceted enterprise" that is "alive and well."[50] Such work includes Radway's 1982 book *Reading the Romance*, for which she interviewed around forty romance readers to explore, in depth, their reading practices, and her 1997 account of the mid-twentieth-century Book-of-the-Month Club, *A Feeling for Books*.[51] In this tradition we also see the work of Danielle Fuller and DeNel Rehberg Sedo in *Reading Beyond the Book*, which investigates mass reading events such as One Book One City programs and mass-mediated book clubs or programs, through methods including surveys, focus groups, interview and participant observation.[52] Megan Sweeney has studied the reading of women in prison in a multifaceted project that included interviews with readers, analysis of the different types of books the women read, and consideration of the processes through which books are approved or censored and circulate within the prison.[53] There is also a substantial body of research into book clubs and their practices.[54]

Some sociological work on reading is marked by a tendency to consider readers in groups, rather than as individuals, abstractions, or extrapolations of the researcher. As I discussed in the Introduction, one of the first questions tackled by sociologists studying reading is a basic demographic one. Understanding the demographics of participation in recreational reading is useful in turning attention to the real-world situation of readers and in pointing to the structural factors that shape reading practices. At the same time, as I emphasized in my Introduction, these groupings can be overly blunt: the questions researchers ask can produce data that obscures the diversity of reading practices.

In addition to demographic analysis, cultural sociologists can produce work on the dynamics of reading as a kind of cultural experience. Griswold wrote in 1987 that in order to keep a focus on meaning, cultural sociology methodologies should begin "by focussing cultural analysis on the point at which individuals interact with a cultural object."[55] Work in this vein includes research by María Angélica Thumala Olave which delves in detail into women readers' own descriptions of the value they place on reading, addressing the "meaning and emotions attached to the subjective experience of the reader," and Clayton Childress's 2019 monograph *Under the Cover*, which traces three related fields of production, circulation, and reception through an in-depth case study of a single novel's lifecycle, including its touchpoints with individual editors, reviewers, and readers.[56]

While such work is granular at the level of the individual, there is still a current of sociological research that focuses on groups. This includes a notable body of sociological research on the question of taste; for studies of readers, this means looking at what readers choose to read, and what they think about what they read. Chapter 3 of this book explores taste in more detail as a component of individual aesthetic conduct, but sociological studies of taste often take a different tack. Such work often uses the model proposed by Pierre Bourdieu in *Distinction*, where he argues that taste is socially structured and distributed. Bourdieu uses the concept of the habitus—a set of socially acquired, embodied dispositions—to explain how tastes are formed and expressed.[57] Research that builds on this model often uses surveys that assess participants' cultural tastes and link these to their demographic categories. An example is Tony Bennett, Michael Emmison, and John Frow's *Accounting for Tastes*, which identifies broad patterns, including correlations between book genre preferences, gender, and class.[58] Understanding the links between taste and demographics can point to influential structural factors at play in book culture, and can disrupt the "we" that is sometimes used too readily by humanities academics to describe reading practices.

However, as I explore further in Chapter 3, Bourdieusian approaches to taste tend to take agency away from individuals by emphasizing the effects of external forces: the family, the education system, institutions, the field, and so on. In such a model, even when readers choose and respond to books with discernment, they are still figured as passive. There is room for a more dynamic approach that sees taste as a set of strategies for negotiating solitary and shared cultural practices. This is especially true since the era of Web 2.0, when the active processes of taste formation became highly visible online. Digital book talk's availability makes it increasingly difficult to ignore as a data source for those who want to understand contemporary reader practices, including those who want to use such data to confirm or complicate academic theories about who reads and how. Just as digital culture is an area where literary studies reaches out to social sciences, so it is an area where the social sciences, such as cultural sociology, can encounter granular data that disrupts established models and categories.

In summarizing recent directions in reading studies, Geert Vandermeersche and Ronald Stoetart identify two clusters. The first is "discourses which seem to hold on or want to return to an 'older' narrative which often entails seeing the university as a protected enclave apart from larger society, a narrow conception of literature as only consisting of print books and a narrowly defined aesthetic, and univocal function for reading." The second group is those who "try to construct new 'scripts' based on insights from multiple disciplines," who acknowledge "the validity of different ways of reading."[59] In this loaded distinction, the second, more interdisciplinary option seems like the better choice. But how to achieve this rapprochement between disciplines, and this outward-looking approach to studying diverse practices of reading? One way is to productively combine literary studies and social sciences through a networked methodology that takes advantage of their shared and overlapping interests to put readers, academics, texts, and material objects in relation to one another, both conceptually and empirically.

An Interdisciplinary, Networked Approach to the Study of Reading

A productive model for studying contemporary readers needs to encompass diverse objects, processes, experiences, actions, and relations to books. Ideally, then, it needs to find some wiggle room in relation to existing disciplinary (and even interdisciplinary) trajectories. In our article "The Epistemology of Ullapoolism: Making Mischief Within Contemporary Book Cultures," Claire Squires and I propose a playful, arts-informed creative approach to studying book cultures, as a way to counter what we see as the inflexibility and insufficiency of frameworks that collect, count, and model aspects of book culture.[60] In our study of the Frankfurt Book Fair, for example, we conducted mini interviews, gatecrashed parties, used fortune telling fish, made collages, and set up our own stand in a disused area of Hall 6 in order to produce situated knowledge of contemporary publishing industry practices.[61] Another form of dynamism comes from actor-network theory and related approaches including pragmatic sociology and institutional ethnography, which have the potential to enrich the investigation of reading by allowing for intercommunication between the concerns of literary studies, book history, and sociology, and by drawing in the activity of a wide range of people and nonhuman objects.

Wiggle room means loosening some structures of thought. One of the barriers to interconnection between humanities and the social sciences in the study of books and reading has been the perceived structuralism of some sociological approaches. The sociology of Bourdieu, for example, is sometimes seen, especially by Anglo-American scholars, as overly deterministic and unable to account for social change.[62] In contrast, actor-network theory and allied approaches offer a more obviously fluid, flexible way for literary studies to expand its scope. Actor-network theory was developed by theorists including Madeleine Akrich, Michel Callon, John Law, and Bruno Latour. Latour, the most closely associated with the theory, was a philosopher, anthropologist, and sociologist whose early work included analyses of scientific practice.[63] As Hélène Buzelin writes, his work and actor-network theory more generally was part of the development of poststructuralist thinking that placed increased emphasis on agency and the dynamics of power.[64] With the 2004 publication "Why Has Critique Run out of Steam? From Matters of Fact to Matters of Concern," Latour explicitly opposed himself to the deconstructionist trajectory of postmodernism.[65] Actor-network theory methodology builds, rather than disassembles. It starts by describing small interactions which build into networks.[66] In *Reassembling the Social* (2005), a key text for actor-network theory, Latour defines "the social" dynamically, as "a very peculiar movement of re-association and reassembling."[67] For reading studies, this is an invitation to look at individual practices first, and build from here to an understanding of what reading looks like in the post-digital era.

Actor-network theory is not without antecedents and did not develop in a vacuum; there are several aligned approaches, especially in the social sciences, that enrich the interdisciplinary study of contemporary reading. Grounded theory, for example, has been used for qualitative research in the social sciences that begins with data (description) and uses it to construct theory, rather than applying theory to situations.[68] Institutional ethnography is another aligned approach. In *The Everyday World as Problematic: A Feminist Sociology* (1987), Dorothy E. Smith suggests that theoretical analyses should "begin with the activities of actual individuals whose activity produces the social relations that they live."[69] Another methodological approach that complements actor-network theory is pragmatic sociology. Luc Boltanski and Laurent Thévenot's work on pragmatic sociology looks to the meaning-making behavior of agents in a network, and shares impulses with actor-network theory (and with other movements such as grounded theory), particularly the injunction to begin with observation and not to impose a preconceived theoretical model on the data gathered.[70]

In this book, I tend to use the language of actor-network theory precisely because it has already been embraced to an extent by literary studies scholars, which suggests a fruitful path for interdisciplinary work. However, the key principles actor-network theory shares with institutional ethnography and pragmatic sociology are where I see the real value of this approach—the focus on building, describing, and connecting.

Three related features of actor-network theory are especially useful for researching contemporary readers: its expansive networks; its attention to materiality (which chimes with work in book history); and its emphasis on description, which decenters the researcher. In relation to the expansive range of phenomena encompassed in networks, the inclusion of nonhuman actors is particularly productive. This is one of the aspects of actor-network theory that has been valued and put to use by literary studies scholars to date, including in the fields of ecohumanities and ecocriticism as well as in contextual accounts that analyze texts within broader networks. For example, Elizabeth Outka uses a Latourian approach to analyze two books, Virginia Woolf's *Mrs Dalloway* (1925) and Oliver Lodge's memoir, *Raymond, or Life and Death* (1916), both of which offer "accounts of World War I soldiers who (allegedly) return from the dead in material form."[71] Outka pursues a Latourian methodology, reading "horizontally" rather than "vertically" (for latent meaning in the texts) to trace the network of associations and actors that shaped the effects of the books.[72] This approach starts with texts, but does not stay within them. It illustrates the generative potential of actor-network theory for bridging the study of books with the study of their readers.

Latour's further theoretical idea that nonhuman actors have affordances that affect others is also productive for studies of reading. For example, I have written with Emmett Stinson about how Goodreads reviewers respond to Indigenous Australian author Alexis Wright's 2013 novel *The Swan Book*; we analyze the formal difficulty of this novel as an affordance that readers engage with emotionally and intellectually.[73] There are a host of other affordances of nonhuman actors that affect contemporary readers, from book covers to hashtags, and paying attention to these illuminates what contemporary recreational readers do.

The inclusion of nonhuman actors in a network allows for the second key advantage of this approach: specific attention to materiality. As noted above, this is a strength of book history that can, via actor-network theory, be added to the analysis of individual texts. In his study of the career of nineteenth-century "media impresario" Andrew Lang, Nathan K. Hensley notes that "the practices of material recuperation and historical particularization that have long been [periodical studies'] hallmark as a subfield" are newly authorized by network-based theoretical models: "it is materiality itself, advocates say, that network thinking has helped bring back to the field of literary criticism."[74] Hensley shows how Lang's networks encompassed writers such as Henry James and Marie Corelli, fields of knowledge from trout fishing to poetry, and institutions from publishing houses to social clubs. These combined to produce texts such as Lang's fairy books, which were published in many versions in the nineteenth century and continue to proliferate as (sometimes dubious) digital products in the twenty-first century.

Just as materiality illuminates past book cultures, it can inform understanding of contemporary readers. Materiality is an important component of what contemporary readers do, as readers engage with print objects, digital platforms, and physical places, from bookstores to libraries to festival stages.

Third, actor-network theory emphasizes description, and where possible allows actors to describe themselves and their relations. Such an emphasis incorporates an openness to new actors in book culture, and new roles and practices for readers. Through this emphasis, literary studies and the social sciences are both required and empowered to let readers speak. Readers and their practices are not immediately placed into categories by researchers, but first noticed and mapped. Latour stresses that while normal sociology offers a convenient shorthand through its categories, sometimes actor-network theory is needed instead, especially in situations of innovation, controversy and uncertainty. In such situations "it is no longer enough to limit actors to the role of informers offering cases of some well-known types. You have to grant them back the ability to make up their own theories of what the social is made of." Famously, you have to "follow the actors themselves," to catch up with their innovations and "learn from them what the collective existence has become in their hands."[75] This is particularly apposite for understanding readers in a post-digital landscape, where readers have evolved their activities.

One of the things contemporary readers do is form groups, in the process of trying out identities. Latour writes that "relating to one group or another is an on-going process made up of uncertain, fragile, controversial, and ever-shifting ties." He suggests looking at how actors fetch resources "to make their boundaries more durable," or mobilize professionals and their paraphernalia. Researchers can also look to the spokespersons and recruiters—the "group makers, group talkers, and group holders"—who speak groups into existence, and to the anti groups that are set up in opposition. Tracking all of this allows delineating groups to be not only the task of the researcher, but the task of actors themselves.[76] For readers, affiliations may relate to who is and isn't a reader, or to other clusters readers might belong to, either in demographic terms or in terms of positions and spaces within literary culture; for example, readers who are also self-published authors, or who are speculative fiction fans. In Chapter 2, I examine these processes in more detail as I examine how readers form networks through the connections they make and break.

For researchers of contemporary book culture, this approach means allowing readers and those with whom they interact—teachers, publishers, librarians, authors, and more—to construct and reconstruct their practices, habits, etiquettes, and expectations, with researchers observing rather than imposing a model upon this world. In building descriptions, "the search for order, rigor, and pattern is by no means abandoned. It is simply relocated one step further into abstraction so that actors are allowed to unfold their own differing cosmos, no matter how counter-intuitive they appear." Latour compares this to painstaking map making, plotting every point no matter how weird it looks. It is important to "leave the actors free to deploy the full incommensurability of their own world-making activities."[77]

This emphasis on description is a post-critical approach. Hensley notes that work that uses "network methodologies" tends to be descriptive rather than critical, and generally has "a bias against normative political approaches."[78] He cites Felski as someone who has done work in this vein in literary studies, drawing on Latour's model. Felski's engagement with actor-network theory is elaborated in a series of publications, including most notably *Uses of Literature*, *The Limits of Critique*, and *Hooked*. In these books, she aims to reduce the authority of critical, suspicious reading in academia and promotes a more expansive view of the ways in which people connect with art.[79] As noted above, Felski focuses upon the primary dyad of the reader (in literary studies) and the text; there is an opportunity to build on Felski's insights, draw in further qualitative research, and test on a wider canvas everything that she has found useful about actor-network theory for understanding the movement and reception of texts. Explaining her project in *The Limits of Critique*, Felski acknowledges that a fuller account would show how "the fate of literary works … is tied to countless agents: publishers, reviewers, agents, bookstores, technologies of consumption (e-readers, Amazon.com), institutional frames … and so on … From such a perspective, the reader-text relationship forms only a small part of a vast and sprawling network."[80] This more sprawling scope is evident in another work of literary studies that makes use of actor-network theory, Amy Hungerford's *Making Literature Now*, which traces some of the networks that produce contemporary American literature.[81] I also want to take an expansive view, but my work differs from Hungerford's by putting readers at the center rather than literary texts or publishers. Scholars such as Felski and Hungerford have provided a manifesto for using actor-network theory in studies of literature—a manifesto that is post-critique, that affirms the pleasure of texts—and this can be extended, using the tools of disciplines such as book history, to more kinds of books, and more readers.

Notably, the larger versions of actor-network theory involve demanding data-gathering. Both Felski and Hungerford embrace actor-network theory but decline to follow its full suite of empirical methods: in *Hooked*, Felski describes her approach as "ANT-ish."[82] I put myself in that category, too—much as I would love to, I cannot trace every connection made by every contemporary recreational reader. My work seeks to reap the advantages of an ANT-style approach through pursuing a "some data" methodology, a middle ground that involves some qualitative methods alongside the academic's own reading. Such data-gathering is essential to avoid taking categories or structures for granted, and to allow for the element of surprise in discovering how contemporary readers relate to books and book culture.

Since actor-network theory holds that the task of defining and ordering the social should be left to actors, not taken up by the analyst, studies of readers should not impose models of reading from within the academy, even generous post-critical models of reading.[83] Scholars need to cede some of their authority to non-professional readers and recognize academia as one regime of reading among many other potential arrangements. Concepts, language, and idiom to describe books and reading need to be drawn from everyday readers' practice; one lively example on social media as I write is a format of posts that present "books I would sell my soul to read again for the first time," a highly emotive form of categorizing a relationship with a book.[84] Latour writes, "This will be an important indicator of quality—are the concepts of the actors allowed to be *stronger* than that of the analysts, or is it the analyst who is doing all the talking?"[85] Allowing readers' own terms and language to rise to the top in academic work is part of de-centering the academic critic in the service of understanding reading as contemporary cultural practice.

The terms readers use to describe their own relations to reading may seem, at times, overwrought, shallow, silly, faddish, or suspect.[86] And yet, as Shai M. Dromi and Eva Illouz argue in their pragmatic sociology account of the symmetry between texts and their readers, "a reader's criticism of a text is important to the sociologist regardless of his or her class, education, or training in literary criticism and whether or not it succeeds in persuading others."[87] Taking statements about reading at face value risks accepting accounts that are disingenuous, deceitful, or just not very interesting. However, as Dromi and Illouz emphasize, the greater risk lies in *not* accepting such statements, imposing other forms of meaning on them and thus potentially missing the richness of the phenomenon being studied.[88] Researchers of contemporary reading need a methodology that is attentive, open-minded, and inclusive: interested in readers' own statements, and the discussions and practices that can build around them.

In addition to the suspicion that everyday statements about reading might not be very interesting, there are other criticisms of and limitations to actor-network theory and related approaches, including post-critique. A ground-up, network approach produces fairly loose constellations of insights that may be difficult to collect and use. Actor-network theory can seem vague. It is not really new, as it has antecedents in all disciplines.[89] These critiques notwithstanding, I believe pursuing this approach is vital in order to set aside some unhelpfully ossified academic attitudes toward reading, and allow the plurality, distinctiveness, and surprises of contemporary recreational reading practices to emerge.

A network-based study of contemporary reading practices comes with numerous advantages in its capacity to account for expansive networks of human and nonhuman actors and their variety of behaviors. But its most productive deployment involves some obligations: notably, the obligation to include some data and to de-center the academic. One further question remains, concerning the de-politicization that is one of the most serious objections raised against actor-network theory and post-critique.[90] Can a network-based approach be properly critical of some of the systems under which contemporary readers operate—of techno-capitalism, of the state, of pernicious cultural hierarchies and persistent inequities and injustices?

Descriptive and Also Critical: Working with Theory That Does Both

There is a need for, and productive overlap between, both descriptive and critical approaches to the study of reading. The dual presence of criticism and curiosity, for example, is evident in Lisa Nakamura's short article on Goodreads, in which she alludes to both the commercial structures that co-opt readers' labor, and also the site's "fascinating thread of vernacular criticism."[91] Descriptive work—such as observing emerging forms of criticism—does not foreclose examination of structural power relations—such as the implications of harvesting readers' data. In my previous research on Goodreads reviews with DeNel Rehberg Sedo, we also combined the critical and the descriptive by using institutional ethnography and feminist standpoint theory to consider everyday readers as a "nonruling group" who devise strategies for interacting with institutions at the same time as nurturing their own local practices.[92]

Description-based models such as actor-network theory, institutional ethnography, and pragmatic sociology can complement more critical sociological modes that have previously been brought to bear on reading studies. For example, pragmatic sociology is not as opposed as it might seem to Bourdieu's more structural sociology. Simon Susen details the strong intellectual connections between Bourdieu's critical sociology and the "sociology of critique" developed by scholars such as Boltanski, despite differences in emphasis and approach. These shared elements include interests in practice, critique, reflexive scholarship, context, and power and a normative impulse that sees sociology as able to change and improve the world.[93] Apparently divergent sociological approaches can be harmonized; for example, the self-interested strategic actions emphasized in Bourdieu's model can co-exist with reflexive actions, through which an individual justifies their actions, showing the kind of critical and moral capacity that Boltanski's model emphasizes. Readers are both affected by structural constraints and have agency to form their own judgments and critiques.

A network-based methodology for reading studies can be alert to both readers' positions within a larger system *and* their capacity to critique and influence that system. A blended descriptive-critical approach resonates with much work on readers from book history and cultural sociology, including work on contemporary reading. Often, for example, a dynamic approach to readers is present in work that makes use of Bourdieu's model of the field of literary production, rather than his more rigid demographic approach to taste in *Distinction*. Bourdieu's model of the literary field accounts for the relations and interactions between multiple people and institutions, who are influenced by their proximity to the autonomous (art-for-art's sake) or heteronomous (market-driven) poles of the field, as well as by their habitus.[94] Research that draws on this strand of Bourdieu's theory holds in view the broad networks in which readers participate: it is these networks that are described, and that are critiqued due to the power relations they impose.

Descriptive-critical research on contemporary reading works by starting with readers, building a description from there, and then critiquing what is found. This is the approach I took in my own previous work in *The New Literary Middlebrow*, where I considered the combination of commercial and cultural aspects in the promotion of books and reading practices.[95] When I began that research, I was inspired by the preceding wave of work prompted by the desire to understand Oprah's Book Club as a new popular reading formation, work such as Cecilia Konchar Farr's *Reading Oprah: How Oprah's Book Club Changed the Way America Reads* and Timothy Aubry's *Reading as Therapy*, which examined the therapeutic reading practices promoted on Oprah's Book Club.[96] This was pragmatic research, following a direction set by readers rather than academia. Aubry articulates his clear focus on "what novels are doing for readers, especially in contexts outside of the university," reminding academics that everyday reading practices may be "more flexible, more capable of accommodating critical, sophisticated modes of thought, and more open to communal aspirations" than is generally acknowledged.[97] To begin with description of readers and then move on to critique is a productive and powerful strategy.

As the twenty-first century has progressed, this pragmatic, reader-centered descriptive-critical tradition has developed through the articulation of a number of models. I mentioned earlier Fuller and Rehberg Sedo's "reading industry," which describes the networks of people, institutions, organizations, and companies that produce temporally specific mass reading events and practices.[98] Hanna Kuusela links Tony Bennett's conceptualization of "reading formations" to describe the situations of popular reading to actor-network theory in her analysis of the reception of a Finnish bestseller.[99] Another network-based model for reading studies is offered in relation to audiobook reception; Sara Tanderup Links conceptualizes "resonant reading" as a network in which readers, materiality, texts, and environment interact, while Bronwen Thomas uses the term "distributed reading" to describe the networked practices of readers on social media.[100] All these different models take seriously the need to describe, from the ground up, specific contemporary reading and book culture practices and use these practices to analyze different forms of power. Like them, my approach is not post-critical, but descriptive-critical. To elaborate how this works, I propose the following crystallization of humanities and social sciences methodologies for studying contemporary readers.

Reader-centered Networks: A Theoretical Model for Contemporary Reading Studies

The pieces are in place for theory to unite literary studies and book history (as well as aspects of media studies, cultural studies and sociology) to study contemporary readers and reading. Complementary strands from humanities and the social sciences can combine within an overarching framework for an expansive, inclusive study of contemporary reader practices. In this book, I mobilize key features of actor-network theory, including its networks of human and non-human actors, attention to materiality, and emphasis on description. I also value the materiality of book history, the attention to different actors of sociology, and the sensitivity to texts of literary studies.

My program for research involves the following principles. These principles can also underpin teaching in the university, offering the opportunity to rejuvenate literary studies through the incorporation of analysis of recreational reading. The first axiom is to start with readers: not with texts. A specific reader or group of readers is the standpoint from which research should take place, and the experience and situated knowledge that come from this standpoint (e.g., that of female readers, young readers, First Nations readers) is what provides this methodology with its critical potential.[101] Examples of this starting point from some of the research I've already mentioned include Sweeney's identification of women prisoners in contemporary North America, Fuller and Rehberg Sedo's identification of attendees at mass reading events across the United Kingdom, the United States, and Canada, as well as those such as Aubry and Konchar Farr, who considered Oprah Winfrey as a reader alongside members of her book club. Once researchers have identified a particular reader or group of readers, they should ask what those readers are reading already. In contrast to the established patterns of literary studies research and syllabus-setting, the academic must cede to readers the authority of choosing what books are valuable and worth studying. Different books will generate different connections and networks of production, circulation, and reception to explore.

Once the focus readers and books are identified, the second step, and the one most closely aligned to literary studies, is to read the book. The text is an actor in networks that cannot be understood without knowledge of the text's plot, language, characters, and style, as well as its material qualities in different formats. Researchers should read with the grain, conscious of what they bring to the reading experience, using all the self-awareness of literary studies.[102] Sweeney, for example, records her own ambivalent feelings about particular urban fiction novels and the genre's role in reinforcing ideologies that fuel inequity, as part of her research into the reading of women prisoners.[103]

The third step is to investigate the networks that have produced this book and its readings. This requires scrutinizing what some other readers think—critics, reviewers, Goodreads users, and book club members, not just other academics. This is where data-gathering comes into play. As noted above, my proposed model includes qualitative research. It is a "some data" approach (as opposed to "big data"). It thus invites the question of what methods might be used most effectively for this kind of approach to studying readers. Which tools or techniques could support this kind of inquiry?

Often, the methods are people-focused. Sweeney interviewed ninety-four women prisoners, multiple times, over multiple years. James Procter, Bethan Benwell and their team recorded dozens of book club meetings.[104] Fuller and Rehberg Sedo ran focus groups, interviews, and a survey with several thousand respondents.[105] There is also a particular synergy between new digital research methods and network-based theoretical models of contemporary reading. In the field of book history, Padmini Ray Murray and Claire Squires have updated Darnton's communication circuit to incorporate digital practices including new opportunities for readers to communicate with authors, publishers, and one another; new research in publishing studies, such as that by Claire Parnell, shows how these communications are shaped by technological affordances and the corporate structures of online platforms, including Amazon, its subsidiary Goodreads, Twitter, and Facebook.[106] Readers' behavior in these digital networks has been analyzed by scholars, such as Lisa Mendelman and Anna Mukamal who conducted topic modeling, most distinctive word analysis, and named entity recognition on Goodreads reviews of feminist novels, and Anatoliy Gruzd and DeNel Rehberg Sedo who studied the Twitter-based book club #1b1t book club and identified the "cultural literacies and skills that readers need to participate fully in the reading group on Twitter," including familiarity with online protocols and knowledge of rhetorical tropes and etiquette.[107]

Computational research methods, such as social network analysis and sentiment analysis, reorient the role of the researcher of books and reading, allowing them to take a step back from the interpretive process and observe the surface level of readers' language and behavior. On their own, though, computational methods risk missing important detail among the vast quantities of data. This is why interviews with readers, observation of events, and close reading of individual online posts also remain important methods. Throughout this book, I advocate for and model a mixture of methods, including digital and computational methods, observational methods, and textual analysis. This combination creates a fine-grained understanding of how readers form and break connections, as they articulate their sense of belonging or detachment, centrality or marginality in the networks of book culture.

Having gathered data, the fourth and final step is to consider readers, the text, and the different statements and practices about the text that arise in their networks in relation to one another. What do these actions and connections say, about the reader, about the book, about others? What is revealed about how culture and commerce sit together, about the aesthetic practices of contemporary readers, about their moral standards, about their desire for social interaction and their need for self-care?

My proposed methodology for studying readers draws on the strengths of literary studies and book history, media studies, and cultural studies, connecting them through the flexible structure of actor-network theory and aligned approaches based on relationality and descriptions of experience. The methodology allows for criticality as well as openness. In pursuing it across this book, I use a number of methods in my primary research, and synthesize these findings with a range of research projects conducted by others that also draw on diverse methods. The range of methods overall includes interviews with festival attendees, sentiment analysis of Goodreads reviews, textual analysis of Instagram posts, close reading of bibliomemoirs, and an embedded focus group of a book club, along with secondary analysis of other research on aspects of reading, from book clubs to social media. A networked view of reading that incorporates textual analysis and data equips researchers and students to make sense of new forms of reader practice that surge into public consciousness and influence the book industry—like the TikTok videos of readers crying that sent Madeleine Miller's 2011 novel *Song of Achilles* to the top of the bestseller lists in 2022.[108] A networked, multimethod approach also keeps in view other facets of contemporary reader practice: the persistence of revered literary critics writing about their reading lives, the ongoing significance of book clubs in readers' lives, the regularity of Twitter protests and Goodreads boycotts, and the deep-seated fascination with solitary reading and desire to turn away from screens.

This is a methodology and an approach that requires expertise across multiple fields and multiple methods. The demands on scholars of contemporary reading are high: knowledge of publishing, of digital media, of institutions, of books. The ambitious program for research begins, as the next chapter explains, with paying attention to how readers form and are formed into networks.

2 NETWORKS OF READERS

A network-based approach indicates that readers can be found in the process of creating that identity by affiliating themselves (strongly or weakly) to the category or group "readers." The identity of reader is not fixed, but is enacted through variable practices. The actions people take to identify as readers are inflected by their other relations and identities: a reader might also be a parent, an accountant, a goth; a book publicist, a festival administrator, or an aspiring writer.[1] In contemporary, post-digital culture, actions that affiliate readers with one another might include reading a book, talking about a book online or to a friend, browsing a bookstore, or going to an author talk. These are context specific, and affected by the other identities readers have. One go-to image of a reader is someone with their head bent silently over a print book. But there are other actions associated with reading, including those arising from traditions that prize oral storytelling.[2] When 22-year-old Amanda Gorman performed spoken word poetry at the inauguration of Joe Biden as president of the United States in 2020, she brought visibility to a cultural practice of reading with a long history and vibrant present, drawing on traditions including hip hop and church oratory.[3] Listening and speaking as reading practices today might mean attending spoken word events, or performing favorite tropes from romance fiction on a TikTok video, or tuning into an audiobook with multiple narrators (George Saunders's 2017 novel *Lincoln in the Bardo* has 166!).[4]

Listening and speaking are activities that can make the networks of readers, and their affiliative groups, apparent and traceable. But even those head-down silent readers are engaged in practices that connect them to networks. For a start, readers visit physical and digital sites that enable them to acquire books: they buy them in bookstores (or receive them as presents that were bought in bookstores), download them from online sites, and borrow them from libraries.[5] In libraries and bookshops, the moment of acquisition can be elongated. It may be preceded by browsing, sometimes undertaken for pleasure in its own right, or a book launch. It may be followed by return visits, or accompanied by chats with staff or other customers. These activities embed the reader in networks of display, conversation, physical maneuvers, negotiations, and transactions. In each situation of book acquisition, readers form relations with other people, organizations, and material and digital objects: right now, I can vividly recall the concrete ramp that leads up to my local library's automatic doors, the self-checkout machines in its foyer, and the black metal stands showing the hot books that month.

In addition to forming networks through acquiring books, readers form networks through interacting with groups that model and discuss reading. Readers learn and practice reading at school and, sometimes, at university. Some go on to attend book clubs, author talks, and festivals, or interact with each other on Goodreads, Twitter, TikTok, YouTube, book blogs, and Amazon. These are the various different networks that readers create and participate in through their practices, the networks that configure what it is to be a reader—and it is these networks, and the reader identities they foster, that are the focus of this chapter.

Each network in which readers participate is structured by power relations that affect readers' visibility, agency, and opportunities to express themselves. In almost every network, for example, authors have more star power than readers (one possible exception is the university, where professors as professional readers carry great sway).[6] Digital change has produced new ways for readers to access authors, but also introduced uneven power relations with the large technology companies that direct and largely control these modes of interaction. At every cultural site, contemporary readers and those with whom they interact—teachers, librarians, booksellers, critics—adjust their practices in light of new technology, from ordering books on Amazon to using Twitter to critique publishers. Readers may be surveilled and aggregated into data points by profit-driven companies, or readers might assert their individuality and subvert platforms to meet their own needs. In all kinds of networks, some readers may be highly active, while others attach more lightly. Some readers might act as bridges between networks, while others are most invested in one and feel excluded from others. The status of authors, readers, and other agents in the reading process is not taken for granted in any network, but is contested.

Readers, then, form relations with people, institutions, and books, and these relations shift, strengthen, and dissolve over time. Through these connections and ruptures, readers are configured with different, sometimes overlapping and sometimes distinct, identities, with varying forms and levels of relative power. In this chapter, I consider three ways in which readers cluster: as reader-consumers, as reader-citizens, and as reader-discussants. These three networks of readers and their continually negotiated relations have implications for the things that contemporary readers do, how they do them, who they do them with, and the effects they have.

Readers as Customers: Navigating Book Retail

When readers acquire a book, they often do this in a store; *contra* the title of an article I discussed in Chapter 1, sometimes reading *is* shopping.[7] To be a reader is, in retail settings, to be a customer. Books are sold in several different kinds of stores, including independent and chain bookshops, online stores, general retail outlets such as discount department stores, street stalls, and mail order businesses.[8] In bricks-and-mortar stores, readers form connections between themselves, books, and other people through the choices they make about what books to pick up, look at, carry to the counter and purchase, and about where to physically move about in the store: to the bargains table, the new releases, or the obscure sections at the back of the store. Online, readers form connections through their search terms, the parts of the site they linger over, the carts they fill, ignore, or check out, and the product reviews they leave.

Bookstores spotlight the constant negotiation between culture and commercialism that characterizes books and the publishing industry.[9] Readers as consumers are figured as part of these discussions: for example, debates about protectionism (such as fixed book prices or restrictions on importing books) may pitch readers as supporters of local books who are prepared to pay a premium, or, conversely, as bargain-seekers.[10] Readers themselves negotiate different aspects of their identity through book buying, which is not always a simple financial transaction but bound up in what Ed Finn calls "networks of literary desire and aspiration as they are expressed through the purchase of a material good."[11] As purchases, books carry a freight of intent, and this is inflected by the site of acquisition. Different kinds of bookstores promote and foster different kinds of reading practices and reader identities. As Julie Rak writes, "bookstores have cultures, and they aim to encourage the production of certain kinds of reading subjects who want to read (and purchase) books."[12] A reader who buys a romance novel from Walmart is positioned in a different way, and forms different connections, compared to the reader who buys new literary fiction from a Waterstones chain, or a secondhand book from The Strand in New York—even though in practice, one individual reader might do all three.

Independently owned and run bookstores are romance-infused. They star in television series (e.g., the long-running UK show *Black Books*), movies (like Meg Ryan's charming New York children's bookstore "The Shop Around the Corner" in 1998's *You've Got Mail*), and novels (Eben Muse has identified 400 novels published since 2000 in which bookstores play a prominent role in the setting or plot).[13] IRL (in real life), independent bookstores can be beloved local institutions that build communities of readers. On the strength of its reputation as a booklovers store, Readings in Melbourne has expanded to a network of eight local stores. Like the Avid Reader bookshop in Brisbane, Gleebooks and Abbey Books in Sydney, and Muse in Canberra, Readings stores are prominent gathering points for local book launches and talks. In America, high-profile independent bookstores include the fabled Powell's in Seattle and The Strand in New York, and author-owned or co-owned bookshops such as Ann Patchett's Parnassus Books in Nashville, and Louise Erdrich's Birchbark Books in Minneapolis-St Paul (which features in her 2021 novel *The Sentence*).[14] Some independent bookstores specialize in a particular genre. Others adopt an activist stance, for example specializing in the works of queer authors (like Hares & Hyenas bookstore in Melbourne, and Little Sisters Book and Art Emporium in Vancouver) or Black authors. A 2023 *Guardian* article noted three recently opened bookstores in California owned by Black women that specialize in the works of writers of color. Octavia's Bookshelf in Pasadena received start-up capital from a crowdfunding campaign after the owner's tweet about wanting to open the bookstore went viral; the *Guardian* article describes the long queue of people waiting to visit the physical store on opening day, showing that even physical stores and their customers are post-digital, interacting online as well as on the ground.[15]

Networks that gather around independent bookstores, particularly bricks-and-mortar ones, participate in what Jessica Pressman calls "bookishness"—the celebration of print books in the midst of a digital age.[16] Customers of these stores align themselves with books as a cultural category, and they do more than make purchases. They receive advice, take in carefully curated displays, attend events, and converse. As Rak writes, "readers come to bookstores to get certain kinds of knowledge, to experience the physicality of a book in terms of its feel, look or smell, or even just to talk to or be with other people who like books."[17] Readers who are customers in independent bookstores attach themselves, weakly or strongly, to a community of like minded bookish people that includes other customers and booksellers. They also make a statement about capitalism by supporting a small business rather than a large corporation or a techno-giant. Affiliating with an independent bookstore is a confident statement that one has the identity of a reader, and imbues that identity with aesthetic, moral, and economic qualities.

Chain bookstores are an evolution of the independent bookstore, and their rise parallels that of the suburban shopping mall in the mid-twentieth century. As Laura J. Miller recounts, the emergence of chain bookstores, with their casual decor, clear signage, low shelves, and bright lighting, made shopping for a book less intimidating for those who don't feel part of an "in crowd."[18] While people who identify strongly with the identity of a reader may feel affinity with independent bookstores, those less confident in taking up that identity may find a chain bookstore a softer entry point to networks of reading. In contemporary book culture, notable chain bookstores include Japan's Kinokuniya, the UK's Waterstones, Barnes & Noble in the US, Chapters Indigo in Canada, and Dymocks in Australia.

Chain bookstores are more standardized in their presentation and their offerings than independent bookstores. Yet they still foster an idea of the reader as a customer with cultural aspirations, and of the bookstore as more than mere retail. In interviews with the staff of three high street chain bookstores in the UK, David Wright found that both workers and managers attributed "an almost evangelical aspect to the role of the bookshop worker, based in part on the belief in the inherent value of books and reading."[19] Bookshops are marked by "an association with a distinctive style of 'soft capitalism' in which the commodity exchange is merely the means to a more romantic end."[20] The connections between bookstore retail staff and customers evidence a sense of their shared construction of reading as a cultural practice. One worker described how, before taking up her position, she "thought I'd be like a customer who took money occasionally."[21] The line between worker and customer blurs; both are figured as operating outside of capitalism.

In the 1990s, big box bookstores such as Borders supersized the chain bookstore model. These were event bookstores that caused a stir when they launched, due to their huge product range as well as their in-store cafes and amenities. A few paragraphs ago, I mentioned the endearing children's bookstore in the film *You've Got Mail*; its proprietor, Kathleen Kelly (Meg Ryan), falls unwittingly for her nemesis, Joe Fox (Tom Hanks), of the soulless superstore Fox's Books that opens nearby. The big box superstore phenomenon was relatively short-lived, with Borders going into liquidation in 2011. The big box bookstores disappeared then in Australia too. Borders stores in Australia had previously been acquired by a company that also owned the Angus & Robertson bookstore chain, and when it crashed in 2011 Australia lost 20 percent of its bookstores, driving some customers to Amazon, and others to independents.[22] The loss of the superstores and some chains also underscored the fact that there are other places that aren't bookstores where people buy books.

At my local Kmart, the book section is tucked between pet toys and office supplies. There's not a lot of variety in the books on the shelves and in the bins—mostly genre fiction, kids' books, and a few recent bestsellers—and they are sold at a deep discount, sometimes for less than half their price at an independent bookstore. Discount department stores, like Kmart and Big W in Australia and Walmart in the United States, are less storied than independent bookstores, but they are also significant book retailers. At these stores, readers are configured as price-conscious consumers who pick up books at the same time as purchasing other household items.

To give an example of the way readers are imagined—or not imagined—as customers of discount department stores, we can consider a rare profile of Big W's book offerings in an Australian newspaper. The journalist Rosemary Neill pointed out that the discount department store retail channel exists outside "the nation's intelligentsia, especially the inner-city literati"; Big W outlets are not typically located in the inner-city locales where many publishing professionals live. One publisher interviewed for the article described Big W as "like a parallel universe," despite the fact that it sells more books than any other retail outlet in Australia, and that its principal book buyer, Meredith Drake, exercises a "startling degree of control" in the industry, including influence over some book cover designs and titles.[23] This depiction of Drake recalls Clayton Childress's account of the literary fiction buyer for Barnes & Noble's 600 US stores, who wields significant influence with publishers including over book cover designs. In Childress's account, this level of influence falls somewhere between independent book retailers, who are not powerful enough to make demands of publishers, and Amazon's arrangements, which are "closer to outright coercion."[24] For publishers, different channels of book retail may indeed feel like "parallel universes"; and readers too may imagine themselves very differently in these different networks. The independent bookstore customer who sees themselves as part of a reading community contrasts radically with the reader who puts a half-price bestseller in a trolley of discount store items and sees themselves as a reader in between their other roles. Identities shift; the one person may sometimes buy a book from one place and inhabit one network, and another day purchase books differently; or they may buy books for themselves one way and books as gifts another way; and so on.

Bricks-and-mortar stores, from Big W to the independents, are negotiated by readers in ways that are embodied. For example, Rak discusses the way readers move around a bookstore to find different genres; in one of the independent bookshops she studied, genres important to the customer base such as current affairs were put at the front of the shop, whereas more specialized genres such as science fiction and fantasy were shelved at the back of the store, because those customers know how to search for and find what they need.[25] Independent bookstores are more likely to follow their own classification systems, whereas a chain—the Canadian chain Chapters Indigo, in her study—is more likely to use signage that follows the standardized classifications that publishers print on the back cover of books. The very physicality of bricks and mortar bookstores shapes how readers circulate, position themselves, and form connections. A different set of movements and connections occurs when the retail experience takes place online.

Online book retailers are spaces where readers form connections. Readers make affiliations when they select an online store to buy from, as well as when they select what format of product to buy (ebook, audiobook, print book) and what other activity they might engage with online (such as leaving a review). Some online sites are digital shopfronts for physical, independent bookstores; this form of ordering became particularly important when Covid-19 restrictions forced many physical stores to temporarily close.[26] Other stores, such as Booktopia in Australia, are online only. The most dominant online book retailer, Amazon, began as an online store with an "ethos of bookishness," but has evolved into a general marketplace more akin to a discount department store—though with bookish corners.[27] Readers who buy ebooks on Amazon or elsewhere (or download them through their library) make decisions that, through file types or digital rights management agreements, link them into distinctive digital networks. Readers who buy print books through online retailers may do so because the prices are cheaper, for convenience, or because they do not have access to physical stores due to distance or limited mobility. Book Depository, for example, was launched in 2004 as an independent online book retailer, acquired by Amazon in 2011 and then closed by them in 2023—its distinctive offering was not only a wide range of titles, but the offer of free postage to customers in 170 different countries, a major incentive for readers for whom it would otherwise be costly to order print books.

Just as shopping at different bricks-and-mortar bookstores allows readers to form a view of their identity as a reader, so too does shopping online. Readers' identities are formed not only through choosing a store and a kind of product, but through the way that online store adjusts its presentation to each user. Readers encounter personalization algorithms that reflect them back to themselves. Online, stores can tailor their appearance and interactions to the user. As Brent Smith and Greg Linden, two of the designers of Amazon's recommendation algorithm, reflect:

> For two decades now, Amazon.com has been building a store for every customer. Each person who comes to Amazon.com sees it differently, because it's individually personalized based on their interests. It's as if you walked into a store and the shelves started rearranging themselves, with what you might want moving to the front, and what you're unlikely to be interested in shuffling further away.[28]

This is significant for understanding how readers form connections in book culture, because it shows an intermediary cultivating identity-formation for readers. Seeing themselves reflected through personalization algorithms, Amazon users may entrench their identities as particular kinds of reader-consumers: as romance readers, say, or fans of a particular author. They may be less likely to be startled or challenged by suggested books; that is, they may form fewer diverse connections with books, authors, and readers.

Readers can build networks and shape their identity by finding and interacting with one another through online book retail. Some connections are active and direct: leaving book reviews, or upvoting the reviews of others. At other times, readers are present to each other (and, indeed, to the store itself and to the public) in more ghostly form, as data. Readers are aggregated through features such as most read lists and average star ratings. Readers also shape the behavior of recommendation algorithms. Amazon's item-to-item collaborative filtering creates prompts such as "customers who viewed this item also viewed" and "frequently bought together"; these show readers the actions and choices others have made, and the connections these have created between books, and with other objects.[29] The exact recipe of an algorithm may be confidential, but the digital aggregations of reader conduct that an algorithm displays nonetheless offer new, and newly visible, ways for readers to affiliate with networks of reading.

The aggregation of reader behavior itself is not new, though. Most obviously, it is a feature of a key mechanism in book culture: the bestseller list. Bestseller lists make reader-consumers' choices visible. As Danielle Fuller and DeNel Rehberg Sedo point out, bestsellers are created by readers, but readers have a range of different reactions to books that are labeled as bestsellers.[30] The bestseller designation is a kind of aggregated word-of-mouth recommendation that will prompt some readers to read a book out of curiosity or confidence that there's something there to enjoy. Other readers will be suspicious of bestsellers, or even of the legitimacy of the term. Bestseller lists are certainly as much marketing devices as they are objective reports. As Rehberg Sedo and I have written, bestseller lists are not straightforward.[31] There are many different bestseller lists, and they use varied methods to gather sales data: some publications use Nielsen BookScan data, based on point of sale information from a range of outlets, but others (such as local newspapers that may not be able to afford a subscription to Nielsen BookScan) base their lists on a specific bookshop's weekly sales. When individual online and physical bookshops produce their own bestseller lists, they reveal connections made between their specific clientele and books.[32] Amazon's proliferating subgenres and microgenres each have their own bestseller rankings, allowing for a niche title to claim a spot as an Amazon Number 1 bestseller and revealing the passions and endorsements of invested fan communities. These different modes of data collection reflect different reader identities: either as a mass of consumers or as patrons of a specific bookshop or subgenre.

Bestseller lists have institutional properties that affect the flow of people and books in networks. There is a hierarchy of authority and prestige for bestseller lists, evident in publishers' promotional references to the most prominent ones, such as those published by the *New York Times* (which themselves sometimes contentiously divide or consolidate into more or fewer separate lists for genres and formats).[33] These industry-leading bestseller lists can be conservative, often including already-popular authors writing in already-popular genres, although, conversely, a breakout bestseller in a new subgenre or format can point to important shifts in reader practices.[34] Bestseller lists also tend to be either nationally bound or to reinforce global hierarchies, dominated in Anglophone markets by titles from the United States or the United Kingdom.[35] Bestseller lists reinforce particular kinds of connections between readers, authors, publishers, and institutions.

Book retail sites and mechanisms showcase readers in the act of forming connections via shopping and purchasing. Readers are configured in this economic matrix as data points, as disembodied sales. But they also act as browsers, and as conscious choosers of where to shop and how to buy. Readers interact with other readers, with staff, with platforms, and reflect on their own past practices and choices. Readers as consumers navigate commercial structures, from e-commerce to bestseller lists to aisle layouts, as they pursue their cultural practice.

Readers as Citizens: Navigating the Education System and Libraries

Other systems and structures that readers navigate as they form networks include those of the state. Since reading is taught and promoted through public institutions—schools, libraries, universities—readers are also fashioned through their engagements with those institutions. For public institutions, readers are present as data, just as they are when consumers, through various success metrics including measures of literacy. Readers also actively form connections with others through public institutions that affect how they use books in their lives. In these networks, readers tend to be figured as citizens, with literacy a foundational pillar of citizenship. A closer look at the education and library systems shows how this works.

While the focus of this book is on recreational reading practices, these are shaped by educational networks. In these networks, people take on the identity of reader-student, an important positioning that shapes how readers behave and interact in many other settings. Adult recreational reading is frequently framed as lifelong learning, in an echo of the educational system, and this understanding grounds aspects of the aesthetic conduct of reading (including the sense that one's life is influenced by books) discussed in Chapter 3, as well as being linked to reading's moral uses, such as the development of empathy discussed in Chapter 4. By cultivating the aesthetic and moral capabilities that will establish them as valued members of society, the student reader is also configured as a citizen.

In the education system, reading is foregrounded and explicit. Reading is both a means of acquiring knowledge about diverse subjects and a skill of its own that is taught. Reading is also not a neutral activity in the education system, but the subject of fierce contestation. In primary and secondary school systems, debates rage around the definition of literacy, and the best way to teach students how to read in order to produce both functional literacy, important for everyday living, and a love for books. Different models are pitted against one another—such as the distinctions educators draw between skills-based literacy tailored to high-stakes assessments, and therapeutic reading for personal development.[36] Much of the anxiety that drives these debates, as with debates about reading in general, is connected to digital technology (particularly multimedia storytelling), and there is a growing body of educational research on the effect of students reading on screens.[37] The ways that teachers present reading set students up to form various connections with books: as sacred objects or things to be dogeared and annotated, as "better" than other media formats (such as movie adaptations) or coexistent with them, and so on.

Different ways of teaching reading shape what reading means beyond school, because school is a highly influential period in people's lives. For many people, school may be the time when they read the books that they remember long afterward. Many "best books" polls, like the *New York Times*' Vote for the Best Book in 2021 and the BBC's The Big Read poll in 2003, produce results weighted toward books read in high school—syllabus favorite Harper Lee's 1960 novel *To Kill a Mockingbird* won the *New York Times* poll.[38] Debates about what texts are included in school curricula—canonical works, Shakespeare, national or local texts, texts that meet criteria of literary excellence, popular contemporary texts— have a deep significance because these syllabi establish the books that people connect to throughout their lives.

The education system creates readers, but it also allows the splitting of reading as an activity from the identity of "reader." That is, it enables people to read without seeing themselves as readers. A few years ago, I was at the pub on Grand Final Day (in Melbourne, this moniker refers to the Australian Football League and merits a public holiday). I asked two teenage girls, daughters of my partner's friend, what they were reading these days. "Oh, I don't read," said the older girl. Her stepmother said, "Come on, you do read! What about at school?" "Oh at school!" said the girl. "We're reading *Freedom Ride*." Because I am really fun at football parties, she and I then talked quite a lot about this book, a 2015 historical young adult novel by Sue Lawson about Indigenous Australian protests in the 1960s. The conversation brought home to me the extent to which reading is a subculture. A young person might or might not choose to identify as a reader, as "bookish"—an aesthetic choice I discuss in Chapter 3. Yet even for those who do not identify as readers, school is a place of exposure to books and reading experiences.

People in the education system form and do not form relations with books and book culture, and they experience power relations as part of this process. One of the features of the education system is that it is hierarchically organized, so that there are evident power relations between students and teachers, as well as in peer relationships among students and among teachers. Government agencies may set curriculum and assessment requirements, and the education system may transmit and replicate other social hierarchies, too.[39] In higher education, one line of tension is academics' struggle to ensure students "do the reading" for class. This is a functional literacy concern that can also, particularly in literary studies classrooms, include concern over the affective relationship between reading and students who report, to quote an article title by Anna Poletti et al., "hating characters, being bored, and feeling stupid."[40] As discussed in Chapter 1, theoretical debates, including varying emphases on affect or critical reading, affect the way reading is modeled and valued in literary studies classrooms. And just as in secondary schooling, there are debates in higher education about the canon, about what is read. Readers may form particular identities as readers of, say, modernist novels, or experimental poetry, or crime fiction and thrillers. Universities can be places where reading habits are explicitly remade.

Across the education system, then, there is a process of forming (or not forming) people into readers. Schools and universities are thus places where readers exist in transition and in relation to others, providing one starting point for the network-based study of readers proposed in Chapter 1. Questions that are prompted in relation to specific reader-learners would include what kind of institution they attend, the particular books they read, how they are taught to read them, and how they feel about those books and their reading. How do they use reading to negotiate relations with each other, with teachers, with the wider world? Do they post Goodreads reviews for school assignments (while using TikTok channels to talk about the books they *really* like?) Examples of such research include surveys of students, or participation observation in online book talk forums with teen readers.[41] But any research at all on readers will be grappling with the effects of educational institutions and the different relations to reading they produce.

The education system is an apparatus of the state; so too are libraries. Contemporary readers act here, borrowing books, reading books, and using spaces. Libraries have significant status as both cultural repositories and public institutions. The Library of Congress, British Library, Library and Archives Canada, National Library Singapore, and National Library of Australia all hold crucial places in their national cultures. Not only do they stand for the importance of reading and readers to public life, they interact with specific readers because they house important archives and collections, administer literary prizes, and host events. Such libraries figure readers as citizens.

This understanding of the reader-citizen filters from national libraries down to smaller, local, or context-specific libraries too. In Chapter 1, I discussed Oprah's Book Club as a prompt for much recent research on readers; Oprah Winfrey famously reflected that, for her as a child, "getting my library card was like citizenship, it was like American citizenship."[42] Smaller libraries have a public mission oriented to the practical needs of the people they serve. Local libraries, for example, are often community hubs, offering noncommercial spaces that include internet access, warm and dry places to rest, children's storytime, and other services alongside books that can be borrowed free of charge. And not just books: local libraries provide a diverse range of reading, listening, and viewing material. Recent moves to abolish late fines speak to libraries' desire to be even more accessible and welcoming spaces to members of the public.[43] Understood this way, libraries are also linked to self-improvement and informal education, historically an important role played by subscription and public libraries.[44] This commitment to accessibility and self-improvement also flows through the smaller libraries that may appear in other state institutions, such as prisons and community centers.

Readers appear as data points when looked at in relation to libraries, just as they do with the education system and book retail. Some historical research, for example, has focused on patron reading records, revealing individual borrowing patterns as well as popular books.[45] This is difficult as a method for understanding contemporary reading practices, as confidentiality requirements generally prevent academic use of borrowing records. However, libraries' lists of most-borrowed or most-requested books offer insights into reader actions in aggregated forms.[46] High-level patterns of use also reveal information about the uptake of ebooks and audiobooks, and about genre preferences as well as individual titles that are popular. Libraries, too, are involved in the commercial book market. Libraries are book buyers on behalf of readers: debates over how ebooks should be priced for libraries reveal the intersection between the networks of reader-citizens and reader-consumers, and the high prices paid by libraries for ebook licensing spotlight how publishers and technology companies' drive to profit disadvantages readers.[47] Yet the commercial battles engaged in by libraries are often in the background and not visible to patrons. In their public role, libraries relate to readers as community members—as citizens—rather than customers, and this shapes the practices that readers form when they visit or interact with these sites. This sense of community extends to the events and book clubs that libraries host, leading into the next section on the sociability of readers.

Reader-discussants: Participating in Book Talk in Person and Online

Readers form connections when they acquire books, when they learn to read, and also when they gather together by choice to discuss books. Such gathering may happen online or offline. Not every reader attends in person book-related events, but thousands do—and these readers move through a range of physical sites. Likewise, not every reader posts about their reading online, but many do, and many more encounter these posts across a range of digital platforms. Sociable book discussions are not usually situations where reading happens, but are rather reading-adjacent. They are opportunities for people to find suggestions for reading, or reflect upon and discuss the reading they have done. They provide information about what some readers read, how they read, who they connect with, and how they experience and enact forms of power. Book-related discussions have, and showcase, power relations, including those between organizers and attendees, between authors and readers, and among audience members. Reading events can be more or less institutionalized, more or less private, online, offline, or both. Here, I'll look at three formations in turn, starting with book clubs.

Book clubs are places where readers talk; where people are encouraged to identify, through their talk, as readers. They have been an important locus of shared reading for hundreds of years, gaining new prominence in the late 1990s and early 2000s due to the phenomenal success of Oprah's Book Club, and continuing today in both face-to-face and digital forms. Book clubs, both now and historically, are often linked to organizations, including libraries, adult education institutions, and bookshops.[48] Even book clubs with an institutional connection, though, are challenging to research because of their informality and privacy. It is impossible to definitively count how many book clubs there are, or how many people participate. Studies in the early 2000s suggested hundreds of thousands of book clubs across the Anglophone world, mostly attended by middle-class women. More recently, a 2019 newspaper article highlighted the vibrancy of book clubs meeting in Indonesia.[49]

What relations do readers in book clubs form? How are book club members situated in relation to each other, to institutions, to publishers and authors, to researchers? Academics have treated them and their links to broader book culture seriously. In an extensive study of contemporary book clubs in Houston, among other insights Elizabeth Long highlights the meaningful, long-term links book club members form with one another through their practices, as well as their connections to other institutions including local bookstores.[50] To select the books they read, book clubs often draw on the recommendations of booksellers, literary critics, libraries, and other institutions. Readers in book clubs have relations to the publishing industry too: for example, publishers market to them directly through book club guides included at the back of novels and through publisher websites.[51] Yet in popular culture, book clubs are often dismissed, not least because they are associated with women.[52] Readers in book clubs thus need to position themselves and articulate the value of their activity to outsiders.

Book clubs lend themselves to in-depth qualitative study; from a researcher's perspective, individual book clubs are almost like a ready-made focus group for learning about reader practices. Book clubs can be studied with varying degrees of researcher involvement, from creating the group, to choosing the text, to participating in the session, to recording it, to interviewing participants afterward.[53] Each intervention has its impacts on the group, and allows different research questions to be explored. Creating book clubs specifically for research is something I have done as part of a team led out of a medical school researching the role of book clubs in fostering well-being. I facilitated one of three book clubs that ran for nine weeks in a local library, in a project that closely controlled what was read and how the discussion was led, and was explicit about some of the power relations in play. I analyze the dynamics of this particular Reading and Writing for Wellbeing group in later chapters of this book. One of the attractions of in person book clubs, for researchers, is the interpersonal relations and practices they model: as Long emphasizes, these include practices of self-formation, often over many years, but they also include the kinds of aesthetic and moral conduct that I elaborate further in subsequent chapters.[54] At the heart of in-person book clubs is a distinctive network enacted through the discussion of reading with known others.

In addition to existing as physical formations, book clubs are also dispersed across media. The increased attention they gained at the turn of the century was partly because Oprah's Book Club was a mass media phenomenon, run initially through television and supplemented in *O Magazine* and online. Book clubs now run on social media platforms, including Twitter, YouTube, and Instagram.[55] There have been several studies of the cultural and commercial impact of mass-media book clubs led by celebrities, from YouTube star Zoella to film mogul Reese Witherspoon.[56] There is less research to date on the members of these clubs, who may be difficult to identify if they interact with the club sporadically, pseudonymously, or relatively passively. Compared to face-to-face book clubs, mediated book clubs create looser networks. Because their members act in many ways like audiences, these large-scale mediated book clubs are perhaps better understood, as Fuller and Rehberg Sedo do, as mass reading events.[57]

Reading events are another way in which readers form networks through discussing books. People take on the identity of readers through their participation in book launches, author talks, and literary festivals. These events tend to be concentrated in metropolitan centers, although there are regional events too, some of which are marketed to locals, and others to tourists.[58] Not only marketing, but the choice of venues affects who feels welcome and able to connect. Some book event organizers work hard to take events outside of traditional places where reading happens; Fuller and Rehberg Sedo note One Book One City events held at pubs, bus tours, ice skating rinks, and laneways.[59] Increasingly, book-related events also happen online. This may happen in parallel with in-person events, through techniques such as livestreaming or live tweeting.[60] Other literary events may be digital only; this became particularly important during the restrictions of the Covid-19 pandemic.

Within the physical and digital spaces of an event, individuals take on various positions: author, reader, moderator, audience member, publicist, arts worker, volunteer. These roles affect each attendee's experience, and its interaction with their reading practices. Publicists and volunteers may see the behind-the-scenes anxiety of a presenting author; authors may feel jittery; audience members may be charmed by an author's charisma and rush to buy their books after the session. Even though they don't usually have speaking roles, audiences are not passive, whether they are on their phones checking messages or tweeting, napping, or gearing themselves up to ask a question at the end of the session. Further, audiences can also include members who have other positions in the arts and play a more explicitly active role at other times.[61] To explore some of these connections and practices in more detail, I want to offer a small case study based on the Melbourne Writers Festival.

Case Study: Forms of Connection and Power in the Audience of the Melbourne Writers Festival

I conducted interviews with attendees at the Melbourne Writers Festival in 2014, a time when social media was in full swing but before the rapidly increased use of Zoom and livestreaming prompted by the Covid-19 pandemic shifted audience expectations and appreciation for in-person events.[62] My interviewees traced the connections they formed as readers and the power relations they experienced at the festival.

During an author talk, the author and moderator hold more power than the audience: this is visually represented through the stage, which situates authors and panel chairs in front of and often above the audience. In my interviews, readers articulated respect for authors. Raelene, a White woman in her sixties, told me:

> The thing that I like about the writers festival is actually the writers themselves. Because I don't regard myself as a high, an intellect, a literate person, so I admire writers greatly because I think it's a hard art, so people who are successful I sort of have them up on a pedestal. I found what attracted me was getting to know the people who were behind the books. So it's a matter of seeing who's there and going to those things. Often I would choose authors I had no idea who they were or what they'd written. I didn't necessarily go to see authors I already knew.

Raelene admires authors as a category, rather than particular authors. She uses the program and a deliberate strategy of serendipity in order to form connections between herself and authors, a process of network building that is supported through the festival.

Given the mediated distance and the power relation between readers and authors, readers can feel thrilled when acknowledged by writers, including over social media. Another of my interviewees, Victoria, described herself as shy but nonetheless created an opportunity to interact with an author over social media:

> it was really exciting because I tweeted a photo from the Tara Moss session on the last day, and she retweeted it, or she favourited it, and I was like Oh my god! And I'm sure it could have just been her publicist or something ... but I got pretty excited about that ... because I didn't ask a question during the session

but I really enjoyed the session … I just put that out there and for that response to happen, it was really, just I don't know what to call it, satisfying or reassuring or, it put a spring in my step maybe. It was just nice.

Victoria is aware of the industrial context of her parasocial digital interaction with an author following the festival session; she knows that a publicist or someone else may be tweeting on the author's behalf. Yet she still experiences a validating, energizing emotional boost as a direct result of her initiative in making a connection between herself and the author. This connection also strengthens bonds between Victoria, the festival, Twitter, and Twitter users who follow Victoria or the author.

Another situation where readers can take initiative is during the question and answer time that follows a talk, during which the event's power relations can be reconfigured or even upended. In some circumstances, this power flip creates discomfort, anxiety, or distress for authors—as when hostile questions are directed by White audience members toward authors of color.[63] In other situations, the power flip has positive effects. Audience member Ann told me about a time when she used a question to redirect a session so that it created the connection with an author she was looking for. Ann had been alienated by a series of questions about writing technique, saying:

> the whole thing about getting up at 7.30 and just sitting at a desk or wherever you get ideas … it's not that I'm *not* interested in it, but, I'm much more interested in the other stories, the life stories … so I asked a question about what [the author was] reading … and it was really fascinating cause this woman from America who I hadn't known before … she'd just finished the Patrick Melrose … and that was *my* discovery from last year.

Ann opens up the question of "who is a reader," showing the instability of this identity by drawing the author into the category of reader. She is delighted when the connection of shared reading (of English author Edward St Aubyn's series about Patrick Melrose) unites the visiting American writer with a member of her Australian audience. Ann used her agency as an audience member to demonstrate the importance of reading to her, and to add to her stock of meaning-making information about reading via forming a connection with another reader, who was an author. She thereby legitimated her reading practice and extended her network. The act of sharing this anecdote with me, an academic researching literary festivals, further extended this network and bolstered its importance.

My interviews also show how readers use festivals as a prompt to connect with friends and family. One of my interviewees told me that she "got into going to festivals with my mum"; another read the program with his friend and when he saw the keynote, "I said to my friend, right, we're going to that." One interviewee who was new to Australia hadn't been able to interest any of her friends in going along with her. In contrast, Carol has long-standing friendships that are built around festival attendance. She told me, "I go with a very good friend, a woman I met as a student social worker 35 years ago, so it's very much within the context of that friendship that we go. We occasionally take other people. We're a bit sort of tragics for the old writers festival. It's a really nice thing to share."

Carol often bumps into people she knows at the writers festival: "there is this really linking thing that happens." Ann described the way that each year she would run "a little bit of a campaign," going through the program and thinking of friends who would enjoy different sessions. She said, "I try and use it as an opportunity to have a special experience with different friends." A group of Victoria's friends, who she describes as "not really that into reading," bought her festival tickets as a birthday present, and she tweeted pictures of the sessions she attended as a way of showing them her appreciation—she thus tweets not only to connect with authors, as in the earlier example, but also to connect with her non-festival-attending friends. These various mechanisms for connecting show the multifaceted capacity of the literary festival to enhance existing relationships and build new ones with family, friends, and coworkers.

While being at a writers festival can expand a reader's network, there is also a tendency toward homogenization that can limit that network's diversity. This tendency is observable in the demographic attributes of those who participate, and also in expressions of a shared, special quality of experience among attendees who are all attached to books and reading. Ann told me that, while she wished "we weren't all so female and old," "it is such a lovely, lovely sense of we're all—these are my people—people who enjoy this world." Phyllis said, "I go along and I think, I have something in common with all of these people." Similarly, Hayley observed that "Even people that you haven't met before, you know that they're interested in literature and books and stuff and so you can always strike up a conversation quite easily." Victoria said, "everyone's there because they love books and writing and it definitely is a nice community" and "you all have a similar sympathy to a lot of ideas and things and that feels nice, it's like a warm blanket or something I think." Miranda said simply, "these are my people!" Ayu, who volunteered with the festival as well as attending events, said, "people will come up to the box office and they'll say 'Oh, are you going to see that as well?' and then they'll just start talking and it's quite beautiful." Carol has also observed a distinctive atmosphere at the Melbourne Writers Festival, "There's a, not elitist, but just a certain kind of … not sophistication even … just a certain calm reflectiveness about the Melbourne one." These observations of a shared sensibility highlight the special quality of belonging experienced in this community, and touch on the fact that this quality is founded on homogeneity.

Social media can reinforce the sense of a festival's strongly bonded community. In recent years, Miranda has live-tweeted festival sessions when she attends on her own, and says "I felt like I met a lot of people through that." She said, "you see tweets from the same people, you follow people, and you build your community that way … it's also been so nice since then, because now my Twitter feed's filled with those people, so when they go to festivals or they're tweeting about books they've read, there's that connection." Twitter is public space, but it can sometimes feel to readers like a smaller, cozy community.

So a feature of the connections formed by readers at literary festivals is that they have felt limits; there is an exclusivity to the network. Victoria said to me, "when the presenters make the kinds of jokes about that literary lifestyle, whether you're a writer or a reader or you just enjoy engaging with those ideas, there's a lot of in jokes." Phyllis had noticed the program expanding in recent years to attract more diverse audiences, and said, "I think that's a good thing even if it means the intimacy might be less." The tension between exclusivity and openness generates a particular quality of experience, as readers both celebrate their similarity to one another, and feel that they should be more inclusive.

The special feeling of book festivals is partly linked to the fact that they operate (to some extent) outside the networks of everyday experience. Raelene called the Melbourne Writers Festival "a tonic" and "a chance to escape really, it's a world I don't know much about, so it was like going on a little bit of a holiday and dipping in." But readers also use these events to recharge, reconsider, and refresh connections elsewhere in their lives. For Penny, a good festival session is "one of those things where you walk out and you're really inspired about writing and life and the rest of it." Book festivals can change readers' perspectives on the rest of life, so that the connections formed have a larger sense of purpose and potentially outward-reaching effects. As Carol said, "The reflection in literature actually opens you up to the fact that it's not just you, that it's a shared human condition and, for me that's what literature is." This sense of being connected to something bigger feeds into the moral aspects of festivals discussed in Chapter 4. It also encapsulates the fact that the festival is valued as a catalyst for the formation of bonds in networks of readers, where readers create an identity for themselves as discussants and participants in a community that cares about books, reading, and ideas.

The Intricate, Visible Networks of Reader-discussants Online

Just like book clubs, events and festivals in the twenty-first century are not only in-person occasions but also spill over, or take place entirely, online. There, they become a subset of online book talk. Online book talk is more than an adjunct to physical events. It is also more than product reviews, although it interacts with commercial activities. Rather, online book talk is a sprawling phenomenon that exceeds these structures and produces networks of its own in which readers are constructed as discussants. As Bronwen Thomas writes in *Literature and*

Social Media, "literary accounts on social media offer users the opportunity to participate, whether that is by commenting, retweeting or simply liking posts."[64] Digital platforms and networks configure the reader as someone who converses about books and book culture.

Online book talk is a reader practice that has been accessible since the late 1990s, when the wider public started using the internet, and has some formal continuities with earlier forms of sharing reading experiences, such as fanzines and book clubs. As noted in Chapter 1, readers have long written about their reading: in diaries, for example, or in personal correspondence, or as marginalia in books. Such traces have been important to scholars of historical reading practices. To illuminate present reading practices, or at least those of the very recent past, we can look to online traces, where people write, record videos, or share photographs about their reading. Readers' online book talk is not just a record of reading practices, but can also intervene in the commerce of the publishing industry through its interface with marketing, or in the domain of professional reviewing as a form of democratized cultural criticism.

Readers move with technology. The networks of online book talk can be historicized, as platforms and sites emerge, surge in popularity, or fade. Readers may be on Twitter, responding to new book releases, prize announcements, or participating in Twitter-based book clubs. They may be on Facebook, commenting on official pages for authors, bookshops, or reading events. They may post and collect pictures of books on Instagram and Pinterest. Readers may participate in online discussion forums, including email lists and list-servs, Google and Yahoo groups, and Reddit threads. They may comment on articles about books from news media sources, such as the *Guardian*. They may run dedicated book blogs, bookish YouTube channels, or podcasts. They may provide content for crowdsourcing book-related platforms such as Project Gutenburg and Librivox, or engage with publisher- or author-controlled websites.[65] They may make collections and lists and leave reviews on LibraryThing, Goodreads, or Amazon. They may write and comment on fanfiction and original fiction on Wattpad, Raddish, or other creative writing platforms.[66]

On each of these platforms, readers articulate their reading: via text, image, video, or audio. That is, these are sites that are about performances of reading, or reflections on reading. This is "writerly" reading behavior. But readers may also participate as quieter discussants, observers of other readers or of authors. These "listening" practices are harder to trace, but constitute an important component of contemporary reading culture, as—through their constant implied as well as actual presence—listeners as well as speakers shape the networks of book talk online.

An individual reader may be most loyal to and invested in one online site. Other readers might cross platforms regularly, and participate in several at once. In her research on online reader responses to contemporary Nigerian novels, Hannah Pardey found a consistency across YouTube, Goodreads, Amazon reviews, and blogs in the language readers used to describe their emotional responses, and in how they linked that emotion to story and character.[67] This shows that there is a consistent vernacular to online book talk. Furthermore, when controversies erupt, they tend to draw in multiple online platforms. It is also important, though, to consider platforms separately. Different sites have different modes, norms, and reputations that affect the relationships and practices of the readers who use them. As José van Dijck has elaborated, media platforms are shaped by their particular organizational structures, governance processes, and business models, and Claire Parnell has shown this at work on Amazon and on Wattpad.[68] Each platform offers distinctive ways for readers to connect to books, describe those connections, and co-constitute relations with publishers, other readers, books, and technology companies. Power is part of each platform; between the user and platform (as enacted through terms and conditions of participation, and through moderation practices), between readers and authors (enacted through behavioral norms and etiquette), and among readers themselves. Even within individual sites, varying networks form: for example, discussion of young adult fiction might be more emotive than discussion of canonical classic texts.[69] With respect to relations among readers online, I have written about "readerly capital" as a term that encompasses the skill and influence exercised by readers who negotiate these online platforms, and which readers possess in different amounts. I have also described some readers (such as leading book bloggers) as "super readers" who are highly influential, with long, strong connections to other actors in networks.[70] These status levels affect the nature of the book talk that happens on each platform, and can also travel with readers across platforms: a book blogger might also be a popular Goodreads reviewer, for example.

Mini Case Study: Goodreads

Over the course of this book, I look closely at a number of digital platforms that readers use, from Instagram to TikTok. Here, I want to consider how readers use a site specifically created for them: Goodreads. There are other reader-dedicated platforms—StoryGraph, for example, founded by Nadia Odunayo in 2019, has a growing fanbase that appreciates its uncluttered interface and effective recommendation algorithms. But Goodreads remains significant, not only as one of the earliest dedicated sites for booklovers, but also because of its industry heft since being acquired by Amazon in 2013. Goodreads was started by a couple, Otis and Elizabeth Chandler, as a way for readers to share their book collections and reviews. When they sold it to Amazon, Goodreads became deeply intertwined with the commercial operations of the book industry in addition to providing a social function for readers. Goodreads and Amazon remain functionally separate sites (although Kindle users are prompted to rate their ebooks on Goodreads at the end of each ebook). However, as a social network where readers follow one another and read each other's reviews, Goodreads complements the recommendation model of Amazon's algorithm-driven purchasing suggestions.[71] Scholars have strong critiques of Goodreads and its role in the book culture ecosystem.[72] Lisa Nakamura, for example, suggests that Goodreads users "are both collecting and being collected under a new regime of controlled consumerism," and that "the tight integration of readerly community with commerce is an absolute given."[73]

While Goodreads does not currently publish data on its usage, as of 2019 it had 90 million members and over 98 million reviews, and a *Washington Post* article in 2021 reported it as having 120 million users—a significant number, though the site is obviously not used by all readers.[74] Most Goodreads users are women.[75] Most come from the United States, and Quantcast reported in 2020 that 77 percent of Goodreads users are Caucasian.[76] Goodreads is a complicated, busy site, with multiple points of attachment for readers, such as creating virtual bookshelves, joining reading groups, and participating in reading challenges. The practice of tagging is one of particular significance. Social tagging creates meaningful "folksonomies" through which people communicate with one another.[77] On Goodreads, tags might be used to attach books to virtual "shelves" or collections, such as "classics" or "DNF" (did not finish). These tagging practices are highly revealing of the relations readers form with books, as well as being a way to communicate with other readers. Tags do not always align with institutional or academic understandings of books; Melanie Walsh and Maria Antonak have shown, for example, that Goodreads users who use the tag "classics" have a more restricted view of what constitutes a classic than school syllabi.[78]

The most detailed Goodreads user reflections on books are usually found in reviews, where readers articulate most legibly the meaning that individual books and authors hold for them. In research with DeNel Rehberg Sedo that analyzed several hundred Goodreads reviews, we showed that most reviews described the experience of reading as well as giving an evaluation of the book; that emotion is prominent in reviews; and that many reviews explicitly or implicitly addressed fellow readers.[79] Goodreads shows readers as discussants expanding their roles in the digital era, shading into and perhaps taking over the functions of other cultural figures.[80] The site demonstrates a shift in power whereby readers now have capacity to influence the publishing industry and book culture through their reviewing and rating practices. As a site that explicitly privileges readers rather than writers, Goodreads repositions the relationship between these two groups. It can look like disintermediation: an author might visit Goodreads to see firsthand what readers think of their book (though authors often warn each other not to do this!). But despite the apparent directness, this is a relationship that has been not disintermediated but reintermediated, routed through the technological affordances of Goodreads and shaped by the commercial imperatives of Amazon. Goodreads is an exemplary site for showing how readers are configured as discussants online, in a network where they negotiate the surveillance mechanisms of contemporary techno-capitalism to find ways of connecting meaningfully with books and each other.

Conclusion: The Networks That Readers Form

It may seem that readers are everywhere and nowhere, but they cluster around specific institutions and platforms where they create and activate networks. In this chapter, I've shown readers in the process of enacting their identities as readers by forming networks, connecting and disconnecting from different people, organizations, and books. I've sketched a number of scenes where this network formation takes place, and which inflect how readers act. First, reader-consumers interact with bookstores of different kinds, online and offline, where they provide sales data, relate to staff or algorithms, move around sites or buildings, talk to or read words by other readers, and form images of themselves and their role in the industry of book publishing and selling. Second, reader-citizens are fashioned through the education system, where they learn how to read but also how to be a reader, which they may or may not choose to do, and then through state institutions such as libraries and festivals that emphasize the importance of the reader as a member of society. Most broadly, reader-discussants, perhaps one of the most common kinds of identity within networks, are configured at sites from book clubs, to festivals, to online. Here, readers work actively to connect with others—and it is in this mode that readers are most vocal in expressing their views.

The networks I've traced here all show the foundational act readers engage in, of making connections: with books, with companies, with organizations, with institutions, with platforms, with authors, with each other, and more. As readers inhabit and traverse the networks they form, they engage in practices that stress-test these connections, reinforcing or weakening them. These practices have both aesthetic and moral aspects, and it is these multiple, multi-faceted, significant aesthetic and moral contemporary reader practices that I go on to investigate in the following chapters. The next chapter, Chapter 3, focuses on how readers in networks engage in aesthetic conduct, using books as models to find their style and understand the shape of their lives.

3 THE AESTHETIC CONDUCT OF READERS

A reader enjoys a book, becoming immersed in its imagined world—or maybe the reader can't stand the book and just wants to finish it. They blissfully inhale the scent of their paperback, caress an embossed hardcover, or raise their eyebrows at the accent of an audiobook's narrator. The reader is bored by the story, but adores the language. Later, they might talk about the book with other people; they might post about it on social media; they might keep it or give it away. Then they choose what to read next.

In this chapter, I show how these actions constitute aesthetic conduct. Contemporary readers experience and express their appreciation or dislike of books, and use those judgments to bring form to their lives, fashioning an identity and way of being in the world. In describing this conduct as aesthetic, I draw upon two key principles from the vast body of scholarly inquiry into aesthetics: first, aesthetic conduct is an activity of the perceiver, and second, aesthetic conduct is socially performed. I contend that contemporary readers' aesthetic conduct is active and it is embedded in networks as an extended process that readers perform to themselves and others. Readers use their aesthetic conduct to navigate institutions, the publishing industry, technology, and their own interiority by making links between their reading and their lives.

This chapter begins by reviewing these aesthetic principles as they relate to contemporary book culture, including through the mode of bookishness. I then analyze three different sites where readers carry out aesthetic conduct. First, I consider the conduct traced by and through bibliomemoirs, which are book-length accounts of reading. I then look at Bookstagrammers and other readers on social media who engage in aesthetic conduct by creating audiovisual and textual content about books. Finally, I turn to a specific book club that I co-facilitated, the Reading and Writing for Wellbeing group, as a site for relatively subtle forms of aesthetic expression. I ask: What aesthetic choices do memoirists, Bookstagrammers, book club members make when they select a book, acquire it, read it, think about it, talk about it? How do people construct a reading brand or style? How do they present their reading as a model for life? And how does this aesthetic conduct express aspects of what reading means, today?

Aesthetics Is Something You Do

In his influential *Critique of the Power of Judgement* (1790), Kant argues that aesthetic judgment is an active process.[1] The activity of aesthetic judgment is divided by Kant into different kinds. One is based on sensory experience and lies in the feeling of pleasure or displeasure. Another, more complex, kind entails reflection, and is thought before felt. It makes use of the higher faculty of cognition and involves an interplay between imagination and understanding to produce a harmonious effect. Positive reflecting aesthetic judgments occur when the perceiver feels a sense of relation between an object and all of nature—between a particular instance and implied universals—which provides a moment of relief in the search to see life as made up of interconnected experiences.[2]

Aesthetic judgment, for Kant, is a human faculty alongside cognition and will. There is no aesthetic quality inherent to objects, only aesthetic conduct, which is (in Christine Ross's gloss) "a cognitive activity of discernment whose unfolding provides affects of (dis)pleasure."[3] This approach to aesthetics is aligned broadly with pragmatism, in that it is centered on the way a person makes aesthetic use of a stimulus. Pragmatic thinking about aesthetics is evident, for example, in recent work in the field of cultural sociology. Antoine Hennion writes that "people are active and productive; they constantly transform objects and works, performances, and tastes," eschewing a view of the amateur (i.e., the person interacting with culture) as passive.[4]

The different kinds of aesthetic judgments are performed by readers as they match their sensory and intellectual engagement with specific books to the world. Considering aesthetics as an activity of readers rather than a property of books was one of the key principles of reader-response theorists. Louise Rosenblatt significantly reoriented the object of aesthetic analysis in literary studies from the text to the reader. She writes,

> It would be less confusing to use the reading act itself [rather than the "art object"] as the general paradigm of the aesthetic experience; it would then become clear that the "object" of aesthetic contemplation is what the perceiver makes of his responses to the artistic stimulus, no matter whether this be a physical object, such as a statue, or a set of verbal signs.[5]

To understand aesthetic experience, that is, look to the reader and their attitude. Rosenblatt acknowledges that this attitude might change by the moment and in relation to context. She distinguishes, for example, between efferent reading—done for information—and aesthetic reading, done for its own sake.[6] In aesthetic reading, "the reader's primary concern is with what happens *during* the actual reading event"; "the reader's attention is centred directly on what he is living through during his relationship with that particular text."[7] The text remains important, as some texts "will yield a greater reward for his attention than others."[8]

The aesthetic moment of reading identified by Rosenblatt can be extended to consider how readers use books in their wider lives. Marielle Macé's essay "Ways of Reading, Modes of Being," which uses the specific phrase "reading as aesthetic conduct," describes reading as a process of being "powerfully drawn towards different possibilities and promises of existence."[9] For Macé, reading literature is a profoundly individuating activity, allowing the reader to construct a personal style, a way of being in the world. There is a resonance, here, with how many contemporary readers and writers see books. The French author of quasi-autobiographical books, Constance Debré, for example, spoke in a 2023 interview about trying to give life shape: "That's why life and literature are so connected: it's the quest for form."[10] Reading provides narrative shapes and models that readers can use as templates for understanding their lives: through language, through plot, through genre conventions. Macé writes that "reading is not a separate activity, functioning in competition with life, but one of the daily means by which we give our existence form, flavour, even style."[11] This sentence is quoted by Rita Felski in *The Limits of Critique*, where she also refers to Macé's writing about how snatches of the books we read make their way into our daily lives.[12] As Jean-Francois Hamel has argued, this view of reading is part of a "pragmatist turn" in literary studies, which he links to William James, that emphasizes connections between art and experience.[13]

And yet, for Hamel, Macé remains "tied to a romantic conception of literature that tends to disregard the social and historical diversity of its representations and uses."[14] Macé's scope is narrow because she focuses on high culture and its transformative effects. This aligns more with literary criticism, and its modeling of aesthetic judgment, than with book history and allied disciplines that highlight the ordinariness of texts as they circulate in people's lives, as well as, as Nan Z. Da has pointed out, the contingency and unpredictability of interactions between books and people.[15] Hamel suggests that Macé is really writing about how *writers* read.[16] This re-produces a hierarchical model of the professional writer or critic as the exceptional "good reader," as opposed to the everyday "bad reader," a framework prominent in twentieth-century discourse, as I discuss in Chapter 1.[17] Fully understanding aesthetics as active means paying attention to a wide range of responses to a wide range of books. Readers aren't only transfigured by great literature; they're sometimes pissed off by a thriller, or charmed by a romance.

A broader view of readers' active aesthetic conduct would embrace not only more kinds of books, but multiple reactions to books: negative emotions such as dislike, low-key states such as boredom, positive affects of delight, and intense experiences of personal transformation.[18] Responses have different qualities, and they also have different strengths. Kant focuses on strong aesthetic judgments, most famously of the beautiful (formally pleasing) and the sublime. In contrast, Sianne Ngai in *Our Aesthetic Categories* (2015) explores weaker aesthetic judgments—the categories of the cute, the zany, and the interesting—arguing that these colloquial terms designate non-cathartic responses that occur as part of, and are symptomatic of the conditions of, late capitalism.[19] Minor affect is undoubtedly part of the suite of aesthetic responses people have to books. At the same time, I suggest (and the examples presented in the rest of the chapter indicate) that the symbolic weight books continue to carry in contemporary culture makes them less likely than other cultural products to be described by nonacademic readers as cute, zany, or interesting. If readers make the choice to articulate their opinion of a book—rather than let it pass through their lives without comment—they tend to describe a strong aesthetic judgment, especially on social media (which tends to amplify emotion). They love a book or they hate it. This is the case even, or perhaps especially, when the books readers respond to are mass-market fiction, such as romance or young adult bestsellers. The beautiful and the sublime continue to be powerful organizing principles in contemporary book culture aesthetics, as readers look for intense, satisfying experiences. Alongside or as part of this search, readers might feel a host of more minor aesthetic sensations, from irritation and boredom to amusement and confusion. Experiencing and expressing a range of reactions to different books is what readers do: the pragmatic concept of aesthetics as an activity of the perceiver is key to understanding the practices of contemporary readers.

Aesthetic Judgments Are Socially Performed

For Kant, aesthetic judgments involve the subjective perception of form, but they are also embedded in social relations; aesthetic judgments are "subjective universal" judgments that appeal to a community of taste. They make a claim of necessity—not that everyone does make the same judgments, but that they should.[20] So aesthetic conduct is not only active, but social.

Sociologists, including notably Pierre Bourdieu, amplify the role of society in aesthetic judgment. In *Distinction*, Bourdieu presents aesthetic judgments as the product of habitus: embodied cultural dispositions and acquired cultural capital. This approach takes account of the influence of social structures, such as family and education, on people's aesthetic judgments.[21] Bourdieu argues that what is deemed beautiful is what corresponds to the taste of a society's dominant class.[22]

Frequently, the aesthetic conduct of contemporary readers is described in terms of tastes, and these tastes are seen as shaped by social structures, by demographic categories. This happens in research, but it happens in everyday book talk too, where tastes in books are pegged as aligning with or rebelling against what "society" deems valuable. As I have written elsewhere, for example, book blogs often cluster around a kind of fiction such as romance or experimental literary fiction and therefore model taste-based reading.[23] Some of these tastes are framed as guilty pleasures, responding to a broader media context in which messages are sent about the validity of different aesthetic preferences. I wrote in Chapter 1 of the unfortunate phrase "pink-jacketed goo" to describe romance fiction; similarly, a 2023 article in the *Economist* offered the backhanded compliment that with the rise in romance fiction's popularity on TikTok, "bookshops no longer stash books with pink covers at the back of shops but put them on tables near the tills; publishers are learning to brave the word 'heartwarming' without embarrassment."[24] Against such bald dismissals, it is no wonder that romance fiction bloggers defend their reading tastes. Sometimes, cues about the tastes of dominant cultural mediators are more subtle, occurring parenthetically or in a clause at the end of a sentence. Once, I sat in the room while a literary prize was awarded. The citation read out for the winning book described it as "never sentimental"; a compliment that implicitly criticized genres of books (such as romance and family sagas) that are described as sentimental, and that not coincidentally are associated with women readers. Readers' aesthetic conduct can involve standing up for maligned tastes. It can also involve attachments to niche genres, categories or styles of writing. Felski, for example, describes reading for shock as an aesthetic mode—"a reaction to what is startling, painful, even horrifying"—that is aligned with the avant-garde; "its aesthetic is modeled on the shout, the electric shock, the wailing scream of sirens on city streets."[25] Aesthetic conduct as preference for a kind of writing is a way readers find like-minded people, and distinguish themselves from others.

Expression of taste is one way of understanding the social performance of contemporary readers' aesthetic conduct. However, Bourdieu's schema in *Distinction*, and similar frames of reference both within and outside academia, arguably overemphasize the social construction of taste to the point where that first principle, the activity of the perceiver, is neglected. Such models are overly static and locked into demographic classifications. More fine-grained approaches consider how taste is dynamically modified through social interactions. Ian Woodward and Michael Emmison, for example, built on Bourdieu's work through a survey that asked participants to define good and bad taste, and found that people often linked taste with the need to manage interpersonal relationships.[26] In *Understanding Cultural Taste* (2015), David Wright breaks down the concept of taste to show that it encompasses *sensation*, a primary sensory experience of the world; *sensibility*, "an orientation towards and away from" things and people in the material world; and *skill*, "a capacity that can be cultivated as people learn how to make judgements and choices within and between these things and people."[27] These shades of meaning show both the personal and the social elements that take place in developing and expressing taste.

Similarly, Hennion's dynamic approach to taste highlights cultural participants' "capacity to transform sensibilities and create new ones, and not only to reproduce an existing order without acknowledging it."[28] Performances of taste are activities in their own right. As Hennion writes,

> When one says that one loves opera or rock—and what one likes, how one likes it, why, etc.—this is already a way of liking it more, and vice-versa … Tasting does not mean signing one's social identity, labelling oneself as fitting into a particular role, observing a rite, or passively reading the properties "contained" in a product as best one can. It is a performance: it acts, engages, transforms and is felt.[29]

Individual aesthetic conduct is modulated through interactions with other people. Aesthetic judgments are susceptible to the influence of these others, particularly members of a group to which a person belongs. In her study of an art group, Hannah Wohl draws on Hannah Arendt's notion of "community sense" to argue that aesthetic judgments are key to group cohesion.[30] She writes that "as individuals assert agreements or disagreements in aesthetic judgments deemed relevant to group identification, their feelings of group belonging are powerfully confirmed or denied," suggesting this is particularly potent due to the capacity for artworks to communicate shared social reality and produce strong emotions.[31]

Seeing aesthetic conduct as socially performed takes an interior process and gives it a network. This is a broader account of readers' aesthetic conduct than that offered by Macé, who Hamel notes presents "a paradoxical privatization of the reading experience," envisioning a reader who is "'hungry for intimacy and self-esteem' as if literary texts were never more than a pretext to withdraw from public space to test one's own style."[32] Framing aesthetic conduct as a withdrawal from community in order to define individuality means ignoring the social aspects of aesthetic conduct—what Hamel calls the "upstream and downstream" of reading, the shared practices of communal attention and interpretation.[33] Constructing a stylistics of existence is, partly, an internal process; but it is also socially performed.

Felski refers to Macé as one of the new French theorists who "offers a fruitful resource in thinking of reading as a coproduction between actors rather than an unravelling of manifest meaning, a form of making rather than unmaking"—yet, as I argued in Chapter 1, this expansion can go further than consideration of the individual reader to include many more actors in the process of readers' aesthetic conduct.[34] Other readers, booksellers, librarians, websites, festival programmers, and so on, as well as the text and author, are involved when readers form and express aesthetic judgments. An understanding of dynamic taste practices is a particularly productive way to view the use of social media by readers. Just like face-to-face group settings, social media platforms such as Twitter and blogs provide tools for self-expression. Wright argues that online culture amplifies the importance of taste; many digital technologies "attempt to capture the affective, sensory aspects of tasting and transform the act of *liking* such that taste becomes even more loaded in contemporary strategies of measuring and managing social life."[35] Performing taste, and communicating aesthetic conduct, is integral to social media, where readers construct public or semi-public ideas of themselves based around what they share, link to, or say.[36]

As noted above in relation to romance book blogs, the social elements of performing taste are particularly striking in relation to readers who are fans of a particular genre, and my research with Kim Wilkins and Lisa Fletcher investigated the expansive social ties that are part of "genre worlds." For some readers, identifying with a genre world becomes part of their presentation of self. Some readers who are part of the fantasy genre world participate in cosplay at conventions, join online forums with genre appropriate avatars and nicknames, and stage displays of book series, merchandise, and aesthetically complementary objects such as medieval knights and dragon figurines on their bookshelves. Readers who love hardboiled crime fiction might frame posters of femme fatales or quotable laconic wisecracks.[37] Such readers interact with retailers, event organizers, other readers, and digital platforms as they use books as prompts for a style of living.

Beyond specific tastes, though, there is another form of aesthetic conduct that contemporary readers perform to themselves and each other. This conduct is effectively caught up in the concept of "bookishness." Unlike genre affiliation, bookishness is an aesthetic affiliation with books in general, as material objects. As Jessica Pressman defines it, bookishness is an aesthetic strategy consisting of creative acts that engage the physicality of the book within a digital culture.[38] Think, earrings made to look like miniature books and sold on the digital marketplace Etsy. Publishers may emphasize the "bookishness" of editions as a deliberate marketing strategy: N. Katherine Hayles analyzes bookishness in relation to Jonathan Safran Foer's *Tree of Codes* (2010), where the pages are extensively die-cut with holes so that the material object is part of the appeal of the book.[39] Bookishness has particular resonance in a post-digital environment, and its most obvious manifestations are on digital sites where people draw attention to physical books.

Aesthetic conduct is strikingly visible online, but it is a feature of all of the networks that contemporary readers inhabit. In each of these networks readers' aesthetic conduct is active, and it is socially performed. I want to look now at a sphere of readers' aesthetic conduct that is relatively old-fashioned and old-media. The bookish delight in books as material objects, and a generalized appreciation of the role of books in shaping one's life and identity, are strongly evident in a particular corner of book culture: bibliomemoirs.

Bibliomemoirs as Aesthetic Conduct

Bibliomemoirs are books about the experience of reading. They have titles such as *Why I Read: The Serious Pleasure of Books* (2014) and *I'd Rather Be Reading: The Delights and Dilemmas of the Reading Life* (2018).[40] As aesthetic conduct, bibliomemoirs articulate reading experiences in unusual detail and depth. They connect reading experiences to larger personal narratives; they model how reading fits into and shapes a life. As critic Pamela Paul writes in her bibliomemoir, "we pass our lives according to our books—relishing and reacting against them, reliving their stories when we recall where we were when we read them and the reason we did."[41] Bibliomemoirs show how reading can provide models for the self a reader is at any given moment, as well as the self a reader builds over a lifetime.

Often reflective, even nostalgic, bibliomemoirs tend to focus on literary classics and children's books. Some offer extended accounts of reading a single book or author—such as Geoff Dyer's *Out of Sheer Rage* (1997), which one reviewer called a "strange, sort-of study of DH Lawrence," and Rebecca Mead's *My Life in Middlemarch* (2014), which focuses on the impact of *Middlemarch* as Mead read and re-read it at different stages of her life.[42] In this, they model conduct that some everyday recreational readers also engage in: María Angélica Thumala Olave, for example, interviewed a woman who reads *Middlemarch* almost every year, saying that it helps her make sense of her life.[43]

Bibliomemoirs may mingle literary criticism, biography, and memoir. Helen Macdonald's *H is for Hawk* (2014) splices together multiple threads including life-writing about author T. H. White. Some bibliomemoirs offer behind-the-scenes glimpses of the reading of well-known authors or critics. Paul, mentioned above, was editor of the *New York Review of Books* before she wrote *My Life with Bob: Flawed Heroine Keeps Book of Books, Plot Ensues* (2017). Other bibliomemoirs are written by book industry professionals, like rare book dealer Rick Gekoski, author of *Outside of a Dog: A Bibliomemoir* (2011).[44] Professional bibliomemoirs promise to take ordinary readers behind the curtains of how and what an expert reader reads. But every bibliomemoir, whether the author is an industry insider or not, is a professional product that circulates and is read and discussed, demonstrating the social performance of reading as aesthetic conduct.

As books that celebrate books and reading, bibliomemoirs are a somewhat self-serving product of the publishing industry where they comprise a steady, though not large, category, with some indications of a rise in popularity. Author Henry Miller's *The Books in My Life* was published in 1952, yet more than sixty years later author Joyce Carol Oates considered bibliomemoirs "rarely attempted, and still more rarely successful."[45] In a long reflective article for the *Financial Times* in 2018, Lucy Scholes argued that bibliomemoirs have recently become more common as a result of a prevailing fashion for personal disclosure. In this respect, bibliomemoirs are contemporary updates of traditional forms such as literary criticism and biography, part of a turn toward personalization in nonfiction, offering an intimacy that is "in tune with today's readers."[46]

Bibliomemoirs have a strong link to everyday reading practices. As artefacts of the traditional publishing industry, in contrast to the digital narratives of reading that I consider in the next section, bibliomemoirs have both status and gravitas. They are marked by a lack of accessibility, because not every reader can secure a contract to publish a bibliomemoir—and indeed, not every reader would go to the effort of writing a book-length account of their reading. The authors of bibliomemoirs are remarkable readers, with unusually high prestige. Yet such books are not just written, but read. Bibliomemoirs are models of reading, rich in "readerly capital": an authority and capacity to influence others in book culture.[47] They are aspirational, speaking to and inspiring the reading practices of others, especially avid readers.

Because of the power relations at play, bibliomemoirs present themselves not just as examples but as guides. The promise of each bibliomemoir is that the reader can, by following the author's example, read like they do. As such, bibliomemoirs fit comfortably within the practices of the literary middlebrow: reverent toward literature, earnest, and emotionally inflected.[48] Like middlebrow institutions of the early-to-mid-twentieth century such as the Book-of-the-Month Club and book-related radio programs, the bibliomemoir is a form of cultural mediation that makes literature accessible to others.[49] One of the ways it does this is through the tool of the list. As Andy Miller writes in *The Year of Reading Dangerously: How Fifty Great Books (and Two Not-So-Great-Ones) Saved My Life* (2014), "In an age of communications overload, we seem to find lists like this irresistible."[50] The list as a tool for managing abundance is very much a middlebrow device, with a lineage stretching back to Great Books projects, and its use has increased in the twenty-first century, reaching an apotheosis of sorts in Alex Johnson's *A Book of Book Lists: A Bibliophile's Compendium* (2017) which collects book lists from a wide range of sources.[51]

The list is also a subset of another organizing principle for bibliomemoirs: the challenge. Such challenges provide a structure for a bibliomemoirs, and recall avant-garde formalist movements (such as Oulipo, or in film, Dogma) as well as, more pertinently, the reading challenges that circulate online, for example, in Goodreads and blogs. Novelist Susan Hill's memoir, *Howards End Is on the Landing: A Year of Reading from Home* (2010), follows her self-imposed challenge to read every book in her home, with no new purchases.[52] Another challenge-based bibliomemoir is critic Phyllis Rose's *The Shelf: From LEQ to LES* (2014), which describes her reading of a single shelf at the New York Public Library.[53]

Challenges and lists are relatable for readers, and so too is the tone of many bibliomemoirs. Miller writes about books in an approachable, often-humorous, reader-oriented manner, for example in describing his "trawl" through Herman Melville's 1851 novel *Moby-Dick,* a book which might fairly be described as "putdownable" … *Moby-Dick* is long, gruelling, convoluted graft. And yet, as soon as I completed it, once I could hold it at arm's length and admire its intricacy and design, I knew *Moby-Dick* was obviously, uncannily, a masterwork. It wormed into my subconscious; I dreamed about it for nights afterwards. Whereas when I finished *The Da Vinci Code*, which had taken little less than twelve hours from cover to cover, I chucked it aside and thought: wow—I really ought to read something good.[54]

Miller offers guidance for everyday readers by modeling aesthetic judgment: *Moby-Dick* is valuable; *The Da Vinci Code* is merely pleasurable. His enthusiasm and generosity toward other readers recall Oprah's Book Club from the 1990s, an institution of the new literary middlebrow.[55] The tone is warm, intimate, and personal, and this is where the distinctive aesthetic conduct of the bibliomemoir lies. A bibliomemoir models not only taste, but the application of books and reading to one's life: the process of self-fashioning through reading. It elaborates the claim that the books someone reads tell you something about the person they are. This conviction is shared by bibliomemoirists and their readers, including reviewers. Scholes, for example, confesses to, like Paul, "peering over someone's shoulder on the Tube in an attempt to catch a glimpse of the screen of their e-reader, or immediately scanning bookshelves when I visit a friend's house for the first time" as a way of getting to know something about them. Bibliomemoirs formalize book talk, offering a kind of one-sided conversation with readers. Three examples, detailed below, show some of the key features of the bibliomemoir as a format: one focuses most on materiality, one addresses childhood reading as formative, and one directly integrates books with ways of being in the world.

Packing My Library, Materiality and Mysticism

One of the most prominent, prolific bibliomemoirists—a writer whose reputation is almost defined by his writing about reading—is Argentine-Canadian author Alberto Manguel. Manguel's bibliomemoirs include *A History of Reading* (1996), *A Reading Diary: A Passionate Reader's Reflection on a Year of Books* (2004), *The Library at Night* (2005), *A Reader on Reading* (2010), and *Packing My Library: An Elegy and Ten Digressions* (2019).[56] It is worth pausing for a moment to note these books as products within a capitalist publishing industry. The economic status of the books as the outcome of labor was highlighted unusually explicitly in one interview, which began bemusedly:

> Alberto Manguel really should be an heir to some sort of fortune, for how could someone like him not be in possession of great sums of cash? … So well-traveled,

so well-read … a worldly man in the old sense, not in any debased, current, broadband sense—an essayist and anthologist and occasional fiction writer. Those occupations do not pay much. It turns out that Manguel needs income, as he told me when I asked. What I thought he did for fun, he in fact does for profit: read, write about reading, and lecture about writing about reading.[57]

I emphasize this quote and the fact that Manguel's bibliomemoirs are steadily selling products in the book industry, because the content of his books is so determinedly noncommercial. These two logics coexist. The book industry enables the dissemination of Manguel's view of what literature is and does, at the same time as commerce complicates some of his more spiritual and moral claims for books and reading. Not only is the author involved in this commercial/noncommercial tension, slipping between amateur and professional modes, but so too are his readers, who purchase or acquire books even as they reach toward a noncommercial sense of meaning through their reading.

Packing My Library, which I'll focus on for a moment, presents a view of the meaning of reading through a focus on the material objects of Manguel's book collection. It recounts his experience of packing up the 30,000-volume library he had established at his home in the South of France; a library that had been profiled in the *New York Times* Home section fourteen years earlier on the publication of his bibliomemoir, *The Library at Night*.[58] In *Packing My Library*, Manguel takes his cue from Walter Benjamin's 1931 essay "Unpacking My Library" and uses the process of handling, disordering, and reordering books to reflect on what they mean to him, and the value of the different libraries he has had.[59] These arrangements of books serve as aesthetic stand-ins for the stages of Manguel's life. He writes,

> My libraries are each a sort of multi-layered autobiography, every book holding the moment in which I read it for the first time. The scribbles in the margins, the occasional date on the flyleaf, the faded bus ticket marking a page for a reason today mysterious—all attempt to remind me of who I was then. For the most part, they fail.[60]

The failure here is important, pointing to something mysterious beyond the pages, but it is partial. The books may not fully recall Manguel's past selves, but they remain talismanic objects. His stories about them are portals: Manguel describes the shelf of books by his cot that he loved to rearrange as a toddler, and the library acquired by his father in Argentina, trimmed in green leather covers. Claire Armitstead, in a review for the *Guardian*, suggests that some of these stories have been repeated and reworked across several of Manguel's bibliomemoirs, becoming touchstones for him and his readers.[61]

It is books as a general category that matter in *Packing My Library*. Manguel has favorite authors he refers to often, including Jorge Borges and Franz Kafka, but the memoir does not feature long expositions or descriptions of specific books. In adopting this wider lens, Manguel activates the aesthetic of bookishness. It is the experience of handling material books and the memories of reading experiences that they evoke that take center stage. As part of his aesthetic conduct, Manguel contrasts his self-confessed desire to possess books with a purer vision of what reading can accomplish. In an allusive style that recalls sermons, he exhorts readers to look for the (Kantian) sublime in books, as windows into ultimate purpose and meaning, writing, "when I'm in a library, any library, I have the sense of being translated into a purely verbal dimension by a conjuring trick I've never quite understood. I know that my full, true story is there, somewhere on the shelves, and all I need is time and the chance to find it. I never do."[62]

There is a mystical sensibility in this description of books-in-aggregate, an idealization that gives them authority. Like Macé, Manguel argues that books direct life:

> we act and feel under the shadow of literary actions and feelings. This contamination, this style of thought, for want of a better term, allows us to believe that the world around us is a narrative world, and that landscapes and events are part of a story that we are compelled to follow at the same time that we create it.[63]

Manguel's use of the first-person plural indicates an assumed audience of avid readers, an approach and tone that potentially excludes some readers.[64] It also has a somewhat proselytizing mission, which becomes stronger toward the end, when Manguel reveals that some time after leaving France he was appointed Director of Argentina's National Library. This raises the stakes of his personal reflections on the importance of reading, turning them into vision statements for a national institution. He achieves this shift by adding a moral agenda to his aesthetic understanding of what reading does, which I return to analyze in Chapter 4. In terms of aesthetic conduct, *Packing My Library* models the attribution of a sublime quality to books through a focus on their material existence as talismanic objects that indicate, but cannot fully capture, the meaning of a person's life.

Childhood Reading and *Storytime*

Manguel's bibliomemoir reflects on the role of book objects throughout his life. Another characteristic of many bibliomemoirs is a specific focus on childhood reading. In her analysis of three memoirs of childhood reading (by Manguel, Michael Dirda, and Karla Holloway), Tully Barnett argues they "serve dual functions, not just as the crux of these autobiographical recollections and life narratives, but as the foundations of careers and livelihoods."[65] That is, bibliomemoirs present a form of professional self-fashioning, through which writers "can establish their credentials as fully fledged members of the literary establishment, can validate and reinforce their inclusion in that establishment, and can nostalgically recall their indoctrination into a mystical world of books."[66] There is a link here to the economic rationale for bibliomemoirs; not only do they make money themselves, they can lead to or legitimize other professional opportunities for the author by shoring up their authority (and model this process for readers who aspire to the same opportunities).

Childhood reading as a focus makes sense, given part of the aesthetic conduct of the bibliomemoir is to show the influence of books on a life. The title of Francis Spufford's bibliomemoir, *The Child That Books Built* (2002), illustrates this neatly, while Alice Ozma's *The Reading Promise* (2011) chronicles the very specific experience of having her father read aloud to her every day from the fourth grade until she left for college.[67] A focus on childhood reading can also align the bibliomemoir, as a form, with nostalgia. There is a resonance, here, between books as objects that can invoke nostalgia in a digital age, and childhood reading as a specific prompt for nostalgia. Writing about journalist Lucy Mangan's *Bookworm: A Memoir of Childhood Reading* (2018), which covers *The Secret Garden*, Enid Blyton's oeuvre, and other Anglophone classics for children, Scholes notes, "if bibliomemoir taps into a collective nostalgia for reading itself amid our current cacophony of digital distractions, then nowhere is this clearer than in volumes such as Mangan's that hark back to a more innocent age."[68]

The childhood reading bibliomemoir I'd like to focus on in some detail is Jane Sullivan's *Storytime* (2019).[69] Sullivan is a columnist and former literary editor for one of Australia's leading broadsheet newspapers, *The Age*, as well as a novelist. *Storytime*, her memoir, is framed as an investigative quest to understand the appeal that certain books had for her as a child in England in the 1950s, and hence to make sense of her lifelong love of reading and her literary career. It is structured into chapters that correspond to twelve books Sullivan loved as a child. Each chapter includes two descriptions of reading experiences: her memory of reading the book as a child, and rereading the book as an adult. Sullivan is bookishly attentive to materiality, describing book covers, illustrations, and bookshops. Each chapter includes an inset box where another author reminisces about the same or a similar book. These interspersed fragments from other writers put Sullivan's journalistic and literary networks on the page, and model the value she places on bookish community.

The active aesthetic conduct in Sullivan's memoir includes her selection of books to write about. These are what Sullivan considers typical of the era, including works by English authors Enid Blyton, A. A. Milne, and Lewis Carroll. Sullivan's bibliomemoir also involves a presentation of her self as mirrored in or shaped by books; she describes how reading about friendship can soothe a lonely child, how reading about posh schools can direct a middle-class child reader's imagination, and how reading about Moominmamma can affirm a child's sense of familial security. *Storytime* sets out versions of ideal reading, including a knowing nod to theories of the sublime: Sullivan writes that, as a child, "books happened to me. I was helpless, I surrendered to them. They immersed me, engulfed me, swept me away into Keats's realms of gold."[70] Each chapter of *Storytime* concludes with a hypothesis about what young Jane was seeking for and found in her childhood reading of that book; for example, "to feel a range of emotions with great intensity" and "to be transported." The bibliomemoir ends by gathering the list of these hypotheses, and concludes that while none suffices and neither can they be put together into "a coherent universal philosophy of childhood reading," together they offer a composite picture of the different aspects of reading that mattered to the child Sullivan.[71] The overall vision of childhood reading she presents is immersive, enchanting, and social (it includes friends, family, and her adult networks).

Sullivan's adult career as a journalist is evident in her interest in authors' lives and the publication histories of books. Yet there is a tension between Sullivan's journalistic interests and her desire to preserve what she remembers as magical childhood reading experiences, when she had none of this information. She expresses distaste for the "annoying reductiveness" of interpreting books as simple transmutations of the author's life, and largely keeps moral questions separate from her aesthetic task in *Storytime*. As a result, *Storytime* skates close to and then veers away from a number of moral issues (such as debates concerning whether Lewis Carroll's relations with children were pedophiliac). In the book's conclusion, Sullivan offers more trenchant arguments about the dearth of books by women and authors of color in her childhood reading ("considering the bulk of what I was reading"; she notes wryly, "it's a wonder I grew up feminist at all"; the absence of stories by and about people of color is something that "today, [she finds] extraordinary and disturbing").[72] The literary journalist Sullivan here expresses a critical position on the reading available to the child Sullivan. As a whole, though, the book constitutes primarily aesthetic conduct, tracing the formation of a self as a lover of books, a member of a bookish social network, and a writer, through her childhood engagement with books.

Aesthetics as a Political Stance in *The Republic of Imagination*

Sullivan's bibliomemoir is predominantly personal; in contrast, Azar Nafisi's *The Republic of Imagination: A Life in Books*, published in 2014, is explicitly didactic and instructional.[73] Nafisi was born and raised in Iran, moving to the United States to attend college in the 1970s, where she was involved in student activism before moving back to Iran just before the revolution in 1979. In the following years she taught literature clandestinely, as recounted in her international bestseller *Reading Lolita in Tehran: A Memoir in Books* (2003).[74] Nafisi moved to the United States permanently in the 1990s when she became a professor at Johns Hopkins University's School of Advanced International Studies. *The Republic of Imagination* is addressed to American readers, encouraging them to value American literature.

In the acknowledgments at the end of the book, Nafisi explains its origin as a writers' festival appearance, and the memoir blends many of the elements that characterize such events: the foregrounding of the personality of the author, attention to the meaning of books as a holistic category, and political engagement (a facet I discuss further in Chapter 4).[75] The book is structured as three lengthy readings of iconic American texts: Mark Twain's *The Adventures of Huckleberry Finn* (1884) (which Nafisi sees as foundational; her original subtitle for the book was "The Progenies of Huck Finn"), Sinclair Lewis's *Babbitt* (1922), and Carson McCullers's *The Heart Is a Lonely Hunter* (1940). Each section blends teacherly exposition of the text with writing about her own life and links to current affairs (the American education system is thoroughly discussed in the Babbitt section, for example). Her book is pedagogical in tone, but also framed through Nafisi's life experiences and friendships, especially with her cousin Farah Abrahimi, who also immigrated to the United States. Abrahimi died from cancer prior to the book's publication, and many conversations in the memoir are presented as taking place during the last months of her illness.

Nafisi's memoir is an example of aesthetic conduct, as it gathers together a lifetime's worth of thoughts on literature and shapes them into a narrative, one that she puts to polemic purpose to advocate for liberalism and humanism. There is a close relationship between aesthetic and moral conduct in this bibliomemoir, since Nafisi's experience of political oppression in Iran drives her view that reading should be valued. She asks, for example, "why do tyrants understand the dangers of a democratic imagination more than our [US] policy makers appreciate its necessity?"[76] She speaks for individualism, and against conformity, commercialism, and ideology. Her points are always grounded in the authority of literature, which she argues gave her, as a young woman, more meaning than political activity did: "Reality was confusing and polarised while fiction was complex, paradoxical and illuminating: that whole vast continent of art and the imagination gave weight and substance to the urgent, emotional, simplified world of protests and demonstrations."[77] Nafisi uses *The Adventures of Huckleberry Finn* to buttress her point about the value of nonconformity, writing that Huck chooses "to be true to that inner self, the rebellious heart that beats to its own rhythm."[78] Nafisi explicitly links this to praise for her cousin Farah, whose commitment to bettering Iran included the choice, at a critical juncture, to leave an activist group: "the group was going too far, and she had the strength to do what few of us can: assert her own private sense of right and wrong and distance herself from the group. It is what

Huck did when he broke from Tom and his band of robbers."[79] Nafisi draws direct parallels between the shapes of narratives and the shapes of societies; between what she reads and how she and her family live. These parallels underscore her bid to restore literature's influence. She wants a nation to alter its aesthetic conduct, to read as she does, and find forms of living in American literature.

In Scholes's words, bibliomemoirs offer a reminder "of why we each of us read great fiction in the first place."[80] The why of reading, and the sharing of these motivations, are key to what I've argued is the aesthetic conduct of bibliomemoirs. Bibliomemoirs show readers with high cultural credibility actively using books— those read in childhood, or classics of recognized value—to fashion a model for how they live and, by extension, how other readers should also live. These memoirs draw explicit links between reading and the style of a life as mysterious, exciting, solitary, communal, reflective, or politically engaged. Bibliomemoirs show, at length, readers integrating books into their broader experiences as they intertwine two trajectories: of reading, and of living. Through them, readers connect books to growing up, to moving country, to watching a loved one suffer, to grieving. Bibliomemoirs perform and model the sense-making work that connects culture to life. They affirm to other readers that reading matters, that reading books can shape experience and render it meaningful.

The Aesthetic Conduct of Readers Online: Bookstagram and Beyond

Bibliomemoirs, as traditional products of the publishing industry, articulate reading as aesthetic conduct from a position of authority that few readers attain. In contrast, online forums offer opportunities for a large number of nonprofessional and professional readers to articulate their reading as aesthetic conduct. Like print publications, digital platforms demonstrate that aesthetic conduct is an activity of the perceiver that is socially performed. As noted at the beginning of this chapter, the performance of taste is particularly striking online, and can be concentrated in visual or audiovisual form as an "aesthetic."

A few years ago, I joined Instagram. I started posting pictures to @popficdoctors, an account created for a research project on popular fiction; my contributions included a shot of a Kindle on a wooden table with autumn leaves scattered nearby, and a "shelfie" that spotlighted a book-reading rubber duck (see Figure 1A and 1B). When I visited England some months later, I met the daughter of a friend of a friend. She was fourteen years old and an active Instagram user, so I showed her my posts and asked for a critical appraisal. "Oh," she said, "you're aesthetic."

The word "aesthetic" has a widespread, ever-evolving vernacular use among social media users. An online tutorial by Instagram user Paper Fury has a section subtitled "Aesthetic." Under it, she writes, "'what the mangled monkey does that even mean anyway????' you grumble because now I'm just getting pretentiously complicated with this tutorial. BUT KEEP YOUR POLKA DOT SOCKS ON. I shall explain."[81] She screenshots a dictionary entry for the word "aesthetic," before going on to explain that on Instagram, aesthetic means "how you want your feed to look." While emphasizing the user's freedom, Paper Fury notes that consistent aesthetics make an account more followed.

This sense of aesthetic as the overall look of a social media account persists, but the word has evolved to carry other senses too. For example, a book may be broken down into its "aesthetic" by an Instagram or TikTok user, who shows images and plays sounds that fit the vibe of a book. Book subscriptions services may organize groups of books by their aesthetic, sometimes using the suffix "core": US company Fairy Loot has advertised books under the headings "piratecore" and "assassincore."[82] Book box subscriptions themselves exemplify bookish aesthetic practice. As subscription services, these continue business models such as the Book-of-the-Month Club; in fact, the most recent iteration of the Book-of-the-Month Club is a book box service.[83] These services offer a regular postal delivery of a new book, along with related products such as tote bags, candles, scarves, pillowslips, bookmarks, art prints, notebooks, lanyards, and badges. Subscriptions may deliver exclusive editions with special features, which some reader reviewers commentate on with the passion of book historians or antiquarians: boxed editions, author signatures, foiled or embossed covers, decorative endpapers, and sprayed edges. Some book subscription services are aimed at specific, genre-based fan cultures, or at audience segments such as children or young adults. Book boxes encourage readers to engage in aesthetic conduct by arranging, experiencing, and sharing the elements of the book box. Most book boxes come with a card and instructions that tell readers to photograph and share, as well as read, the contents. Videos of "unboxing" book boxes are popular on YouTube and TikTok, and components can be arranged into a display to be photographed for Instagram.

In contrast to such heavily styled aesthetics, there is also a rising anti-aesthetic or casual aesthetic, most prominent on TikTok, in which users share what looks like unfiltered glimpses into a reader's or writer's life. This homey, intimate "un"aesthetic is exemplified by the woman who posted a sixteen second TikTok video of her 74-year-old father at his desk, and turned his backlist title into a bestseller as readers virally shared, hearted and commented on the video.[84] All this variety of aesthetic conduct of readers, supported by and interwoven with publishers and book retail services, finds a quintessential stage on social media platforms. These platforms are aesthetics made manifest, to the point where they become sites for playful, hyperbolic, or deadpan aesthetic conduct.

Readers who use books to construct a visible, traceable "stylistics of existence," to adopt Macé's phrase, may spread their activities across multiple platforms, adjusting the nature of their content and engagement to suit each platform. Many choose to maintain one platform—Goodreads, Instagram, or a blog, for example—as a base,

 **popficdoctors**　　　　　　　　　　　　　　　•••

 Liked by **hexebart** and **others**

popficdoctors The latest member of the #popfiction
team #shelfie #literature #bookstagram

View 1 comment

2 March 2017

 **popficdoctors** •••

 Liked by **sue_driscoll** and **others**

popficdoctors Beth's Sunday afternoon reading
#crimefiction #australianauthor #books

13 March 2016

FIGURE 1A AND 1B Two of my "aesthetic" posts on Instagram.

linking other social media accounts back to their main home. Each platform supports and limits different forms of aesthetic conduct, from Goodreads' shelf displays to the customization options that enable book blog designs to visually reflect their genre affiliation.[85] Aesthetic conduct on bookish social media accounts is also bound up in techno-capitalism and the economics of content creation and influencing, as readers' stylistic choices feed into marketing practices and as different platforms rise and fall as drivers of book sales.[86] To illustrate some of these dynamics, I'll focus for a moment on Instagram, an established, image-based social media platform.

As of 2022, Instagram was more popular than TikTok, Snapchat, Pinterest, and Twitter but less popular than Facebook, YouTube, and WhatsApp, with 1.5 billion users each month. Two-thirds of Instagram users are under the age of thirty-four.[87] Of all the online forums for the sharing of reading experience, Instagram is perhaps the most obviously visually aestheticized. Instagram was originally designed to share photos, and still carries space and formatting restrictions that make it easier to share photos than written content.[88] Instagram encourages highly image-conscious, stylized use.[89]

On Instagram, readers interact with book objects, the platform, and other users to present and refine an aesthetic of reading. The term "Bookstagram" has evolved to gather together some of these users and posts. In an introductory blog post for readers curious about Bookstagram, user Laura defines it as a niche corner of the internet for book lovers.

> Using the hashtag #bookstagram, you'll find millions and millions of book-related photos posted by people from all over the world. It's an online community of bookworms who love to share pictures of what they're reading, their favorite books, their bookshelves, the libraries, and bookshops they're exploring and more. All manner of bookish people are on bookstagram, including authors, bookworms, booksellers, bookshops, libraries, book prizes, and more.[90]

In an academic context, Kenna MacTavish defines Bookstagram as "a community organised by the hashtag #bookstagram," and a Bookstagrammer as an active, ongoing participant in this community with "a profile that communicates an overwhelmingly bookish aesthetic."[91]

Bookstagrammer accounts range from the professionalized, with hundreds of thousands of followers, through to more grassroots, everyday reader accounts with fewer than 100 followers. My 2023 search yielded over 85.5 million posts tagged with #bookstagram (up from 44 million when I searched in 2020) as well as over 16 million tagged with #bookstagrammer (up from 6 million in 2020). These numbers are lower than for general hashtags such as #selfie or #love, but still significant. Notably, the Bookstagram community is multilingual, as Thomas notes: "One of the obvious attractions of Instagram for book lovers is that the images can be enjoyed regardless of language, and while posts tagged with #bookporn or #bookstagram are predominantly in English, the communities engaging in the activities are clearly multilingual."[92]

Unlike the explicitly aspirational platform Pinterest, where users collect images that inspire them, Bookstagram purports to show everyday reading practices.[93] Yet it is nonetheless (perhaps even more so) a practice that fashions and presents the self. Maarit Jaakkola cites Erving Goffman's 1959 book *The Presentation of Self in Everyday Life* when she describes Bookstagrammers' conduct as the creation of a "reading self" based on "systematically performing cultural engagement online"; impression management that takes place in public and is intended to be seen by others.[94] The construction of a reading self through Bookstagram posts may involve alignment with a genre—romance fiction, young adult fiction, and poetry are prominent on this platform—or the development of a distinctive style of writing in the captions. Most centrally, aesthetic conduct takes place through the creation of visual content.

Users make a series of choices about how they present images of books, selecting images, props, photo styles, filters, captions, and more.[95] Searching the hashtag #bookstagram shows at a glance the popularity of particular formats and styles of image. Books are often held in hands. Sometimes they are stacked (spine out). Sometimes they are shelved (spine in, or color-coded). Sometimes books are placed among related objects to create a still life presentation. Users who achieve an overall "aesthetic" for their account do so through consistent choices relating to filters, style and props. Thomas writes that while "the book as an object of display and even fetishisation can be found everywhere on social media" it is Bookstagram that most clearly "demonstrates how curation on social media can be a creative activity relying on considerable craft and artistry."[96] The aesthetic act of arranging and photographing a book object is often detailed work, involving a combination of digital and material practices. While there is variety in these practices, there is also a dominant vernacular type of post. As MacTavish has written, the most common visual brand on Bookstagram is a kind of middle-class, feminized domesticity, featuring "domestic props such as a cup of coffee, tea, plants, candles, socks, and cereal" in intimate household settings to "create a representation of everyday readerly experience."[97] This visual mode recalls other institutions of the new literary middlebrow, especially in its mass media forms.[98]

Trends on Bookstagram circulate through the affordances, including the algorithms, of Instagram. Sometimes an individual user's conduct is directed by algorithms or other aspects of the platform's technical design, and sometimes it resists the platform. For example, Jaakkola notes that despite Instagram's restrictions on written text, many book reviews on Instagram have a focus on text, including reviews and book talk alongside the image. She suggests this kind of use seems to "resist the platform policy by intentionally mis-interpreting the caption norm and turning the written text into the primary mode of communication."[99] Such acts of resistance bring home the space of agency that exists for readers as they engage in aesthetic conduct online.

Features of Instagram that have been embraced by users include liveness and interaction, which intersect with the site's commercial influence. Kathi Inman Berens has written of these dynamics in relation to the phenomenon of Instapoetry—short poems published first on Instagram, and sometimes later in print. Some of these have been startling economic successes in print form, such as Rupi Kaur's *Milk and Honey* (2014), but Berens notes that "stripped of liveness, printed Instapoetry ends up looking banal. Its treacly insights, absent the warm glow emanating from fans inside the app, harden into branding." The best approach to understanding the success of such books, she suggests, is to see them as "brought into being" by social media transactions: "the reader being converted into a datastream is not a byproduct of reading poetry. It is part of the poem itself."[100] At the same time, she reminds us that tracking readers and their data is not just a social media phenomenon, but part of the print book industry. Instapoetry shows that commerce is an element—but not the totality—of the social media networks of readers, and this mingling of sociality, creation, and monetization intersects with and feeds into the book industry as a whole.

Tracking readers is an established practice, but hashtags make this easier (and more self-directed) than ever. The aesthetic conduct of Bookstagrammers includes not only making posts, but labeling them with the #bookstagram hashtag. Hashtags create paths through a platform—users can search for, follow, or add a hashtag to their post to find and connect with others who have the same interests. Using hashtags can brand a post (and, over time, a user's account) as bookish, as well as increasing visibility and popularity on the platform with other booklovers. Some hashtags are used to create events or challenges that different users can join, enhancing the sociality of the site and helping to generate new content. Jaakkola's study indicates that the most engaging forms of participation for Bookstagrammers are book reading and reviewing campaigns, such as readathons and book challenges, which in fact often originate from other platforms such as Goodreads.[101] Fuller and Rehberg Sedo find this in their interview with book influencers on YouTube, too—straight reviews are seen as less appealing than themed posts that bundle books (such as top 5s, or books that made the user cry) which are more personal and more directly invite engagement with viewers.[102]

Bookstagram events and conversations are analyzed by Jaakkola, who shows that they emphasize reading experiences that are "alleged to be individual, idiosyncratic and unique." Reporting on reading challenges, tallies and experiences makes the experience of reading "more meaningful and helps assess one's identity and capabilities as a cultural consumer or citizen."[103] Jaakkola concludes that Bookstagrammers are best thought of as "individualized experts of their own reading experience, mediating their intellectual, emotional and aesthetic ephemeral experience regarding the book product they happen to have received or stumbled upon." Hashtags sort posts into groups, but they also enable aesthetic conduct that illuminates the individual reader.

The use of hashtags is a reminder that the aesthetic conduct of readers on Instagram is highly networked and socially performed. My own brief fling with Bookstagram was driven by the academic imperative for research "engagement," although our forty-four posts and seventy-six followers hardly transformed the image of the university as an ivory tower (an image with an aesthetic, now I come to think of it; to say nothing of the "dark academia" aesthetic trend that was all over social media in 2022).[104] The professional metric of "engagement" (also known sometimes as "impact") is a reminder of the networks that users of Bookstagram create. Importantly, there is a dominant affective quality to these networks. The discourses of Bookstagram tend toward encouragement and openness, with a focus on helping others choose books to read, and critique can be softened (much softer than, say, on Twitter). For Jaakkola, this softness is important because individual posts are best understood as occurring within the context of "fan communities or scenes."[105] That is, Instagram is not simply public (as, say, Twitter can be seen as a town square) but is experienced as a more intimate community. Bookstagram functions as an extension of domestic space; it is a way of taking something private and making it public, but not too public.

And yet, despite its softened and semi-private communal aspects, the Bookstagram community *is* public, and it is not just a fan space but a commercial space. Jaakkola's neat account of readers presenting themselves as having "stumbled upon" books, quoted above, shows how Bookstagram can elide its intersections with marketing. A 2017 article in the *Huffington Post* focused on Bookstagrammers who work in the book industry, interviewing a publisher, a book blogger/publishing intern, a literary agent, a marketer, and an author— all young women.[106] The variety of these professional and semi-professional activities shows the different overlapping roles that readers assume online, and the potential for Bookstagramming to work in concert with the publishing industry as well as being part of the economy of social media. Bookstagram is also linked to other institutions that participate in the commerce of the book industry, such as the education system (which keeps backlist titles alive through steady sales) and the broader media and entertainment industries. Thomas notes that the most frequently mentioned writers on Instagram tend to be those featured on school curricula or in high-profile film and TV adaptations, such as Shakespeare and Tolkien.[107]

The aesthetic conduct of Bookstagrammers feeds directly into, and can be almost indistinguishable from, marketing. For example, Bookstagrammers have been credited with exerting influence on book cover design, as contemporary publishers seek to create objects that photograph well by using clear, bold typography and bright colors.[108] Thomas notes that many trends on Instagram support the marketing activities of publishers, writing that "[b]ook hauls, book porn and bookstagramming can of course be easily co-opted for commercial purposes."[109] In her study of the #bookreview hashtag on Instagram, Jaakkola notes that "a considerable amount of #bookreview material on Instagram is actually supportive material rather than original reviews."[110] Yet the symbiosis of book marketing and Bookstagramming is not total; MacTavish's analysis found a counter-practice where a book may be presented in an aesthetically pleasing manner with the hashtag #bookstagram, while the accompanying caption is critical of or disappointed in a book.[111] Bookstagram's very concentrated form of aesthetic conduct, focused directly on representations of book objects and of reading, is enmeshed in affective communities, commercial trends, and economic structures, but not in straightforward ways.

Aesthetic conduct on social media evolves at a fast pace, and it can be complex for readers to decide how and whether to use different platforms. Writing for *GQ* magazine in 2023, former BookTuber Barry Pierce described how he felt when he discovered BookTok. "It was like entering a parallel universe," he wrote, "where reading wasn't just something that someone did for fun, it was a lifestyle, an *aesthetic*."[112] In a confessional mode, Pierce writes,

> Way back in the 2010s there used to be a community of book lovers on YouTube. The collective, known as BookTube, was very much a precursor to today's BookTok. Some of the pillars of BookTok (books hauls, unhauls, challenges, reading wrap-ups) were pioneered on BookTube and, for a while at least, it was a cosy and wholesome corner of the internet. I used to be a BookTuber, one of the bigger ones actually, it's kind of the reason why I was able to have some legitimacy when I transitioned into writing about books as a career.

Pierce writes that he "stopped making BookTube videos because the community had become overrun by commercialism," bemoaning the way in which, on BookTube, "The act of reading became replaced by the act of being a *reader*. Actual reviews became few and far between and many of the smaller, genuine readers on the platform jumped ship." He then writes, "it feels like BookTok has got to the same place, only much faster." He quotes author Stephanie Danler, who wrote that TikTok is "not a social media app but an entertainment app. On it, you can't just show a book by Clarice Lispector. The successful accounts *performed* being a 'woman who reads Clarice Lispector.'" This judgment diminishes the intimacy of social media while highlighting its performativity; but as the growth of BookTok shows, there are readers who find these forms of participation satisfying.

Readers build the networks that sustain them through the platforms they are drawn to, using these digital sites to express aesthetic conduct. Like bibliomemoirs, but with more accessibility, Bookstagram and BookTok offer public stages for the articulation of aesthetic conduct. These stages are digital platforms, but public articulations of taste can also happen in person, which is the focus of my next section.

Notes from a Reading Group: Aesthetic Conduct Face-to-Face

As I remember it, the sun was pouring through the west-facing windows of the Richmond library. The other members of the reading group and I were taking a mid-session break, nursing cups of tea and biscuits as we sat on the vinyl lounges. The warmth of the sun seemed to cast a spell that eased the formality of the preceding hour, in which this group of people, who barely knew each other, had read a poem: Seamus Heaney's Blackberry-Picking. "Late August, given heavy rain and sun," it begins, "For a full week, the blackberries would ripen./At first, just one, a glossy purple clot/Among others, red, green, hard as a knot./You ate that first one and its flesh was sweet/Like thickened wine: summer's blood was in it." Blackberries are an invasive weed in Australia and August isn't fruit ripening time, but we'd put that aside. Something about the imagery of the heavy sun and the fruit seemed to connect with people and spill over in the break room. We started sharing memories of childhood summer adventures, feeling our way from the poem to reflections on our lives: a magic intertwining of storytelling, self-understanding, and communication.

In-person events that are centered on books and reading prompt aesthetic conduct; not just expressions of taste, but attempts to understand life through the model of art. Such conduct depends upon, and can affect, the bonds in networks of people, organizations, and books. In Chapter 2, I discussed interviews I conducted with attendees at the Melbourne Writers Festival that illustrate the different networks that readers form. Some elements of this network formation constitute aesthetic conduct. For example, Victoria, who used Twitter to connect with non-attending friends and authors, also has an annual ritual of emailing her work colleagues when the program comes out. She told me that by doing that, "you kind of learn that you've got similar interests as other people. Because I think people's literary tastes are quite different, or can be surprising sometimes." Her desire to connect with those in her workplace and prompt future discussion was expressed in aesthetic conduct, a display of her taste and bookishness through selecting sessions to highlight to her colleagues.

Using taste in books to connect with peers also happens through book clubs. Simply belonging to a book club is a kind of aesthetic conduct: a declaration of bookishness and perhaps, if it's a themed club, a commitment to reading a particular kind of book. I've belonged to a lot of book clubs, but my most longstanding one is a dedicated Jane Austen group that reads her novels aloud (a chapter or two each month) with occasional bonus Austen-themed social catch-ups. Being a part of this group is a kind of aesthetic conduct for me (I'm a Janeite!), as are our acts of reading, discussing, picnicking, and board-game-playing. In every book club, members perform aesthetic work through creating and joining the group, setting up protocols for their meetings, and choosing and discussing the books that they read.[113]

In this section, I want to explore the aesthetic activities of one book club I've been involved in; really, more a reading group than a book club since it focused on individual poems and short stories. This is the group that met that sunlit afternoon in the Richmond library. It was part of a project called Reading and Writing for Wellbeing run in 2017, modeled on a program from the Hearth Centre in Birmingham, UK. We recruited members for three reading and writing groups by advertising through a local community library. I co-facilitated one group with a colleague from the University of Melbourne's medical school, who also conducted initial interviews and ran psychological and physical tests that aimed to measure the health effects of the group on participants. Unlike some of the other reading practices and formations discussed in this chapter, this group had an institutional (rather than commercial) context; it was run by university researchers in collaboration with a local public library. On one view, this was an artificially created reading group with a heavy-handed institutional framing. Yet within these parameters, the group prompted several subtle forms of readers' aesthetic conduct. It is a case study in the small, quotidian, evanescent components of aesthetic conduct that can mark everyday engagements with reading. This group offered examples of common forms of readerly aesthetic conduct in book clubs, as well as conduct that was heightened due to the particularities of the group, such as the moderation of aesthetic judgment according to a group's power relations.

With around a dozen people, the group I co-led was quite large. Most participants were female, over forty, White, and English-speaking (another group in our project was more culturally and linguistically diverse, with Mandarin-, Spanish-, and Italian-speaking participants). We ran our groups during the working week; some of our participants were retired, some were working irregularly due to health issues. Participants expressed a range of levels of confidence when discussing literary texts. Some were very vocal (including both men in the group I led), and others needed encouragement to contribute. Over the course of twelve weeks, the group gradually established norms for talking about reading. Our groups followed a specific model.[114] All texts were read aloud during the session, so there was no homework and reduced pressure on participants who may have low literacy. We read our out-of-copyright texts from photocopied handouts, precluding discussion of the materiality of book covers, formats, and editions. Each session began with the facilitator reading out loud a short story or poem, without any introductory material or information about the author. While the group had a focus on well-being, the aim was to advance this through the creation of a specifically aesthetic experience: to offer group members the opportunity to enjoy and think about a literary text. There would then be a discussion of the text's themes and its historical and social contexts. The text was sometimes read aloud again, by the facilitator or a volunteer from the group. After a break for a cuppa and biscuit, there would be either a second text to read and discuss or a writing exercise and discussion. The sessions ran for around two hours. The works we read were mostly classic, canonical poems and short stories, such as Guy de Maupassant's "The Necklace" (1884) and Robert Frost's "The Road Not Taken" (1916).

Group participation was itself a primary form of aesthetic conduct. Members took on a certain bookish position through their attendance. Each member had learned of the group through their subscription to a public library newsletter, where this group was advertised as a university study. Many participants expressed curiosity about the research, and a sense of academic importance ran through the sessions. One member, for example, approached me and my co-facilitator after an early session with lots of questions about the purpose and value of the group. During discussions, however, group members tended not to present themselves as literary experts and instead deferred to facilitators. There was a power imbalance in this group that affected the aesthetic possibilities for participants.

The power imbalance was built into the structure of the group, not just because the facilitators were academics, but because the facilitators chose the poems and short stories, replicating an educational model where teachers are familiar with a text and participants may not be. Normally book groups choose their own texts, and this is one of their defining and most fulfilling tasks.[115] Members of this group were aware that it ran in a different way and was part of a University study. Of note, perhaps, is that this group decided to keep meeting *without* the facilitators after the conclusion of the program, choosing their own texts. During the program, participants often asked facilitators why we had chosen particular stories or poems, perhaps due to their interest in the fact that the group was a research project. Indeed, the grounds for choosing texts were academic: our method was to replicate the selections used by our model, the Hearth Centre in the UK, which themselves had been chosen with an eye to including various well-being-related themes for discussion (such as death, relationships, and family dynamics), to which we added some Australian content. In discussion of texts, participants often demonstrated concern about whether they had got the meaning of a poem or short story "right," indicating that an educational tenor pervaded the group (despite my efforts as a facilitator to encourage and welcome a wide range of responses to texts—itself a pedagogical gesture!). The educative mode of the group was also evident on the handful of occasions when participants said that the discussions had helped them understand the works better—and, in some cases, like them more. The group thus provided participants with a prompt for reflecting on how bookish they felt themselves to be. Bookishness was a form of aesthetic conduct participants expressed through showing up, and through how they discussed texts and referred to other participants and the facilitators.

Expressing Aesthetic Judgments in Group Discussion

Perhaps because group members didn't choose the texts themselves, one of the most common forms of aesthetic conduct in the group was the articulation of rejection or dislike. Previous research on book clubs suggests that members' judgments about whether or not they like a book are affected by a range of factors, including the dynamics of the group.[116] The articulation of negative aesthetic judgments in this group often had an emotional component. Some texts were experienced as depressing: after one poem was read aloud there was a long pause, before a group member broke the silence by saying "what's the Lifeline number?" (referring to a service for crisis support and suicide prevention). Sometimes there was robust disagreement about whether a piece was bleak, philosophical, or funny, showing the way these emotional judgments can overlap or blend. The experienced difficulty of a text also produced emotional reactions which led to judgments about the work. Susan Sontag's "The Way We Live Now" (1986), a story about the impact of AIDS on a group of friends, was one that I read aloud. The story has an unusual structure and multiple perspectives, and I stopped fairly often in the first half to check in with the group about how they were understanding and experiencing it. I was struck by how often group members expressed dislike and irritation toward the story and its characters: an emotion-laden aesthetic response that, in other research, I also observed in Goodreads reviews of a challenging text.[117] This form of aesthetic conduct was partly to do with participants' perceived expertise, but also involved responses to specific authors, styles, and characters.

Beyond the question of liking or disliking the texts, discussion in this group tended to bounce off the text into broader discussions about life: the importance of trust or optimism, the complexity of friendships and relationships, what it means to save face, give advice, become involved in politics or activism. Reading "Blackberry-Picking" prompted discussions about relationships between spouses, as well as those childhood reminiscences that continued as participants sat in a sunny corner of the room during the tea break. "My Country" (1908), a classic Australian poem by Dorothea Mackellar, led to a discussion about nationalism and the Australian landscape, including contrasting perspectives on patriotism. These discussions sometimes incorporated moral reflection, as I'll elaborate in Chapter 4, but sometimes it was primarily aesthetic: linking a creative work to life, seeing in individual poems and stories models that did or didn't fit a reader's understanding of the world

One of the features of this group is that it included time to write as well as to read. In every second meeting, group members wrote poems using a prompt based on the reading: for example, addressing the same theme, or using the same language devices. Often, participants became very absorbed in the writing exercise and did not want to stop. This writing was a form of aesthetic conduct, in that it involved making artistic objects as a direct response to reading. Participants were invited to share their writing with the group afterward by reading it aloud, which was another form of aesthetic conduct. This component of the group discussion was explicitly framed as supportive rather than critical, and responses were generally enthusiastic. Nonetheless, some people chose not to read their writing aloud. Sometimes, people told the group their writing was too personal to share. One participant told me she wasn't comfortable sharing her work because the group was daunting, especially compared to her long-established writing group. This shows the importance of trust as a foundation for sharing aesthetic conduct in a face-to-face setting.

A clue as to what is required for full aesthetic participation in the reading group came from a piece of participant feedback. This member wrote, "in the beginning I … couldn't find myself to speak. From about halfway through I started to relax. I started to feel more comfortable amongst people I didn't know … Even though we were just reading … it took my mind off everything else and I could fully immerse in it."[118] The capacity to fully engage in an aesthetic experience is here valued as one of the outcomes of a reading group, an experiential immersion that was only possible after the norms of the group had stabilized. Wohl argues that expressing aesthetic judgments is part of the process of group cohesion: that "individuals experience feelings of belonging and distinction through the communication of aesthetic judgments in face-to-face interactions."[119] For this newly formed reading and writing group, the process of building trust through the gradual sharing of aesthetic conduct was just beginning and still often tentative. These inhibitions contrast with the lower barriers to participation for social media users and bibliomemoir readers (although the social risk can be higher for people who are active creators online or write their own bibliomemoirs). There are different thresholds for readers' aesthetic conduct, which may be more private or more public, with greater or lesser risks (and rewards) for belonging and group cohesion.

This account of one reading group illuminates manifold aesthetic acts undertaken by readers. In contrast to bibliomemoirs and social media, this case study shows the lightness of touch that can accompany aesthetic conduct. Aesthetically prompted behaviors often sit below the threshold of obvious artistic production, but are nonetheless active, social, and creative. Members of the Reading and Writing for Wellbeing group listened to stories and poems, voiced their appreciation or dislike of them, linked them to issues in their lives, and responded with their own creative writing, which they did or didn't share with one another. Their articulations of tastes were dynamic and moderated through the prism of group discussion. They did all this in the context of a time dedicated to aesthetic experience. While this time was set apart, it was also ordinary—an activity at the local library, taking its place among other activities in a week. Maybe that's why reading Seamus Heaney, a poet attuned to the aesthetics of the everyday, unlocked some magic. In another poem, "Digging," Heaney describes his father cutting turf, the sound of the spade rasping outside his window. The poem ends with Heaney linking that activity to his own as a writer: "Between my finger and my thumb/The squat pen rests./I'll dig with it." There are myriad small, daily ways in which readers and writers express themselves aesthetically. The reading and writing group I've described in this section shows the layering of these aesthetic acts, through which people use books and reading to understand themselves and their lives.

Conclusion: The Aesthetic Conduct of Contemporary Readers

This chapter has argued for an understanding of aesthetics as something that readers do, and do for others. Bibliomemoirs perform and model a bookish life, illustrating what it looks like to be a reader and how it can shape experience. Bookstagram, a corner of the internet where aesthetics are almost painfully obvious, sets up opportunities to play with images and objects that communicate a reader's style and passion. Book clubs allow readers to test their responses to narrative, working out their aesthetic judgments in a group discussion and drawing links to their lives. Readers explore and respond to books as aesthetic stimuli. They engage in aesthetic conduct that takes a range of forms: online and offline, strong and weak, public, semi-public, or private. Their conduct encompasses and spreads out from the moment of reading to include pre-reading and post-reading activities. Such aesthetic conduct is, in Hennion's terms, a "pragmatic self-formation," where the articulation of "attachments, tastes, ways of acting, and pleasures" is "an activity in its own right."[120] Through their conduct, whether on social media or at a book club, readers align themselves to, or distance themselves from, cultural tastes, and form their views on authors and books, articulating their responses in a process of self-fashioning and self-presentation.

The active, socially performed aesthetic conduct of contemporary readers takes on some common modes. As this chapter has shown, a reader may engage in practices that create alignment with an aesthetic of bookishness—identifying and presenting oneself as a reader, a person who likes books. Participating in the aesthetic of bookishness might mean owning lots of print books, valuing the feel and smell of print books, confidently attending book-related events, or buying book-related merchandise from t-shirts to candles. Books may be carefully arranged, photographed, and presented on Bookstagram, or tagged and annotated and filmed for BookTok. In bibliomemoirs, bookishness may emerge in the author's self-description as a lifelong booklover whose life has been shaped by reading. In book clubs, negotiating the aesthetic of bookishness may involve articulations of comfort with reading, and displays or disavowals of expertise. This chapter has also shown how readers can aesthetically align themselves with particular genres, whether that's romance, young adult, speculative fiction, or literary fiction. Aesthetic alignment with genre is relatively obvious on social media, but this chapter has also drawn out aesthetic affiliation through bibliomemoirs and book clubs with literary classics, poetry, short stories, and children's literature as categories of books and reading.

Alignment with bookishness or a genre are relatively broad modes of aesthetic conduct. Within or alongside these modes are aesthetic acts that relate to specific books: choosing them, experiencing the reading of them, liking or disliking them. This interaction with specific books can happen in (apparent) solitude, as readers encounter styles or ideas and fit these to their understanding of themselves and the world. It can also happen socially. Bibliomemoirists describe books at length in published works, Bookstagrammers use images and captions to describe books for their followers, and book club members articulate their opinions of books to one another, face to face. As participants in networks, readers make meaning and present their selves through their interaction with books.

To different extents, these acts of aesthetic conduct are inflected by (even embroiled in) commerce, the commodification of taste, and neoliberal self-fashioning. Reading memoirs may articulate noncommercial messages about reading even as they comprise products of the publishing industry. Bookstagram is strikingly embedded in book marketing, and TikTok drives sales. The book club I ran was framed through an institutional setting—public libraries and a university—and used public domain texts, and so was markedly educational and therapeutic rather than commercial in tone. Readers undertake aesthetic conduct as part of an intersecting mix of activities that includes their negotiated participation in state and capitalist systems.

Aesthetic conduct also intersects with readers' moral conduct, as I've hinted at but not fully developed in this chapter. A bibliomemoir that is nostalgic for the children's literature of a bygone era might be conservative or critical; one that values a nation's classics might invoke patriotism or resistance. A book club that reads a short story about AIDS discusses changing social attitudes toward sexuality. A Bookstagram account that showcases books by Black women has a progressive agenda. Both aesthetic and moral conduct are pragmatic processes through which contemporary readers make books and reading mean something in their lives. Just as contemporary readers use their reading to inform their style and understand the shape of their lives, they also use their reading to challenge or reinforce their beliefs about right and wrong. The next chapter directly addresses the moral agency, acts, and force of readers.

4 THE MORAL FORCE OF READERS

Morality, a sense of right and wrong, is an inextricable component of interactions among people, and is thus woven into the networks of reading. Readers form and express moral judgments about characters, authors, publishers, and other readers, as well as those outside a book's world—neighbors, politicians, colleagues, or family members—who they may see reflected in what they read. I use the word "moral" here in a capacious, everyday sense that overlaps with ethics and can sometimes, when organized and collective, shade into political action.[1] In this chapter, I propose that for contemporary readers, morality works on three levels. First, reading itself is framed as a morally weighted activity. Second, moral judgments are formed about the plots and characters of books. Finally, readers act morally in relation to book culture and the publishing industry, judging the actions and statements of authors and publishers. As moral actors, readers move fluidly between forms of moral conduct, and exercise their agency, influence and power in multiple arenas.

Like aesthetic conduct, moral conduct is active. Appreciating this means working against any tendency to see readers as passive. Insofar as books are associated with morality, it is often authors rather than readers who are seen as morally active. Writing involves taking a public stand, and can seek to persuade readers of a moral viewpoint. Notable examples of overtly moralizing books include Harriet Beecher Stowe's *Uncle Tom's Cabin* (1852), which mobilized antislavery sentiment in nineteenth-century America, and Rachel Carson's *Silent Spring* (1962) and Tim Flannery's *The Weather Makers* (2005) which were rallying points for environmental activists.[2] Contemporary novels, too, sometimes explicitly tackle moral issues. To take just three, US-based examples: Angie Thomas's bestselling 2017 young adult novel *The Hate U Give* focused on police killings of young Black Americans; Jodi Picoult presented the moral dilemma of having a second child to be an organ donor for their sibling in *My Sister's Keeper* (2004); and Lionel Shriver's *We Need to Talk about Kevin* (2003) dramatized the perspective of the mother of a school shooter. These writers and their books are individualized and high-profile; in contrast, their readers are often posited as an abstract mass.

But the work of writers has impact through the responses—through the activity—of readers. For some readers, this might be reflection and contemplation. For others, it might be more outward-facing and urgent. In our analysis of online reviews of six bestsellers, DeNel Rehberg Sedo and I found readers often articulated moral positions in response to *The Weather Makers*.[3] One Amazon reviewer wrote, "This is a MUST READ for anyone interested in saving the planet. But be prepared—you'll actually have to do something to be a part of the process."[4] Miranda Jeanne Marie Iossifidis and Lisa Garforth's in-depth study of two online reading groups that read Jeff Vandermeer's speculative climate fiction, *Annihilation* (2014) showed readers' affective and imaginative engagement with ecological horror as they grappled with the novel's creepy mood and minimalist characterization.[5]

The different platforms available to readers for moral discussion, with their particular affordances, norms, and levels of privacy, shape how readers act. Imogen Mathew's analysis of online reader reviews of *Am I Black Enough for You?* (2012), a memoir by prominent Indigenous Australian author, academic, and activist Anita Heiss, showed a stark difference between reader reviews on Goodreads and Amazon; many Goodreads reviewers were supportive, modeling empathy and ethical reflection, but many Amazon reviewers were aggressive and trolling.[6] Calls to arms, reflections, statements of sympathy, and hostile insults are all forms of reader action. That they occur after a book has been written does not make them of secondary, or lesser, importance. Writing and reading are co-constitutive, co-creative processes, and this is as true when it comes to promoting or resisting social change as it is when it comes to creating aesthetic experiences.

The contemporary reading environment is infused with the potential for moral judgment and action. The sections in this chapter trace different arenas or settings where readers engage in moral conduct, drawing on empirical examples from contemporary reading practices. First, I consider how readers frame reading itself as a moral activity by looking at how book clubs and festivals promote a positive view of reading as liberal, open-minded, and supportive of social cohesion. Second, I look at the use of reading to form moral judgments about people and actions through responses to characters and plots, paying particular attention to the link between reading and empathy. Finally, I consider readers' expression of moral views about the conduct of agents in book culture by examining the growth of this moral practice online, where reader reviews and social media posts can be used to articulate views about the behavior of authors, publishers, and other readers. This includes displays of not-reading, or reading boycotts—so-called "cancel culture." What readers do, as this chapter demonstrates, is integrate their reading with their moral concerns; using their choices about what and how to read, and their reflections on the books they read, to form moral judgments and call for changed behavior from themselves and others.

From Dissipation to Worthiness: The Moral Freight of Book Reading

When readers read, they engage in an activity that has long attracted moral judgment. Historically, this has sometimes been a negative judgment, particularly when novels are involved, and particularly when the people reading are women. Women's novel reading in the nineteenth century was figured as morally dangerous: a gateway to indolence, dissipation, seduction, and addiction.[7] Even today, some forms of reading are deemed morally suspect. In Chapter 3, I wrote about taste as a form of aesthetic conduct, but it also has a moral dimension. The reading of popular fiction, especially romance, is often cast as the equivalent of eating junk food—at best, an indulgence, at worst, something to be ashamed of. Shaming was a notable feature of commentary on the megaselling success of erotic novel *Fifty Shades of Grey* (2011); an exemplary (self-deprecating) reflection from a *Guardian* journalist was headlined "Fifty Shades of Shame."[8] Awareness of the ongoing moral judgment of popular fiction is also evident in book blogs where readers defend beloved genres as guilty pleasures—one of my favorites is the romance blog "Smart Bitches, Trashy Books."[9] In his work on taste, David Wright points out the moral connotations involved in acquiring good taste and judging others' bad taste, processes that become avenues for imagining an idealized version of the self.[10] Pursuing this ideal, readers are subject to praise or scorn, and a moral cast is added to their reading choices.

But despite this history and the lingering, negative moral judgments directed at popular fiction, on the whole these days book reading is most likely to be framed as a moral good, particularly in comparison to screen-based activities. Broadly, the positive moral expectations of reading fall into two overlapping categories: first, the expectation that reading will make you a better person, and second, the expectation that readers will make society a better place. Danielle Fuller and DeNel Rehberg Sedo note the "historically persistent ideas about the socially transformative and civilising effects of book reading."[11] Such sweeping judgments have been gendered, just like the disapproval of reading: in her account of the rise of the novel, Terry Lovell writes that "an identical 'civilising power' is attributed to literature and to women."[12] Research on the history of women's reading groups reveals that they often pursued a progressive social agenda alongside their literary aspirations. Elizabeth Long shows, for example, that reading, in many nineteenth-century literary societies was allied to an agenda of educational development and the establishment of libraries and kindergartens.[13]

This socially progressive vision of women's reading in the nineteenth century had its limits, including exclusions based on race and class. Dramatizing this, *Anne with an E*, a television adaptation of *Anne of Green Gables* (a story cherished by many booklovers) included an episode about a reading society focused on education for girls, which excluded Anne due to class prejudice against her as an adopted orphan on a farm, rather than a middle-class town girl. Yet book clubs could also work against exclusion. Elizabeth McHenry's work on African American literary societies in the nineteenth century focuses on the Black upper and middle classes and shows how reading and discussing books was used "as a means to assert their civic identities and intervene in the political and literary cultures of the United States from which they were otherwise excluded."[14] McHenry argues that association with literary culture was seen as central to the aim of "racial uplift and social reform," including through political agency.[15] The phenomenon of the literary middlebrow that emerged in the early-to-mid-twentieth century also had a strong ethical component, part of its earnest belief in self-improvement, so that socially progressive ideals were often pursued alongside and through middlebrow culture's conservative aesthetic forms.[16]

The broad expectation that reading can make society better is particularly pointed when readers interact with state and educational institutions, one of the networks of reading I discussed in Chapter 2. Many of these institutions place strong moral frameworks around the act of reading. For example, Wendy Griswold notes that the United Nations Declaration of Human Rights and its Convention on the Rights of the Child both align literacy with moral development: linking education to, for example, "the strengthening of respect for human rights" and the promotion of "understanding, tolerance and friendship."[17] Harvey J. Graff has problematized this alignment, arguing that literacy education was used to induct the working class into the (secular, non-familial) moral community required by industrial capitalism.[18] Whether the morality invoked is a universal ideal and/or a tool for capitalism's development, this association between literacy, the good of the individual, and the good of society persists.

In a bibliomemoir I analyzed in Chapter 3, Alberto Manguel builds the aesthetic link between books and his life into a moral point about the benefits books and reading hold for society. Reflecting on his appointment as the Director of Argentina's national library, he maintains that "all literature is civic action: because it is memory."[19] That is, books have a moral task as the bearers of history. Accordingly, a national library has an obligation to hold representative material— he noted nothing at that stage had been done to collect material relating to native communities, gay, lesbian, and transgender histories and the feminist movement in Argentina.[20] Gunter Leypoldt has written of the dual value systems that readers participate in: "one rooted in the everyday, the other in a sort of moral economy." Reading can be everyday recreation, relatively free from judgment, but can also, especially when cued by institutions, be invested with a sense of moral importance "when what we read has the authority of 'serious' or 'great' art."[21]

When books and reading become heavily freighted with obligation, the urge to react against moral duty—to read "just for fun," for pleasure, or for aesthetic goals alone—can be strong. This is when the separateness of aesthetic conduct may be invoked. Literary studies scholar Nicholas Dames articulates this urge, writing that

> the psychological processes of novel-reading … are continually being recruited into contemporary debates about literature and civic virtue, which not only potentially distort and misrepresent the actual rhythms and practices of novel-reading, but also construct dubious ethical hierarchies (which are often hierarchies of taste, or class) of kinds of novel consumption.[22]

The ethical hierarchies that govern reading—and their conservative, gendered, classed limitations—are real, and Dames is right to caution against the analytic collapse between reading and virtue. However, from the point of view of recreational readers, the two cannot entirely be disentangled. As Jason Tougaw notes in his review of Dames's book, "the connections between an ethics and an aesthetics of reading" are of particular interest to nonspecialists; for readers, the moral aspects of book reading will always be present in the penumbra of their cultural engagement, and will sometimes be central.[23] Book reading today is morally infused with a positive sense of civic responsibility and social improvement. The moral loading of reading is perhaps most clearly demonstrated in book events.

Book Events and the Liberal, Open-minded Reader

Literary festivals are imbued with morality. Announcing his retirement in 2023 after fourteen years as director of the Edinburgh Book Festival, Nick Barley spoke of his pride in creating an event that was "a forum for thoughtful conversations between writers and readers" marked by a "quality of discourse for which we are rightly celebrated."[24] This claim gathers writers and readers into a shared, morally worthy project, with the word "thoughtful" doing a lot of work. It's a very typical way to frame what a writers festival is. As I've written with Claire Squires, media discourse presents book festivals "as a location for considered public discussion and political debate, a liberal arena."[25] We highlighted a

British newspaper's account of the UK Hay Festival's satellite events in countries such as Denmark, Peru, and Columbia, which blithely noted, "it doesn't really matter where it takes place; Hay is about conversation, ideas, thoughts large and small."[26] Hay Festival was famously called the "Woodstock of the mind" by Bill Clinton; the tagline for the 2021 Toronto International Festival of Authors was "Reshaping the world through stories."[27] The act of attending a writers festival signals participation in these grand, society-shaping, storytelling projects, and adherence to a set of underlying values. Being a reader, as figured through statements such as Barley's, is a morally loaded identity. It means conversing thoughtfully; it means pledging allegiance to a suite of norms including tolerance, respect, and freedom of speech.

It's not only literary festivals that frame readers this way. Many reading events are shot through with a sense of moral purpose that connects reading to self-improvement (including moral improvement, becoming a better person) and social progress. This moral loading, marked by an earnestness that I've argued elsewhere can be understood within the frame of the middlebrow and building on the nineteenth-century tradition noted above, is what distinguishes attending an author talk from going for drinks with friends at a pub.[28] The moral value of festivals and book events is not just marketing spin, but integral to how they are understood by both organizers and attendees. Fuller and Rehberg Sedo's comprehensive study of mass reading events such as One Book One City programs included interviews with arts administrators who were optimistic about their ability to effect social change. Fuller and Rehberg Sedo write that "what all the events in our study have in common is an unquestioned acceptance by those producing and managing them of the idea that reading and sharing books is a worthwhile pursuit."[29] Reading events arise from and reinforce the belief that reading is a force for good.

The broad worthwhileness of reading manifests in specific events and discussions that showcase moral judgment. In her book on literary festivals, Millicent Weber refers to the work of Fuller to explain that festivals showcase vernacular (rather than scholarly) reading practices, including reading for moral purposes such as political commitment or empathy.[30] This is evident in the programming of festivals: the 2022 Edinburgh Book Festival, for example, featured sessions on climate change and trans writing. Other festivals are specifically set up to redress inequity; in the introduction to this book, I mentioned new African literary festivals launched recently, including the Abantu Festival in South Africa, which centers Black reading cultures, and the Feminart Art and Book Festival in Malawi. Sometimes, the different norms that writers festivals showcase conflict and erupt into moral controversy: protests attending the appearance of writers who disparage sex workers; walkouts for a White writer defiantly wearing a sombrero; sexual misconduct allegations leveled against writers.[31] Book-related events can be stages on which moral issues are worked through, not least by prompting clashing views. But the events themselves are undergirded by liberal ideals.

Writers festivals proceed on the basis of a shared conviction that reading can achieve positive change in the world through creating connections between like-minded people. This came through in one of the interviews with Melbourne Writers Festival attendees that I discussed in Chapter 2. Carol spoke to me about a session with the writer Kate Holden, whose memoir describes heroin addiction and sex work; Carol had brought along a young friend with a connection to these experiences, and told me, "this was really kind of a turning point for her and Kate Holden was incredibly open to her and took, maintained communication with her for a long time. And that's one of my things about writers festivals, about sort of reading and the kind of capacity to do good in the world." Here, the writers festival is the catalyst for an interpersonal connection that affirms a larger ideal, the power of books and reading to improve the world.

The capacity for reading to forge social connections is explicitly activated in book-related events, and this is understood by participants as a moral good. Fuller and Rehberg Sedo write about the citizen reader: the reader who finds a sense of belonging in shared cultural practice that may not be available to them through other routes (e.g., the state). They write, "the citizen reader, as we have conceived of her, is not necessarily a person who volunteers her time and gives back to her community in material ways; rather, she is a reader who engages with shared reading events in order to feel part of a social network that is visible in a public domain."[32] Fuller and Rehberg Sedo summarize their account of such readers: "these are people who read to belong."[33] Their concept of the citizen reader points to the way participants use events to create experiences of connection and community that they understand as valuable and worthwhile.

If writers festivals and book events provide short-lived, ephemeral experiences of connection, book clubs can offer a more secure, enduring sense of community. As Long's research has shown, book clubs can be long-lasting forums for the discussion of participants' lives, including through the use of shared reading to raise and work through moral issues.[34] This is particularly evident when book clubs read explicitly for empathy, or choose controversial books, and I give more detailed examples of this practice below. At this stage, I want to point out that simply joining a book club indicates a moral intention. This is most clear when book clubs adopt a particular theme or focus. The very names of some book clubs indicate a moral component, so that signing up to them is a statement about what the member believes reading is and can be. For example, the Blackfullas Book Club on Instagram promotes books by First Nations authors in Australia. Actor Emma Watson started "Our Shared Shelf" as an explicitly feminist book club on Goodreads; announcing it, she said, "As part of my work with UN Women, I have started reading as many books and essays about equality as I can get my hands on … I decided to start a Feminist book club, as I want to share what I'm learning and hear your thoughts too."[35] A number of other book clubs also explicitly promote women's interests and writing by women, such as those headed by Reese Witherspoon and Jenna Bush Hager. The base act of participating in such a club is a moral act, but joining any book club signals a belief in the power of reading, and talking about reading.

The "citizen reader" who attends book-related events or joins a book club has a moral conviction that community is good, that it is good to belong to something larger than yourself, and that reading can provide this through the formation of networks. The very act of declaring oneself a reader through attendance at a book event has moral implications through an implied commitment to reasoned debate, inclusion, and respect, and points to the moral force that readers can exert. Once readers see themselves as morally involved in the world through the act of reading, they bring that moral sensitivity and capacity to individual books. From a morally loaded base position comes the formation of specific moral judgments based on a book's plots, characters, themes. This is the second level of readers' moral activity to which I now turn.

Judging Characters

"What would you do for someone you love?" asks the tagline for US author Jodi Picoult's 1996 novel *Mercy*. "Would you lie? Would you leave? Would you kill?" If some readers are already inclined to see a moral value in the activity of reading, this can be supercharged by books that directly invite the moral judgment of the reader. The questions that blurb *Mercy* call the reader to weigh in on dilemmas faced by the novel's characters: a man who kills his terminally ill wife at her request; the police chief to whom he confesses; and numerous other residents of their small town, with their own perspectives on love and justice. Each element of this book, from the core quandary of euthanasia that sets the plot in motion to the enticing second person address of the blurb, encourages moral involvement. As one reviewer on Goodreads responded, "This [book] covers mercy killing, which is such a controversial subject matter … Picoult is a master at weaving in so many emotions and questions, leaving readers debating and thinking about the story long after putting the book up."[36] Books such as this interact with readers by prompting engagement—interest, emotional investment, comparison, and deliberation. The judgments readers make may be critical of characters or supportive; may confirm what readers already believe or constitute a re-assessment of moral views.

A similarly explicit invitation was issued by Australian author Christos Tsolkias's 2008 novel *The Slap*, which features both an ethical hook—the novel begins with a man slapping someone else's child at a suburban barbecue—and a structure that showcases eight different characters' perspectives on this scenario. This structure, which mapped neatly onto the book's later adaptation as an eight-episode television series, encourages readers to judge the sharply distinguished characters. A reader might feel sympathy for protective mother Rosie, or find her annoying; is she a good mother or a bad one? Books such as *Mercy* and *The Slap* not only invite moral reflection during reading but are designed to be discussed. I remember how many people talked to me about *The Slap* when it was published in Australia. It was water-cooler fodder, what the industry calls a "book club book" because it's so discussable. But any book, and especially any popular book, can set the stage for moral responses to characters. My thirteen-year-old daughter is re-reading *The Hunger Games*, and was grumbling to me about how one-sided BookTokkers are in their support for Peeta over Gale in the book's central love triangle. A whole series of videos compares one character to the other; referring to Peeta's hotness and Gale's war activities, one pithy take contrasts Peeta, "a boy who likes to drop baby bombs," with Gale, "a boy who likes to drop bombs on babies."[37] Ouch, the judgment.

The conversations surrounding individual books point to the highly networked situation of readers as they exercise moral judgment. In speaking up for the principle of symmetry for analyzing texts and readers, Shai M. Dromi and Eva Illouz note the "multivocal and conflictual" process of making and justifying moral cases through reading, in which "moral claims are expressed, evaluated, and negotiated by texts and through texts by readers."[38] For them, characters and readers as well as writers and critics are all "social actors endowed with moral competence."[39] This is a vision of a network in which readers and fictional characters work through moral dilemmas in relation with one another.

Books introduce readers to different kinds of people and situations, and the immersive quality of reading, created through techniques including first-person narrative, enables readers to imaginatively experience different ways of being in the world, and test their moral views. The moral judgments readers form of characters in relation to the plots of books can spill over to broader discussions, and involve reflecting on people outside the text. As María Angélica Thumala Olave writes, fiction "offers readers occasions to reflect upon their position and commitments towards others."[40] This reading practice invites consideration of the powerful concept of empathy.

Empathy and Anti-empathy

The belief that novel reading cultivates empathy is widespread and powerful. US president Barack Obama opened his 2016 interview with novelist Marilynne Robinson by saying, "the most important stuff I've learned I think I've learned from novels. It has to do with empathy."[41] Indigenous Australian author Claire

G. Coleman said of her debut speculative fiction novel, "The entire purpose of writing *Terra Nullius* was to provoke empathy in people who had none."[42] The idea of growing as a person through the cultivation of empathy links this moral conduct to the identity of the reader-learner that I discussed in Chapter 2, and there can be a pedagogical cast to discussions of empathy. Fantasy writer Ursula Le Guin, for example, wrote that fantasy texts for young readers (which often dramatize, and complicate, a battle between good and evil) are tools that train the imagination "into foresight and empathy."[43] In my earlier book, I studied a number of articles by educators who used the Harry Potter novels to develop ethics (part of the critical literacy movement, which promotes social inclusion and care for others); for example, by drawing parallels between Harry Potter characters and deaf children.[44]

The link between literature, empathy, and a more just society is a crystallization of the moral claims made for reading in general, an instantiation of reading's liberal and humane qualities. To take one example, philosopher Martha Nussbaum has argued for the power of empathy developed through novel reading to improve public discourse and address racism and socioeconomic inequity.[45] To take another, in the bibliomemoir I discussed in Chapter 3 Manguel argues for "what readers have long known: literature, better than life, provides an education in ethics and allows for the growth of empathy, essential to engage in the social contract"; he suggests "a national library can act as a school for empathy."[46] Similarly, in the bibliomemoir *The Republic of Imagination*, Azar Nafisi makes a number of universal pronouncements about the value of reading, including the declaration that "many things change with time, but certain basic human traits remain eternal: curiosity and empathy, the urge to know and the urge to connect."[47] The capacity to enhance empathy is one of the key ways in which reading, as a category, is figured as morally worthwhile.

Empathy is a meaningful concept for readers, but academically it lacks precise definition. The word has only existed since the 1800s. Some useful working frameworks are drawn from science; for example, empathy has been split for analytic purposes into cognitive empathy (understanding another person's perspective) and affective empathy (experiencing another's feelings and emotions).[48] This second kind signals the strong relation of empathy to emotion, which readers might experience in strong or subtle, positive or negative forms, either during reading or in reflection and discussion afterward.

Scientific studies of empathy and reading conducted to date are enticing, but do not yet point to convincing, absolute conclusions about the link between them.[49] Rather, an emerging scientific consensus finds a relationship of correlation rather than causation, and not directly between reading and empathy, but between lifelong reading habits (generally measured through recognition of authors) and theory of mind (the ability to attribute mental states to others). More specific scientific claims about the effects of fiction reading are often very narrowly framed, using methods that are highly empirical and positivist in a way that does not capture the multiple dimensions of reading. For example, one study claimed to find differences in readers' responses to literary fiction and popular fiction, using a research design that greatly simplified the contrasts between these two forms of writing and producing findings that have not been replicated.[50] While there are differences between literature and genre fiction in terms of industrial production and formal style, readers' experiences of the two cannot be neatly distinguished. There is a multiplicity operating across book culture and its readers that resists simplistic divisions; many readers read more than one type of fiction, and exercise multiple modes of engagement for any given book that might change moment to moment, from reading for plot to enjoying escapism to focusing intently on language or characters. To understand empathy's importance for readers, it's necessary to complement scientific research with insights from the humanities.

For example, empathy connects with aspects of how reading is understood by literary scholars. Writing in the 1990s, Andrew Bennett observed two prominent strands in reading theory: attention to historically situated readers, for example women and LGBTQIA+ readers; and recognition that there is no singular self who reads, that the self splits when reading.[51] The idea of reading for empathy intertwines these strands, as the (historically situated, specific) self who reads inhabits the thoughts of another, the character.

In *Hooked*, Felski explains empathy as one (and not the only) way that readers identify with characters.[52] A loose version of empathy is also at work in *Uses of Literature*, present in her categories of "recognition" and "knowledge" as everyday motivations for reading. With regard to reading for recognition, Felski writes that this entails both recognizing oneself in a book and recognizing others: "Our sense of who we are is embedded in our diverse ways of being in the world and our sense of attunement or conflict with others ... We are fundamentally social creatures whose survival and well-being depend on our interactions with particular, embodied others."[53] In terms of reading for knowledge, Felski writes that reading can be revealing of other people and other social worlds through its inculcation of "deep intersubjectivity," a concept Felski adapts from George Butte and elaborates as attunement to perceptions of ourselves and others, a subtle form of knowing which she notes has often been gendered female.[54]

Humanities and social sciences scholarship can also point to the cultural specificity of empathy as a moral justification for reading. Empathy is a cultural practice, materially connected to experiences of emotion that vary with historical contexts. Feelings are constructed and shared within specific social and cultural settings, and both the display of those feelings and the interpersonal connections fostered through them will also be culturally influenced.[55] In particular, as Suzanne Keen argues in *Empathy and the Novel,* reading for empathy is associated with the middlebrow reader, who is predominantly gendered female.[56] This accords with my own research for *The New Literary Middlebrow,* where I discuss empathy as related to the emotional and earnest dimensions of middlebrow literary culture; increased empathy can be conceptualized as part of the personal and social development that occurs through middlebrow reading practices.[57] In her research on the middlebrow and the Book-of-the-Month Club in the mid-twentieth century, Janice Radway describes "personalism," a term she distinguishes from abstract, dispassionate understandings of individualism. Personalism is individualized, but is a mode "of both affect and empathy. People felt—and they felt for others."[58] When understood as part of a middlebrow practice, personalism produces a kind of reading that is an "event for identification, connection, and response"; this is an intense experience, where readers feel "with greater force and fervor than one might be permitted in ordinary daily life."[59]

Noting the cultural specificity of empathy also means being alive to some of the ways in which readers might resist empathy. Just as some readers value the cultivation of empathy as a moral act, others may resist empathy, also on moral grounds. While in general empathy is morally weighted as good, there is also skepticism toward words like "empathy" and "well-being" (as considered in Chapter 5) and their cooption into a neoliberal agenda of self-improvement that leaves larger structural social problems and inequalities untouched.[60]

There are multiple ways in which empathy may be resisted. Empathy can be seen as a problematic emotive force that fosters superficial commonalities— for example, leading people to identify with characters who resemble them.[61] Another objection to empathy is that it is overly reliant on emotion, as opposed to rational compassion. In her article for *The New York Review of Books,* "The Banality of Empathy," novelist Namwali Serpell refers to Paul Bloom's book *Against Empathy*: "With a simple thought experiment—you pass by a lake where a child is drowning—Bloom shows that emotional empathy is often beside the point for moral action. You don't have to *feel* the suffocation, the clutch of a throat gasping for air, to save someone."[62] This leads to Serpell's deeper objection that empathy is, in fact, a *substitute* for action. Empathy makes people feel good about themselves without requiring real change. Serpell argues forcefully that

> The empathy model of art can bleed too easily into the relishing of suffering by those who are safe from it. It's a gateway drug to white saviorism, with its familiar blend of propaganda, pornography, and paternalism. It's an emotional palliative that distracts us from real inequities, on the page and on screen, to say nothing of our actual lives.

A similar argument against empathy is developed in Sarah Sentilles's *Draw Your Weapons*.[63] Sentilles suggests that not only is an empathetic reaction to an artwork always belated, because the pain is over, but it can also slide into a feeling of virtue for feeling empathy. Timothy Aubry's analysis of Amazon reader reviews of *The Kite Runner* suggests that "if not in the tragic narrative itself, then in their own compassionate reaction to it, many readers find a self-validating basis for hope."[64] Serpell's and Sentilles's critiques are strong, but to me Aubry's research suggests a possible, productive role for empathy. Even if empathy doesn't directly produce social cohesion, reading for empathy allows readers to form a view of themselves that they admire and clarify their moral values, with potential implications for their behavior in other contexts. Reading for empathy may be a substitute for action, but it may also be a step along the way to action.

As part of their moral conduct, readers may embrace or reject empathy. It is important for researchers to remain open to the meanings that readers assign to their own practices. If we think of these different views—one, that reading promotes empathy and this is a good thing, and two, that reading does not produce meaningful social change—then it is important, as per a pragmatic sociology approach, to treat them symmetrically. They are both ways of understanding what reading does. Empathy has different meaning for readers in different contexts, and I want turn now to look more closely at how readers in book clubs mobilize the (nebulously defined, fluid) concept of empathy as they realize the moral potential of reading as a practice.

Reading for Empathy in Book Clubs

In book clubs, there is often an imperative to springboard from the book to discuss broader social issues. The group context allows for and encourages interpersonal moderation and testing of moral judgments. The "discussability" of book club books often relates to their ability to inspire disagreement and contrasting judgments of characters, which may be defended or adjusted through the process of a group discussion. In their work on book clubs, C. Clayton Childress and Noah E. Friedkin argue that responses to a book are rarely homogenous and that readers influence each others' evaluations of texts in localized processes of interpretation and understanding.[65] In their case study of a particular group's discussion of one novel, they found that the process of interpersonal influence in the group created shifts in how individual readers responded to issues of gender and race raised by the book.[66]

As discussed in Chapter 3, one of the research projects I have been involved with was a Reading and Writing for Wellbeing group in a local library. As part of this, I had the chance to witness how readers responded to texts; these responses were often to characters, and involved expressions of antipathy or empathy toward them. Group dynamics made the process of expressing these responses more complex. I noted, in Chapter 3, that early insecurity about participation in the group often seemed to be directed into negative aesthetic evaluation. This was intertwined with negative moral judgments of characters—bristling at them, dismissing them, even being angry at them. Susan Sontag's 1986 story *The Way We Live Now*, about a group of friends supporting a friend with AIDS, drew particular hostility from readers, not only for its complex formal structure but because of their frustration at the behavior of the characters.[67] Empathetic responses became more common several weeks into the program. As the weeks went on, I more frequently heard people say, "I relate to that"— such as remembering blackberry picking from their own childhoods, when we read Seamus Heaney's poem on that topic. Such linking, through the sometimes maligned concept of "relatability," is a foundational part of empathetic reading. In this group, readers both refused and chose to read empathetically. They found characters likeable and unlikeable, they mused on moral dilemmas, they compared depictions of awkward relationships and of childhoods to their own lives, and they chimed in with their views on moral issues raised, such as patriotism and war. As a newly formed group, this was often done somewhat hesitantly, as part of the work of staying psychologically safe in a new face-to-face social setting with an institutional attachment.

Relatability is key to reading for empathy, but so too is otherness. Some book clubs specifically read for difference, to expand their knowledge and sense of connection to different people in the world. Robert Clarke and Marguerite Nolan have researched book clubs that discuss books about Indigenous Australian history.[68] Following interviews with members of clubs that read Kate Grenville's 2005 historical fiction novel, *The Secret River*, Clarke and Nolan found that within overarching agreement about the novel there was also considerable dissensus, both explicit and subtle. Furthermore, this disagreement was highly valued as members "appreciated hearing perspectives that differed from their own."[69] This was part of each club's aim to learn and grow through their conversations about books. Varying attitudes to the connections between social contexts and books emerge in other studies of book club discussions of novels that address racism. Fuller and Rehberg Sedo's study of UK book clubs that discussed Andrea Levy's 2004 novel about Caribbean immigrants, *Small Island*, found that some readers made detailed links to contemporary instances of discrimination, while others demonstrated only a "gestural empathy" toward the novel's characters.[70] James Procter and Bethan Benwell's *Reading Across Worlds*, which analyzed discussions of books addressing racial themes including Zadie Smith's *White Teeth* (2000) and Monica Ali's *Brick Lane* (2003) from twenty-seven book clubs, including six outside the UK in Jamaica, Canada, Nigeria, India, and Trinidad and Tobago, found that book club members discuss race and ethnicity in ways that signal empathy, establish solidarity, and present a moral account of oneself, while remaining somewhat ambivalent and uncertain about racial topics.[71]

Empathy is a reading practice that is also modeled and taught within the university in some contexts. For example, Sandra Phillips and Clare Archer-Lean consider how the reading of Aboriginal and Torres Strait Islander literature might be decolonized through an overt engagement with readers' moral frameworks.[72] They report on the design of a reflective standpoint journal assessment task, defined by four principles: recognizing the multiple forms and genres of Aboriginal and Torres Strait Islander writing; acknowledging the standpoint of the reader; acknowledging the contexts of production and distribution of a text; and, finally, understanding cultural sensitivity as "enacted through empathy to worldview and a deferring to Aboriginal and Torres Strait Islander epistemologies as authority."[73] This reader-centered pedagogy uses empathy as part of a project to open up reflection on First Nations texts.

But what about First Nations readers—does empathy work in different directions, and if so, how? A study of the Murri Book Club in Townsville, Australia, by Maggie Nolan and Indigenous cultural engagement officer Janeese Henaway, offers insight.[74] The Murri Book Club, made up of First Nations Australian readers, eschews an overtly moral purpose. This is evident in their expressed desire to not read serious books. As Henaway reports, many of the book club members worked in roles

> where they were representing their cultural origins and dealing with social, political and cultural issues within their organizations on a daily basis ... we did not then want to go to a book club and have heavy discussions on Indigenous issues. The group predominantly wanted a light, entertaining and enjoyable experience. Although we're Murris, we are also readers. From that moment, we decided not to structure the book club in the usual way and just to let it evolve naturally.

This turn away from heavy moral discussion is itself enmeshed in moral considerations about readers' lives outside the club. It is also networked in relation to other book clubs that members had heard about. The model on which the club was originally based, the Reading for Reconciliation book club in Brisbane, reads books "selected to educate its members about Indigenous history and perspectives." Nolan and Henaway write that "members of the Murri book club had heard through the 'Murri grapevine' that, although the Brisbane-based Reading for Reconciliation group was hoping Indigenous people would participate in the group, an Indigenous reader who joined the group 'felt uncomfortable, like they were on display.'" There was a desire for the Murri Book Club to offer members "a break from being 'an Indigenous professional', without having to, as one member of the group put it, 'leave your Indigenous identity at the door.'" Instead, the Murri book club modeled alternative reading practices—such as drawing diagrams of books, selecting books based on their cover, and a general agnosticism as to whether chosen books were popular or literary. One key difference between the Murri book club and mainstream book clubs, Nolan and Henaway suggest, is "that the Murri book club seems less governed by what we might call middlebrow reading practices."

Nolan and Henaway write that the Murri Book Club is deeply aligned with a core Indigenous Australian value of relatedness, and that the group prizes this over the accumulation of cultural capital. The attention to relatedness may suggest the group also values reading for empathy. Nolan and Henaway note that current research often seems to assume that cross-cultural empathy works only in one direction: "the capacity of white people to empathise with people of colour." They suggest that the Murri book club offers an example of empathy beyond this one direction, quoting one member as saying, "I love reading because it helps to think about and understand other peoples' feelings, and when you understand other peoples' feelings you can empathise with them more." It's not clear if this empathy was felt across the group, and the group's rejection of other middlebrow norms suggests that empathy is differently configured here than in other venues, such as major writers festivals, due to the cultural specificity of the group and its chosen reading practices.

Empathy is a powerful concept available to readers—one they can embrace, reject, or adapt to their own situation and needs. It is one of the tools readers use as they engage in moral conduct by reflecting, to themselves or others, on characters in a book. Building on the base conviction that reading is a liberal and open-minded cultural activity, readers who respond morally to the plots, themes and characters of books actively make connections between books, themselves, and the broader world around them. This can be even more overt in the third kind of moral conduct I examine: direct intervention in book culture and the publishing industry.

"Disappointed to Say the Least": Online Book Commentary and Reader Activism

Coloring books aren't usually controversial.[75] But in January 2023, negative reader feedback led to author Colleen Hoover and her publisher, Atria, withdrawing a coloring book based on Hoover's international megaselling novel *It Ends with Us*. This 2016 title became a sensation on the back of TikTok, reappearing on the *New York Times* bestseller list in 2021 and staying there throughout 2022 and 2023.[76] The same platform (as well as Instagram and others) was used to criticize the coloring book as an inappropriate spinoff, given that the theme of the novel is domestic violence. In a video with over 220,000 likes and more than 2000 comments, Charls from @charlbookshelves expressed herself as "disappointed to say the least," noting the mismatch between the themes of the novel and the format of a coloring book—as she said, "what moments are you going to be coloring?"[77] In a release announcing the cancellation of the coloring book, Hoover explained that it was meant to represent the empowerment of the main character, but accepted that it looked insensitive.[78] Hoover's success is very much due to her strong reader fanbase (known online as the CoHort), and her responsiveness to their moral judgment is a hallmark of contemporary book culture.

One of the most striking phenomena of contemporary book culture is moral disapproval of the conduct of authors and publishers, and it usually happens online. Readers exercising moral judgment through online commentary has become a regular feature of digital book talk: of readers' reviews and book-related discussions on Twitter, Amazon, Goodreads, YouTube, TikTok, and so on. It is particularly evident in relation to Young Adult fiction, romance fiction, and speculative fiction, but occurs across genres and sectors of book culture. Social media allows for a new directness and immediacy in the relationships between readers, authors, and publishers; one where the readers' voice, and capacity to influence, is not dependent on professional critics or journalists as mediators. Prior to social media, forums for debates about issues in book culture were marked by highly uneven power dynamics. For example, writers' festivals have long been more likely to feature men speaking on the stage and women listening from the audiences; in contrast, about 75 percent of Goodreads reviewers present as women.[79] A 2014 panel of children's authors at established US industry event BookExpo did not include any women or people of color; in response, Korean-American author Ellen Oh launched the #WeNeedDiverseBooks campaign on social media. Digital platforms and social media provide avenues for the redress of gender and racial inequities in book culture. This is the case, even though online platforms have their own power relations, including the power technology companies have to regulate or permit speech. Online space is often hostile toward people with marginalized identities. The effects of trolling and discriminatory algorithms on women, LGBTQ+ people, and people of color, and the co-option of their unpaid labor to generate profits for tech companies, are well documented.[80] Yet online spaces nonetheless create opportunities for expression, including moral judgment of authors, publishers, and other book industry organizations, that were not available in traditional publishing and criticism venues.

Readers' moral judgment is inflected and shaped by the digital platform where it takes place. Sites are not only repositories, but active online communities with their own ethical norms.[81] These norms are still in some flux, particularly when new platforms emerge. Each new social media platform sparks a process of determining how it will be used, offering a new potential sphere of reader action, a shift in power dynamics, and consequent cascading discussions over the appropriate use of newly amplified voices. Furthermore, online platforms have shown themselves to be potent fomenters of controversy. Combined, the flux and the susceptibility to conflict of social media enable and augment the moral conduct of readers.

Social media also leaves traces, so that this moral conduct is unusually visible. In my own research to date, I have focused on case studies of responses to particular books as a way to manage the sheer volume of book talk across social media sites and forums. I have drawn on digital methods, like sentiment analysis, word frequency analysis, and social network analysis, as well as close reading. Both types of methods, and indeed the combination, are appropriate within an overall methodology that is attentive to the everyday, surface meaning of statements by readers, including moral statements. Several years into Web 2.0, we can start to see these case studies combine into a bigger picture, one that shows clearly how prominent moral responses to books, authors, and publishing are in contemporary reader conduct online. This prominence, alongside the frequency of this kind of reader conduct, opens up the possibility of reader-led change in response to moral issues.

There is a kind of controversy in online book culture, for example, that has become almost paradigmatic. Consider this example. In 2016, Harlequin distributed advance review copies (ARCs) of *The Continent*, a young adult novel by Keira Drake. Distributing ARCs is a standard marketing strategy to build buzz for a major new release. The buzz, in this case, turned out to be critical. ARC readers used social media to raise concerns about the book, objecting to its depiction of a White girl who brings peace to warring tribes as a white savior archetype, and to its use of stereotypes associated with Native American and Japanese cultures.[82] *The Continent* was withdrawn by the publisher, and its author undertook revisions before a new version was released eighteen months later.[83] While this incident drew considerable attention, it's not isolated. A number of other children's and young adult books have been withdrawn, with the author's agreement, following reader feedback about racism, including, in 2019, *Blood Heir* by Amelia Wen Zhao and, in 2021, *The Adventures of Ook and Gluk: Kung-Fu Cavemen from the Future* by Dav Pilkey.[84]

In those cases, objections focused on the books themselves, especially their characters. But sometimes the moral judgments of readers crystallize around the figure of the author. This is one of the features of online discourse, where debates can become highly personalized. Focus on the figure of the author is not limited to digital culture, though. At writers festivals and live events, for example, the body of the author is an important mediator of the book. Online, a different kind of intimacy is deployed as readers take moral action based on an author's actions or statements.

Sometimes, readers criticize the match between author and the book, either through charges of cultural appropriation or simply for the missed opportunity it represents for authors of marginalized identities. For example, Twitter users responded to the publicity for the 2020 novel *American Dirt* by Jeanine Cummins with anger that this high-profile book about the experience of Mexican immigrants was written by a white, non-immigrant author.[85] The moral outrage stirred by *American Dirt* was part of a broader movement, the #ownvoices campaign that called for more diversity in the publishing industry by increasing the number of books where the author and the protagonist share a marginalized identity.[86] The use of this hashtag shows readers as active campaigners for structural change in the publishing industry. In a way, it is an extension of the "resisting reader" theorized by literary studies scholar Judith Fetterley in 1978. Fetterley wrote of the need for the feminist critic "to become a resisting rather than an assenting reader and, by this refusal to assent, to begin the process of exorcizing the male mind that has been implanted in us."[87] Social media has democratized this role, as everyday readers showcase their practices of resistance to books that occlude or dramatize violence against those with marginalized identities. In her later work, Fetterley focused on raising the visibility within literary studies of works by nineteenth-century women. So, too, have everyday readers and writers (and academics) in contemporary culture, not only by spotlighting #ownvoices books that exist but by raising a call for more of them to be written and published. There is a connection, here, between the work of the activist literary scholar and critic and the work of contemporary recreational readers.

"Authors Are Real People": Reader Responses to Author Behavior

Sometimes readers respond to author conduct, rather than their books. The online response to Kathleen Hale's debut novel, *No One Else Can Have You*, a 2014 work of young adult fiction, was initially positive, but was transformed after Hale wrote a confessional piece for the *Guardian* about physically tracking down a reader who left her a one-star review on Goodreads.[88] (Hale used the term "stalking" to describe her own actions; indeed, in 2019 she published a collection of this and other essays titled *Kathleen Hale Is a Crazy Stalker*.) Hale's expression of aggression toward an online reviewer was a lightning rod for readers online to express their disapproval of Hale and support for the reviewer.

Readers expressed their views in distinctive ways across digital platforms. The most emotional language, according to the sentiment analysis I conducted, was found in book blogs, while Goodreads reviews and comments "below the line" of a news article on the *Guardian* were less emotive.[89] Bloggers took a leadership role in many of the online debates by creating forums for discussions and offering longer analyses, showing their authority within online book communities.[90] On

Goodreads, readers were less emotional in their language but more absolute and action-based: one Goodreads user, for example, deleted their original review and replaced it with the text, "Review has been removed, because what this author does in real life when you leave a negative review is not okay and I don't want to support that kind of behaviour."[91]

In the Hale case, readers led a moral campaign against an author who had intervened in a specifically reader-centered practice, Goodreads reviewing. In other online moral controversies, readers participate in debates that might previously have played out among authors and professional critics, and which still feature these voices most prominently. This is particularly the case on Twitter, which is much used as a platform by authors, academics, and journalists. An example from the world of literary fiction is the CanLit (Canadian Literature) controversy known by the hashtag #UBCAccountable, which preceded, but then spoke into, the broader #MeToo debate.[92] In 2016, over ninety well-known Canadian writers, including Margaret Atwood, Joseph Boyden, and Michael Ondaatje, wrote an open letter asserting that fair process had not been accorded to Steven Galloway, a professor of creative writing at the University of British Columbia who had been accused of sexual misconduct. The letter, stored on a website, used the hashtag #UBCAccountable, and sparked intense debate across multiple media venues.[93] In response to this letter, readers and writers used online platforms to express their view that Atwood and her co-signatories were silencing present and future complainants by placing the symbolic weight of the country's leading writers behind the accused man. Some of the letter's signatories, including Madeleine Thien, Rawi Hage, and Lisa Moore, removed their signature. Others defended their position, on Twitter and through opinion articles in other media outlets, like Atwood's 2018 piece for *The Globe and Mail*, "Am I a Bad Feminist?"[94]

The controversy highlighted how power is expressed through different media. As Canadian author Zoe Whittall reflected, "those of us who spoke out against the letter mostly did so on Twitter, but the signatories, some of whom were among the biggest names lining bookshelves across the country, had access to major newspapers and magazines."[95] Some of those big names, including Atwood, pitched themselves as less powerful than Twitter users; Atwood likened the wave of Twitter commentary to the Salem witch trials.[96] Further power dynamics were cast into relief when Galloway sued the graduate student complainant and dozens of Twitter users who retweeted her, in a defamation case that was still before the courts in 2023.[97] This high-profile Canadian example is one of several, particularly at the height of the #MeToo movement, in which writers and readers alike debated the moral issue of sexual harassment in book culture and the publishing industry. Other controversies include the departure of *New York Review of Books* editor Ian Buruma following criticism of his decision to publish an article by Jian Gomeshi, who has faced numerous allegations of violent sexual misconduct, and accusations of harassment made against writers Junot Diaz, Sherman Alexie, James Dashney, and Jay Asher.[98] Social media affects power relations by reconfiguring the distinction between active and passive participants in book culture, expanding the scope of influence for readers as well as non-celebrity writers and industry professionals.

Digital media notably creates opportunities for people to join together in their moral conduct, and sometimes reader responses online move from individual moral judgments to collective political action. The term "cancel culture" has been used—in increasingly bad faith—to describe mass online actions against high-profile figures. Such actions are political because they are directly, consciously about the exercise of power: who has it, and how it should be used. A striking example of collective reader criticism is the response to J. K. Rowling. Rowling has written a series of tweets that undermine transgender people, support anti-trans activists, and mock trans-inclusive language.[99] Rowling was criticized by readers on Twitter and on Goodreads, where reviews for Rowling's 2020 novel (writing as Robert Galbraith) *Troubled Blood* objected to the stereotyping involved in Rowling's creation of a cross-dressing serial killer, and linked this to her views on trans women. A similar dynamic has been seen in responses to Chimamanda Ngozi Adichie's statements about trans women and culture (including her statements in support of Rowling); readers and writers, including non-binary writer Akwaeke Emezi, have criticized Adichie as anti-trans.[100] While there is power in these responses, the authors at the center also maintain power. For example, in 2022, Rowling (again writing as Robert Galbraith) published the 1,024-page novel *The Ink Black Heart*, featuring a character who is bullied online for her views about gender and sexuality. The incredible length of this book, and its publication by Hachette, a major multinational publishing house, demonstrate the size and reach of the platform that is available to Rowling as an actor in contemporary book culture.

The powerful using mainstream media and the less powerful (including readers) using social media to debate moral issues has become an established dynamic, but this is sometimes unsettled. Not all authors are as powerful as Atwood, Rowling, or Adichie. Published authors may have more prestige than readers, but many are also financially insecure, vulnerable to the decisions of risk-averse publishers, and apprehensive about the effects of reader criticism. Authors who are used to treating social media as their own peer support network might not appreciate the ramifications of criticizing a reader online. Misapprehension about how authors are expected to use social media goes some way to explaining the controversy that surrounded *New York Times* bestselling author Sarah Dessen in 2019. A local newspaper had run an article about Northern State University's Common Read program, in which all students read a book chosen by organizers. The article quoted a former student who said she had joined the organizing committee specifically to stop them choosing a book by Dessen: "She's fine for teen girls ... But definitely not up to the level of Common Read." Dessen posted a screenshot of the quote (with the student's name scribbled out) and called the student's criticism "mean and cruel," writing, "authors are real people." Other authors responded to Dessen, including one who wrote, "fuck that fucking bitch" (to which Dessen replied, "I love you").[101] The online debate that followed included readers' criticism of Dessen, who was seen as punching down by singling out a reader (the name of the student was easily discovered and shared online). Dessen later deleted her tweet and apologized. The initial moral conduct, in this case, is by the author; the reader had made an aesthetic valuation which the author and her allies objected to because it was personally hurtful and, as some tweets explained, because it seemed to dismiss the reading tastes of young girls. This author's intervention was then responded to through the moral conduct of other readers, who highlighted what they considered a misuse of power.

Not Reading as Strategic Moral Conduct

I wrote above that sometimes the content of the book is irrelevant to readers' moral conduct. Sometimes, the absence of the content of the book from discussions becomes, itself, a focal point: when readers respond to the controversy surrounding an author by specifically deciding not to read their book.

Not reading is more than the absence of reading. It is a broad suite of practices that take place both online and offline. In her chapter "Not" of the edited volume *Further Reading* (2020), Lisa Gitelman outlines three contemporary forms of not reading: computational analysis of textual corpuses; experimental books that cannot be read; and strategic not reading.[102] It's this third kind that involves readers' moral conduct, and which I focus on here.

Strategic decisions to not read exist in relation to a person's past reading, and their present practices and networks. In actor-network terms, not reading breaks (real or potential) connections; it can also form bonds of solidarity with others who choose not to read a particular book. The breaking and making of these connections are most evident when the choice to not read is explained. A narrativized not reading is a strong action, because it involves admitting to not reading, and therefore carries a risk of seeming uninformed and losing status. Justifications for not reading may articulate a number of reasons, including the aesthetic reasons of not enjoying a style or genre, but are especially forceful when they make a moral case. Further, not reading has the most impact when it is unexpected. For example, Bethan Benwell, James Procter, and Gemma Robinson in their study of not reading note that "not reading in a book group context is arguably an activity which is at odds with the identity category 'book group member' and for this reason is invariably accompanied by *accounts* which either involve apologies or justifications for the practice of 'not reading.'"[103] Not reading that disrupts a reader's established aesthetic and moral conduct is very powerful.

Professional readers rarely model not reading, but one notable example is academic Amy Hungerford's account of not reading *Infinite Jest* (1996) by David Foster Wallace.[104] Hungerford is a literary studies academic, a context that is important in establishing the prima facie expectation that she would read a well-known work of twentieth-century literature. Her argument against reading *Infinite Jest* hinges on the moral responsibilities of literary studies as a discipline, and it is an argument not just for not reading, but for publicly explaining this decision. She writes, "here is why refusal is so important. Sometimes scholars will need not just to silently make their choices without acknowledging the choices forgone, but to refuse, in a reasoned and deliberate way, to read what the literary press and the literary marketplace put forward as worthy of attention."[105] She concludes that the consequences of following the lead of the publishing industry, which is overly focused on a small number of titles by "well-promoted stars," are that future generations of students "will inherit the sort of narrow archive that still structures modernist studies."[106] A further argument for not reading *Infinite Jest* is presented in Chapter 6 of her book *Making Literature Now* (2016), where Hungerford draws attention to aspects of Wallace's earlier works and behavior that seem misogynistic.[107] There are intellectual and aesthetic reasons for wanting to read widely, but Hungerford's refusal to read gains most strength from the moral case she makes for increased diversity in the books and authors that gain attention and recognition.

While Hungerford is a professional reader, her articulated moral argument authorizes the not reading practices of recreational readers—and it's worth nothing that *Infinite Jest* is regularly flagged as a problematic book by readers online. It is often featured, for example, in the meme of the "red flag bookshelf," in which social media users post lists of books that would count as a "red flag" or warning if encountered on someone's home shelves. In his analysis of this meme, Edmund G. C. King argues that "the 'problematic' bookshelf emerges from these discussions as a social signalling device, with titles and authors acting as proxies for their readers' assumed ideological and political orientations."[108] Readers critique one another as well as authors and publishers via their discussions of other people's bookshelves, and express moral conduct through disavowing or disconnecting from books and authors—through not reading them.

Moral justifications for not reading are particularly prompted by controversial books. Benwell, Procter, and Robinson study examples from the turn of the twenty-first century in which "not reading is an intensely *productive* site of cross-cultural negotiation and conflict": protesters at the set of the film adaptation of Monica Ali's *Brick Lane* (2003), who believed the novel and film promoted racist stereotypes of Bangladeshi people, and religious protests against Salman Rushdie's *The Satanic Verses* (1988). For protesters, not reading the novel was badged as an expression of "principled identity"; "not reading was understood either as an elected or an extreme response to the work of art deemed distasteful, insulting, or blasphemous." In these controversies, "discourses of reading, not reading or partial reading are deployed to perform moral work."[109]

Not reading also has a strong association with controversy in online spaces. Readers may make online statements about not reading to protest against an author, or defend readers' rights to speak online. In April 2021, for example, author Lauren Hough posted a series of tweets criticizing Goodreads "assholes" who gave her book a four-star (rather than five-star) review. "Grow up," she posted, above a screenshot of two readers debating whether to round a 4.5-star review up or down.[110] In response to Hough's dismissive attitude toward Goodreads reviewers, thousands of readers gave her book one-star reviews. This outpouring might look disproportionate. It's highly likely that most of the people leaving one-star reviews did not read Hough's book. But not reading is part of the moral repertoire of readers. Like the Goodreads responses to Kathleen Hale, the one-star reviews for Hough were an assertion of readers' freedom to express themselves without interference from authors. Readers, like other social media users, adapt platforms for their own purposes—including using stars or other codes (such as tags) to express their judgment of an author's behavior. Not reading, and the use of codes to announce this, forms part of the wide array of practices used by readers online that exceed the protocols of professional critics, and constitutes a form of moral engagement with book culture.

Qualitative data from readers confirms the significance of not reading as moral conduct. In her 2016 survey of 396 readers of speculative fiction, Michelle Goldsmith found that a high proportion of readers would not read the work of an author whose social media presence demonstrated behavior that the reader did not like.[111] Speculative fiction has long been marked by competing conservative and progressive factions, and these tensions have been heightened online.[112] The statements and behavior of speculative fiction authors lead to both positive and negative moral judgments by readers, who act on such judgments by, for example, buying an author's books, signing up to their newsletter—or choosing to boycott their work. Fifty-seven percent of Goldsmith's respondents said they chose not to read or purchase a book due to their negative opinion of an author's behavior. She writes that "many readers saw their purchases as an indirect endorsement of the author as an individual or their views on specific topics"; or in the words of one reader, "it's related to the idea of voting with one's dollars." Misogyny, racism, homophobia, and transphobia were all listed by readers as reasons not to buy or read a book by a particular author. Women were more likely to explicitly acknowledge influences on their book purchasing; Goldsmith notes that "qualitative responses indicated that this was likely due to certain types of bigotry, such as sexism, being more personal to female readers. This is evident in responses such as, 'I am unlikely to pick up anything from [Author] as he has made it clear that I am one of the kinds of people that he particularly hates.'"[113]

Not reading, then, especially when articulated and defended, can be a moral judgment, a component of the moral conduct exercised by readers. Not reading constitutes a direct and radical intervention in the moral landscape of book culture. The power of not reading is derived from the fact it constitutes a refusal to engage in other moral practices associated with reading, like open-mindedness and empathy. A reader who deliberately doesn't read is using one of their strongest actions, adding it to the suite of other forms of moral conduct in which readers engage.

Conclusion: The Moral Force of Readers

As I write this chapter, a wave of political actions is underway to ban books, mostly those with LGBTQ+ themes, from US libraries. Government censorship on religious and political grounds is a feature of contemporary book cultures in China, Singapore, Malaysia, the Philippines, and elsewhere. Moral judgments are, indeed, an inextricable component of book culture—and readers participate in moral conduct. This chapter has focused on the different roles that contemporary readers play as they express moral judgments and contribute to debates about reading in general, about individual books, and about authors and publishers. Such judgments, I have argued, are a core component of what readers do.

As the chapter has shown, it is in relation to the moral force of readers, rather than their aesthetic conduct, that the shifting power relations of contemporary book culture become most apparent. Social media and digital platforms have facilitated new ground-up expressions of readers' moral views. This is a cause of concern and fear for some. Readers can be pitched as puritanical censors, as vigilantes, as pushing on the levers of capitalist machinery to suppress the creativity of authors. Such discourse can aggregate readers into a monolithic force: Australian critic Rosemary Sorensen, for example, has written of "Twitter's book burning mob."[114] But the full picture is more nuanced. For a start, there is an open question about who has power in these situations, and the extent to which high-profile authors and large publishers continue to have more influence than readers. Even if we acknowledge that there has been a rise in reader power, this is not only exercised through extreme statements and actions. Periodic outbreaks of collective action are just one component of how readers exert influence through their moral judgments. Readers are not monolithic, and they do more than get angry—they express varying points of view on debates, ask questions, and show interest. Controversies are striking, but they sit on top of a steady, varied stream of readers' expressions of moral views online.

And moral conduct continues to occur offline too. Digital technologies have provided a new, visible arena for the expression of moral judgments from readers, but these complement a range of other moral behaviors, from taking on the liberal identity that comes with participating in a writers festival, to reflecting on the actions of characters in a particular book, to discussing books and authors in person and online. What is clear is that some readers are active, and morally engaged in book culture. The books readers read interact with and prompt the large moral questions that animate readers' lives. Books are catalysts for moral reflection and discussion; like aesthetic conduct, the moral conduct of readers shows how readers link books with their lives.

5 PRIVATE READING AS SELF-CARE

Some of the most special reading moments happen alone. For me, that includes afternoons spent as a teenager in the window seat of my bedroom, reading or rereading door-stoppers like *Lord of the Rings*. Or, if not actually alone, I've been able to feel alone, willfully ignoring those around me: pulling my Kindle out of a tote bag at the beach, registering the sun and waves and adjacency of my family, then plunging into *The Brothers Karamazov* or the latest Sarina Bowen hockey romance.

Not all reading is like this. Sometimes, reading is distracted or half-hearted, with fleeting, if any, moments of absorption. But even if the privacy of reading is partial and occasional rather than universal, it still has an importance that needs reckoning with. The private moment of reading is, for many, the heart of its value. The preceding chapters of this book have shown that readers engage in a myriad of social interactions—but reading also provides experiences of interiority, when the physical world falls away. While I have felt joy and fascination in talking about reading with others, and adored reading aloud and being read to, alongside those activities there is an unassailably private component to what reading is and means for me. This chapter delves into the private dimension of reading, and argues that, for some readers, in some circumstances, it constitutes a form of self-care. Reading for self-care is a distinctive project that sees readers marshaling and configuring some of their aesthetic and moral practices in order to create private, intimate experiences that restore and deepen a sense of self and provide resources for living.

I have saved this chapter for last because this way of understanding reading is so seductive that it can eclipse all the other things that contemporary readers do. But by this point in the book, it is clear that reading isn't only private. The inward dimensions of reading overlap with outward-facing aesthetic and moral conduct in the constellation of reader practices. Furthermore, private reading itself is fashioned in relation to wider social imperatives. The value of private reading is communicated through schools, through media articles, through events and more.[1] In the academy, private reading is a concept that carries significant investments. For example, the discipline of book history long told a story about the development of silent, solitary reading. The story went like this: silent reading emerged in early modern European societies as part of a gradual move from orality in antiquity to literacy in medieval times.[2] The shift from reading aloud communally to reading silently alone was a function of both increased education and technical innovations (such as the use of spaces between words) that made reading more accessible. The story continues: the development of the printing press in Europe and the further spread of both print objects and education led to private reading becoming more common and gaining cultural resonance as a central component of the Enlightenment. Personalized reading practices became linked with increasingly democratic access to knowledge and the growing sense of a private life that exists alongside the public sphere.[3]

This evolutionary narrative, however, has been disturbed by the book historical counterview that silent reading existed in ancient times, too. As R. W. McCutcheon writes, *contra* the conventional understanding of silent reading in antiquity as the preserve of a few exceptional individuals, "a substantial body of research in this field flatly rejects the contention that ancient readers were unable or unwilling to read silently."[4] McCutcheon presents evidence—such as the presence of punctuation in antique texts—that suggests silent reading could well have taken place in antiquity, and moreover notes the dearth of absence that silent reading was rare: his position challenges "the linear, supersessionist, and teleological model that underlies much of the narrative history of the book."[5] As such research shows, stories about private reading can be too smoothly put to work in support of liberal-humanist projects. Narratives about private reading should be interrupted by evidence of granular, uneven, surprising practices. Private, silent reading is not the ultimate achievement of Western democracy, but rather a practice that exists alongside others and is shaped by what's around it.

In contemporary culture, private reading is often romanticized, but it is not a simple opposite of either technology or capitalism. Private reading is inflected by commercial structures and the individualizing logics of capitalism, not least of which are neoliberal discourses of self-care that frame well-being as a matter of individual responsibility. Contemporary private reading also occurs in active relation to digital technology. Like the other components of contemporary reader conduct discussed in this book, the privacy of reading is supported through online as well as offline practices. Private reading may align, imaginatively, with a preference for print formats of the book and non-technological settings: reading at the beach, in the bath, in bed. But perhaps those print books were bought online— or perhaps it is an e-reader that is providing a shroud of privacy.

Researching something private is a methodological challenge. All accounts of reading experience are after-the-fact, partial, and edited for a particular audience. This is true of research that asks readers, directly, about their experiences of reading. It is also true of research that looks at traces of reading practice, including traces from history and digital traces in the contemporary period. For historians who must already piece together ideas about people and societies from scraps of archival evidence, a further leap to imagine the interiority of the reader is understandably one they are usually reluctant to make. As I showed in Chapter 1, Robert Darnton is a reference point for this foundational disciplinary hesitancy to make inferences about reading experiences; Susan K. Martin notes that Darnton's sentence "the experience of the great mass of readers lies beyond the range of historical research" has "become almost a catchphrase."[6] Caution intact, book historians have continued to carefully assemble evidence of reading: the multinational Reading Experience Database, for example, is an open access resource which has collected, digitized, and tagged vernacular accounts of reading from 1450 to 1945.[7] Interpreting this evidence remains the challenge; as Martin explains, the cryptic nature of partial notes and recollections can perversely "compound the elusiveness of the act of reading."[8]

In the contemporary moment, the same difficulty around fragmented piecemeal evidence attends research on reading. Consider, for example, the methodological challenges involved when interpreting online book reviews. Are they written by humans or AI? By real readers or sock puppets (stand-ins for the author or publisher)?[9] Out of love or as school assignments? And how to read so many? Amid these evidentiary questions, finding the private reading moment can seem daunting—although, as DeNel Rehberg Sedo and I have argued, there is evidence of intimacy and profound individual moments in the vernacular style of Goodreads reviews, which use emotive language and describe reading experiences nearly as often as they evaluate books.[10]

Beyond analysis of online book talk, other social sciences research also uses evidence to argue for interior experience. Cultural sociologist María Angélica Thumala Olave uses survey responses and interviews to argue that, for contemporary women, "the pleasures of reading fiction support processes of self-understanding, self-care, and ethical reflection." Thumala Olave's analysis of readers' accounts of what reading means to them grounds her argument that reading contributes to the "search for the meaning of life and to making life liveable" and helps with the management of physical and emotional pain.[11] Research in book history and cultural sociology can point to private reading moments, extract them from totalizing narratives through the use of evidence, and begin to describe their meaning, but these disciplines have not yet fully developed their account of private reading experiences.

Scholars in literary studies who engage with the private reading moment present a different set of possibilities for understanding contemporary everyday readers. In *Uses of Literature*, Rita Felski writes, with a nod to William James, that "to propose that the meaning of literature lies in its use is to open up for investigation a vast terrain of practices, expectations, emotions, hopes, dreams, and interpretations."[12] Felski's four everyday motives for reading—reading for recognition, enchantment, knowledge, and shock—invite phenomenological ways of thinking about the private interactions between readers and books, but she stops short of qualitative research on readers. Felski writes of "the sheer impossibility of getting inside someone's head to judge the quality of their aesthetic pleasure."[13] How can something as personal as private reading be studied? This is the most thorny methodological question of this book, but an interdisciplinary, actor-network informed approach still holds.

The method I pursue in this chapter is an analysis of key discourses about private reading circulating in media that frame the practice's personal impact on readers. I am interested in the overarching modes that characterize popular, public descriptions of private reading. Such accounts appear on social media, particularly the public-facing accounts of bookstores and publishers, as well as in mainstream news media such as the *New York Times*. My method is somewhat risky, because these accounts can be strongly normative, simplistic, and trite, but the risk is worth it for what it reveals about how private reading is valued. Popular articles about reading provide frameworks and vocabulary through which everyday readers can articulate and understand the value of their private reading experience. For the researcher, they provide a structure for analysis that complements other methods for investigating reading experience.

Recognizing discourses about private reading as legitimate parts of book culture is a way to hold space for the mysterious and unknowable. We can mark out, sketch, and keep present the contours of private reading as an important, elusive, but not invisible practice. I pursue a networked approach that puts individual reading practices into relation with media outlets and book industry organizations as well as academics and critics. In what follows, I analyze three principal modes that are used to depict the private reading experience. The first is eroticism, understood as sensuality, desire, and satisfaction: describing private reading using eroticized language is a mode that appears everywhere from bookshop social media posts to author interviews. The second is deep reading, a science-inflected understanding of the value of uninterrupted, sustained reading and its benefits for the reader that has strong media cut-through. And the third is mindful reading, a mode that describes private reading as a meditative practice and as belonging to a suite of practices designed to enhance wellness. All three modes speak up for private reading as a form of self-care, and a way of nurturing the self. Each mode contributes to understanding reading as a cultural practice by articulating aspects of private reading—the sensual, the deep, the mindful—that have meaning for recreational readers.

The three popular accounts of contemporary private reading as eroticized, deep, and mindful arise from the media rather than academia or the archives, de-centering the researcher and giving priority to popular understandings of contemporary reading. This expansive, explicit use of actor-network thinking prioritizes how agents other than academics articulate the value of private reading and has the potential to provide insights into what contemporary readers do, and imagine themselves to be doing, in their private moments. Media accounts of erotic, deep, and mindful reading are attempts to make sense of private reading practices and their value that sit alongside all the articulations of individual reading experience previously discussed in this book, from Goodreads reviews to book club discussions.

These media accounts are pervasive and influential. They are crafted: not organic, in the wild or romantically close to real reading. They are also not especially nuanced. If anything, media discourses about the value of private reading are more normative and totalizing than most academic accounts. But their very force invites not only serious attention but disagreement, creating analytic space and thereby avoiding the flattening that can attend conventional academic accounts about reading. The project of maintaining and collapsing critical distance is nowhere more intriguing than in relation to the first discourse I want to consider, the erotic force of reading.

The Eroticization of Private Reading

There is a popular media discourse that describes reading in terms of desire. Consider this caption to an Instagram post: "A book is like a key that fits into the tumbler of the soul. The two parts have to match in order for each to unlock. Then— click—a world opens."[14] This description of a deeply private moment—a reader's soul being unlocked by a book—appears on a 2019 Instagram post by Melbourne bookstore Readings, alongside a photo of a man with his head bent over a book, against a backdrop of bookshelves. The quote comes from page 218 of US author Brad Kessler's 2009 memoir, *Goat Song*, but the real context here is contemporary book culture. The quote-about-reading-plus-image-of-bookshelves format is one of several recurring types of posts that Readings uploads to Instagram, and its purpose is to express bookishness, a generalized—and in this case eroticized— love for books.

With its erotic imagery of keys unlocking tumblers, the Kessler quote invokes passion. This way of describing cultural experience is not limited to books. There's a quote that circulates on the internet attributed to Maria Augusta von Trapp of *Sound of Music* fame: "Music acts like a magic key, to which the most tightly closed heart opens."[15] There is a way of understanding cultural experience that is erotic, where erotics is broadly defined as to do with sensuality, emotion, longing, and satisfaction. This is evident in contemporary articulations of the value of reading; in a July 2022 *Guardian* feature on "What We're Reading," for example, author Hannah Giorgis writes, "I read romance novels year-round, but something about the sun shining for more than three consecutive days makes me want nothing more than to lie in the grass with a whole pile of them."[16] A 2022 book review published in Melbourne newspaper *The Age* begins by referring to "that aching feeling after finishing a good book," the language of heartache.[17]

This erotic discourse, which both reflects and shapes the private practices of readers, is present across media (especially social media), is bound up in the commerce of the book industry and especially its use of digital platforms, and also feeds into and out of academic and intellectual theorizations. The sensuality of cultural experience, for example, is the core claim made by Susan Sontag in her 1996 essay "Against Interpretation," the famous last line of which invites us to replace hermeneutics—or intellectual interpretation—with an "erotics of art."[18] Sontag writes against formalism and in favor of sensuousness, experience, and feeling as ways of appreciating and valuing art.

Within literary studies, eroticized reading also finds its place. In *Uses of Literature*, two of Felski's ordinary motives for reading, "recognition" and "enchantment," have eroticized elements. Her language is most eroticized with respect to enchantment. She begins her chapter on enchantment by citing Joseph Boone's description of close reading, writing that "for Boone, close reading is about intoxication rather than detachment, rapture rather than disinterestedness. It is, above all, about learning to surrender, to give oneself up, a yielding that is not abject or humiliating, but ecstatically and erotically charged."[19] Felski herself writes of enchantment as "total absorption in a text, of intense and enigmatic pleasure," of "a state of intense involvement, a sense of being so entirely caught up in an aesthetic object that nothing else seems to matter," of being "soaked through with an unusual intensity of perception and affect." "Rather than having a sense of mastery over a text," she writes, "you are at its mercy. You are sucked in, swept up, spirited away, you feel yourself enfolded in a blissful embrace. You are mesmerized, hypnotized, possessed. You strain to reassert yourself, but finally you give in, you stop struggling, you yield without a murmur."[20] This is playful exaggeration, but it contains insight in its striving to describe a particular kind of reading experience.

A focus on the erotics of reading, inside and outside the academy, can produce a normative expectation that reading is satisfying. Deidre Lynch cautions against this tendency in *Loving Literature* when she cites Daniel Boyarin's observation that "naturalising accounts of the privatised, eroticised reading of fiction that make that reading practice seem a 'given of being human'—a bit like sex, in short— sometimes fill him with a 'feeling of inadequacy.'"[21] It is important to remember that there are other experiences of private reading that are not eroticized, even as erotic reading is idealized, including through overstatement, within and without the academy.

One popular reference for the erotic force of reading is Virginia Woolf, whose brand in contemporary book culture embraces multiple strands, including her feminism, her evocative stream-of-consciousness prose, and her association with the bohemian Bloomsbury group. She also stands for a passionate relation to reading. In diaries and letters, Woolf wrote about books in erotic terms that her biographer Hermione Lee describes as playfully opposed to phallocentrism: Woolf's was "an erotics of being flooded, fertilised, 'getting full' of a book."[22] Woolf's feminized erotic mode remains vital today, to the point where it can be parodied. One affectionate example is the briefly active, but widely followed, Twitter account, Bougie London Literary Woman: in the words of its profile, "a 20-something seabird adrift on the tides of London. Can be found devouring literature, swimming wild and scribbling." An exemplary tweet reads, "A eureka moment in packing for my weekend away! I shall eschew all clothing to make more room in my trunk for books, and go nude but for an overcoat and a sharp brogue."[23] Another confides, "I'll never reveal my most cloistered secret … how many of my books I've purchased purely on the basis of their intoxicating smell."[24]

Clandestine nakedness, secrets, and solitary sniffing: this is an individualized erotic. There is an asocial element to the eroticization of private reading. Roland Barthes builds up to this point in *The Pleasure of the Text* (1975) as part of the distinction he draws between pleasure and bliss.[25] For Barthes, reading can sustain a consistent selfhood through providing pleasure, but it can also, more dramatically, provide a temporary experience of loss of selfhood—an experience of asociality—through bliss, a translation of the erotic French term *jouissance*.[26] Bliss cannot be found in mass culture (because "the model of this culture is petit bourgeois"); a popular text like *The Count of Monte Cristo*, for Barthes, "is my pleasure, but not my bliss: bliss may come only with the *absolutely new*, for only the new disturbs (weakens) consciousness."[27] Barthes's distinction between pleasure and bliss is hard to see as anything other than a hierarchical distinction between kinds of books, aligned, pretty much, with modernism and its famous injunction to "make it new."

A broader account of bliss would encompass the different types of erotic experience that reading can provide. It seems counterintuitive, for example, to exclude romance fiction and its passionate readers from any account of the private pleasures of reading. For some readers, genre fiction or mainstream fiction, not experimental literature or poetry, may prove most intensely satisfying. This is a reminder that our private reading experiences are socially conditioned. Earlier in this book, I mentioned Janice Radway's reflection on how this process occurs, in her account of reading and enjoying middlebrow Book-of-the-Month selections, even while learning at university that these were texts to be dismissed.[28] That's why it's particularly ironic that bliss, Barthes's highest form of erotic experience, is in his formulation an asocial experience. Barthes holds that bliss in reading is personal and therefore can only be studied psychoanalytically, not sociologically. He emphasizes "the asocial character of bliss: it is the abrupt loss of sociality, and yet there follows no recurrence to the subject (subjectivity), the person, solitude: everything is lost, integrally. Extremity of the clandestine, darkness of the motion-picture theatre."[29] But not everything is lost in eroticized reading.

The Mediated Intimacy of Reading

Blissful reading experiences are personal, but they are not asocial—even when they feel like it. Publicly shared efforts to describe the pleasure of reading (to say nothing of the many people required to place a book in a reader's hand) point to the private reading experience being something other than the loss of the social self. The individualized erotic of reading is more completely understood as a form of mediated intimacy. This is not just the mediation of the publishing industry and the other situations of reading outlined in Chapter 2, from education systems to online fora. Rather, the private reading moment itself is mediated by and formed in relation to the book, and the implicit presence of the author. Consider, for example, another post on the Readings bookstore Instagram account. In this one, the bookshelves image is captioned with a quote from UK author A. S. Byatt: "Think of this—that the writer wrote alone, and the reader read alone, and they were alone with each other."[30] This sense of two alonenesses meeting is at the core of the erotic force of reading. The pleasure of private reading is found in this distinctive, heightened experience of one-on-one intimacy—the capacity of the book to construct an experience of aloneness that is simultaneously an experience of communicating with another.

Woolf is relevant here too. In a *New Yorker* article called "Can Reading Make You Happier?" author Ceridwen Dovey quotes Woolf, referring to her as "the most fervent of readers." Woolf wrote, as Dovey paraphrases, that a book "splits us into two parts as we read:" "the state of reading consists in the complete elimination of the ego" while also promising "perpetual union" with another mind.[31] Dovey builds a lineage for the understanding of reading as both solitude and intimacy from Woolf, promulgating it in the *New Yorker* for contemporary readers as a means of understanding the value of their practice.

Another interweaving of individualized and interpersonal reading occurs when people refer to Proust; a favored touchstone for contemporary readers, as evident in Alain de Botton's bestselling bibliomemoir, *How Proust Can Change Your Life* (1997).[32] In a post for her blog *Brain Pickings* (now *The Marginalian*), Maria Popova dwells in length on Proust's views about reading. Popova's post, titled "Proust on Why We Read," begins, "how is it that tiny black marks on a white page or screen can produce such enormous ripples in the heart, mind, and spirit? Why do we lose ourselves in books, only to find ourselves enlarged, enraptured, transformed?" Popova goes on to say that "one of the truest and most beautiful answers to this perennial question comes from Marcel Proust," when he writes that reading is "an intervention that occurs deep within ourselves while coming from someone else, the impulse of another mind that we receive in the bosom of solitude."[33] In this account, the connection to the other mind is just as much part of the private reading experience as solitude is.

One of the effects of reading's mediated intimacy is that the reader can feel seen, understood, and acknowledged by a book (and implicitly its author). In her work on reading for recognition, Felski writes of the moment when "suddenly and without warning, a flash of connection leaps across the gap between text and reader; an affinity or an attunement is brought to light … I feel myself addressed."[34] Felski describes such reading as part of a "drama of self-formation," quoting feminist critic Suzanne Juhasz as writing, "I am lonelier in the real world situation … when no one seems to understand *who I am*—than by myself reading, when I feel that the book *recognizes* me, and I recognize myself because of the book." Felski writes, "Reading may offer a solace and relief not to be found elsewhere, confirming that I am not entirely alone, that there are others who think or feel like me. Through this experience of affiliation, I feel myself acknowledged."[35]

Can all kinds of books prompt this sort of mediated, intimate experience? With apologies to Barthes: yes. Bookish discourse extends this quality of intimacy to all books. Numerous media articles and quotes circulating online imply that the experience of intimacy in reading is broadly accessible, because it is linked to the use of imagination rather than to the literary quality or artistic accomplishment of the book. For example, 1,829 users on Goodreads have "liked" this quote from Carl Sagan's 1980 television series, *Cosmos*:

What an astonishing thing a book is. It's a flat object made from a tree with flexible parts on which are imprinted lots of funny dark squiggles. But one glance at it and you're inside the mind of another person, maybe somebody dead for thousands of years. Across the millennia, an author is speaking clearly and silently inside your head, directly to you. Writing is perhaps the greatest of human inventions, binding together people who never knew each other, citizens of distant epochs. Books break the shackles of time.[36]

The materiality of the book object as the conduit for this intimacy recalls the ecstatic language of Manguel's bibliomemoir, discussed in Chapter 3. It is also modeled by essayist Rebecca Solnit, a writer who has dwelled in detail on the intimacy of private reading. As with bibliomemoirs, many of her essays depict reading as aesthetic conduct that shaped her identity and profession as a writer. Solnit's accounts, published not only in book form but on websites such as *LitHub* and discussed on blogs such as *The Marginalian*, are particularly phenomenological and aphoristic, in ways that capture some of the media discourses of eroticized reading. Solnit writes of the interplay of solitude and sociality in her account of her own development as a writer, by describing her early reading experiences. "Like many others who turned into writers," she says, "I disappeared into books when I was very young, disappeared into them like someone running into the woods."[37] But this solitude was not total; she writes that readers live "through books, in the lives of others that are also the heads of others, in that act that is so intimate and yet so alone."[38] She elaborates on the meaning of this as a writer, who must remember that "the object we call a book is not the real book, but its potential, like a musical score or seed. It exists fully only in the act of being read ... A book is a heart that only beats in the chest of another." Her fullest explanation of this intimacy from the point of view of the writer is worth quoting at length:

> writing is saying to the no one who may eventually be the reader those things one has no someone to whom to say them. Matters that are so subtle, so personal, so obscure that I ordinarily can't imagine saying them to the people to whom I'm closest. Every once in a while I try to say them aloud and find that what turns to mush in my mouth or falls short of their ears can be written down for total strangers. Said to total strangers in the silence of writing that is recuperated and heard in the solitude of reading ... Is it that the tongue fails where the fingers succeed, in telling truths so lengthy and nuanced that they are almost impossible aloud?

I've included this long quote as an example of the eroticized discourse of private reading as intimate communication. It rings true for me as a reader. I have valued reading because it feels like access to other people's interiorities. My favorite author, Alice Munro, writes short stories that feel exactly like that to me; like I understand a character, and an author, at a level that isn't possible any other way. The narration of interiority allows a reader to discover what a character is thinking, remembering, or dreaming about, even if that character doesn't tell anyone else in the story. It's a privileged witnessing. A connection can happen that feels like one interiority reaching out to another interiority. The things I think, feel, and imagine but do not tell anyone are mirrored by a character (and therefore with the writer—the person who understands) through reading. And, like a dream, no one has to know about this connection, about what part of you has responded to what part of another, unless you choose to express or act on it, now or later. Such reading helps the reader know themselves.

Power, Politics, and the Eroticized Reading Experience

The perception of an intimate connection not only helps readers understand themselves, but fosters their sense that it is possible to know another. This links with empathy, an aspect of reading discussed in Chapter 4 on the moral conduct of readers, and it has political dimensions. In her essay "Uses of the Erotic: The Erotic as Power," Audre Lorde describes the erotic as "self-connection shared."[39] The foundation of this is sensuousness and emotion; Lorde writes of the erotic as "the open and fearless underlining of my capacity for joy. In the way my body stretches to music and opens into response, hearkening to its deepest rhythms, so every level upon which I sense also opens to the erotically satisfying experience, whether it is dancing, building a bookcase, writing a poem, examining an idea."[40] While reading is not one of Lorde's examples, it is a close fit for her concept of the erotic satisfactions of cultural and intellectual life.

On this foundation of sensuous emotion, Lorde sees the potential to build political action. In another essay, "Poetry is Not a Luxury," Lorde links feeling with agency: "The white father told us: I think, therefore I am. The Black mother within each of us—the poet—whispers in our dreams: I feel therefore I can be free."[41] Lorde explicitly calls for political action associated with erotic experience, writing that "when we live away from those erotic guides from within ourselves, then our lives are limited by external and alien forms"; in contrast, being in touch with the erotic makes people dissatisfied with numb acceptance, "less willing to accept powerlessness." For Lorde, "recognizing the power of the erotic within our lives can give us the energy to pursue genuine change within our world ... For not only do we touch our most profoundly creative source, but we do that which is female and self-affirming in the face of a racist, patriarchal, and anti-erotic society."[42]

Lorde's celebratory account of how erotic experience can empower political action is tempered by a note of caution. She writes that "this erotic charge is not easily shared by women who continue to operate under an exclusively european-american male tradition"; the erotic is stifled when it is constrained within misogynistic or otherwise dehumanizing systems.[43] This is affirmed by the findings of other researchers of women's cultural experience. For example, Radway argued that women's reading of romance novels can siphon off their discontent with their domestic arrangements, allow them to reinterpret relationships, and ultimately enable them to return to and live within a patriarchal, repressive system.[44] Lauren Berlant's account of the "intimate public" frames it as a space of shared cultural consumption in which feelings operate "juxtapolitically"—alongside, and therefore instead of, political action.[45] Berlant's model has been applied to the sphere of reading by Danielle Fuller and DeNel Rehberg Sedo, who see it at work in some aspects of the reading industry, which offer experiences of belonging outside political structures.[46] Eroticized reading is not always political. Yet, as I discussed in Chapter 4, readers do sometimes find moments to act collectively, or use their reading to push for social change. For all the constraints they operate under, readers can find moments of political agency. Some of these moments are activated and inspired by eroticization—one way this happens is through playfulness.

Political action can be pursued, intriguingly, through affectionate parodies of eroticized reading. In her behind-the-scenes account of creating the Bougie London Literary Woman Twitter account, Imogen West-Knights describes it as borne out of female intimacy and shared humor. She writes, "my friend and I used to spend our evenings staying up too late drinking tea, and inventing characters for fun. It's difficult to explain why we do this, but we do. I guess that's the nature of close friendship: you do odd things together."[47] The Bougie London Literary Woman was not just a joke: their intention was to "poke some fun at ourselves and our social circle"—"class was on our minds; the clue was in the name." Another clue to the political dimensions of Bougie London Literary Woman was the creators' decision to identify the account as run by women (the bio reads, "a man is not behind this account dw [don't worry]"). West-Knights writes that their initial decision to make the account anonymous

> made some people self-conscious about how to engage with it. If the parody
> is affectionate, identifying yourself with it feels safe, but if it's malicious,
> identifying yourself with it might end up making you look like the butt of a
> joke in the long run. And gender definitely came into it. It seemed important
> to us, right at the beginning, to say outright that we were not men, sneering at
> women on the internet.

The Bougie London Literary Woman account formed a playful alignment with eroticized reading in order to build solidarity among women, and critique the alignment of literary culture with the upper and upper-middle classes.

The sensuality of reading has also been parodied by Claire Squires and myself in our pseudonymous comic erotic novella about the publishing industry, *The Frankfurt Kabuff*. At one point heroine and publishing consultant Beatrice Deft is in a taxi with police officer Caspian Schorle:

> In the back of the cab, she could feel the heat from his body radiating towards
> her. His muscular arms were tightly crossed, making his shoulders bulge against
> his dark blue uniform. She wondered what kind of books he read.[48]

The frank linking of sexual attraction and reading in *The Frankfurt Kabuff* mischievously riffs off popular associations between reading, desire, and sensuality to perform political work, connecting characters who become allies working against harmful forces in book culture (specifically, neo-Nazis; the inclusion of far-right publishing groups has been a contentious issue for contemporary book fairs, and has led in some cases to violence).[49]

Bougie London Literary Woman and *The Frankfurt Kabuff* are written by publishing professionals and academics, not everyday readers. But the same playfulness is a feature of recreational reader practices, too—consider the over-the-top emotional reactions filmed for BookTok, where young women (usually) gleefully overdo their swooning in a form of heightened communication. In a piece I wrote for the *Sydney Review of Books*, I described BookTokker Simone, who begins a video by announcing excitedly that she is about to read Sally Rooney's *Beautiful World, Where Are You* (2021), then dramatically cuts to Simone "a couple of hours later," lying on her back, stunned, holding the book to her chest and looking at the sky while a ballad plays. Caption: "this is how it feels to read any Sally Rooney book imo."[50] Intense emotional reactions to books are also evident in another BookTok trend from 2023, where readers crushed on Joseph Kafka and especially his *Letters to Milena* (1952). One video shows a young female reader, eyes peeking over a paperback with young Kafka on the cover, and an overlaid caption that reads "when he calls you pretty but Kafka said ≪ in a way you are poetry material; you are full of cloudy subtleties I am willing to spend a lifetime figuring out ≫." The video cuts to her falling over in a swoon.[51] The relishing of emotion on BookTok isn't always political or even critical. In fact, extreme emotion tends to work in concert with the algorithms that drive digital platforms because it spurs high engagement. But there's an element of self-awareness and play in these eroticized accounts of reading that opens up agency and a space of possibility, that makes connections with others, and that in all its funny silliness constitutes a form of self-care—play is nourishing.

The mode that describes private reading as an erotic, sensual experience shows reading folded into personal desires and satisfactions. This popular way of discussing private reading, which is evident across social media, newspapers, TV, and more, points inward, but also intersects with the work and reflections of authors and theorists, as well as the algorithms that support techno-capitalism. The intensity of eroticized reading can attract likes and shares; it can become a (hyper) human point of connection in a commercialized online sphere. It can also be a tool for playful parody and satire, introducing a little critical distance from book culture. And at other times this mode can be deeply earnest—a straightforward, if sometimes metaphorical, account of the personal needs that reading fulfills. The romance and sensuality of eroticized reading undergirds other ways in which private reading is valued, including the apparently more scientific discourse of deep reading.

Deep Reading

The *New York Times* article "How to Be a Better Reader," first published in February 2020 and updated to a snackable format in 2022, offers seven bite-sized tips. The third, after "Choose the Right Book" and "Make a Reading Plan," is to slow down and "Read More Deeply."[52] The concept of deep reading is a powerful and widespread way in which the value of private reading is described. This dominant twenty-first-century framework for understanding reading invokes an interest in how the brain works. It is a scientific mode, often linked to children's brain development and pedagogy. It is also strongly interested in (and often reacts against) digital technology. But despite its prevailing scientific, educational, and technological tenor, this mode rests on a substrate of the same romantic attachment to reading discussed above. It builds on and complements an eroticized view of reading, while also gaining force by drawing on neuroscience. This explains why deep reading is an ideal that people attach themselves to fervently.

The term "deep reading" was proposed by essayist Sven Birkerts in his 1994 book *The Gutenberg Elegies: The Fate of Reading in an Electronic Age*.[53] Birkerts was writing at an important moment when the World Wide Web was gaining traction, inspiring reflection on how digital technology would alter cultural practices. Against a backdrop of multimedia and internet-based entertainment (and, specifically, in contrast to listening to books on cassette), Birkerts claimed a special status for reading:

> Reading, because we control it, is adaptable to our needs and rhythms. We are free to indulge our subjective associative impulse; the term I coin for this is *deep reading*: the slow and meditative possession of a book. We don't just read the words, we dream our lives in their vicinity.[54]

Birkerts combines the scientific language of "subjective associative impulse" with the richly imaginative phrase "dream our lives," which invokes a romantic understanding of reading (on the same page, Birkerts writes more erotically of "the slow, painful, delicious excavation of the self by way of another's sentences"). Both the scientific and eroticized elements remain evident in the way the concept of deep reading has been taken up as an object of interest in the twenty-first century.

Deep reading's blend of the scientific and the personal has proven attractive to scholars who advocate for private reading. Such scholarship draws on science to make claims for the essential humanness of private reading. Anne Mangen, professor at The Reading Centre, University of Stavanger, writes that "it is an inevitable consequence of the human architecture that the processes involved in, and required for, reading necessarily preclude extensive socialising being carried out simultaneously."[55] She contends that contemporary academic accounts of reading fetishize the social at the expense of the solitary, and that the "social turn" in literacy studies and the rise of new media has led to a situation in which words such as "social," "network," "openness," and "immediacy" and "flux" are "cool," whereas terms such as "solitary," "sequentiality," "linearity," "closure," and "fixity" are seen as outdated.[56] Mangen quotes Philip Gough, who wrote in 1995 that the common sense understanding of reading was as private:

> Let us grant that Literacy is "socially embedded." Congresses, parliaments, and school boards discuss it; the meaning and import of literacy is surely a matter to be socially negotiated. But I would argue that the act of reading, that is, literacy itself, is one of the least social of human activities … Ordinary reading … strikes me as one of the most private, unsocial things which people do. We often do it alone, and if we do it in the presence of others (as in libraries or aeroplanes), we

interact with others only at the cost—the interruption—of our reading. I think that reading is most naturally construed as an act which is primarily not social, and it distorts our ordinary language to call it so.[57]

Gough was reacting against the emphasis on sociality in the "New Literacy" proposed in the mid 1990s. As this thread of literacy scholarship has expanded to include more forms of interaction including with digital media, resistance and attachment to older ideas of reading have also continued. One of the most prominent current researchers in this area is Maryanne Wolf, author of *Proust and the Squid: The Story and Science of the Reading Brain* (2000) and *Reader, Come Home: The Reading Brain in a Digital World* (2018). A quote from a piece co-written by Wolf and Mirit Barzillai indicates how the concept of deep reading is interwoven with child development, and with an interest in print versus screen formats:

> By deep reading, we mean the array of sophisticated processes that propel comprehension and that include inferential and deductive reasoning, analogical skills, critical analysis, reflection, and insight. The expert reader needs milliseconds to execute these processes; the young brain needs years to develop them. Both of these pivotal dimensions of time are potentially endangered by the digital culture's pervasive emphases on immediacy, information loading, and a media-driven cognitive set that embraces speed and can discourage deliberation in both our reading and our thinking.[58]

One of the surprising aspects of this quote is that one might think of deep reading as a unified experience—a wholeness that is the opposite of digital fragmentation. But Wolf and Barzillai articulate deep reading as an "array," a multitude of processes that can succeed one another very quickly or very slowly.

In addition to fragmentation versus wholeness, the question of speed—of fast versus slow—takes on interest in this strand of research. The cover blurb for Wolf's book, *Reader Come Home*, speaks of the "'slower' cognitive processes like critical thinking, personal reflection, imagination, and empathy that comprise deep reading." Yet literal slowness is perhaps not quite the point, as readers enact processes at different speeds. While deep reading may be articulated in terms of valuing slowness, the real issue seems to be distraction and the protection of a special kind of reflective thought. One of the aspects of deep reading that is prized may be its capacity, in Birkerts's words, to support "subjective associative impulses"—daydreaming, extrapolating, thinking around the text—but this is seen as different from the distraction of the internet, which leads the reader away from the text.

Expressing deep reading as slow, as the opposite of speedy digital culture, is an attempt to articulate and preserve what is special about reading. At times, such arguments tip into prejudice against digital media forms. For example, Robert P. Waxler and Maureen P. Hall suggest the internet is inhuman, or dehumanizing, when they write that "deep reading requires human beings to call upon and develop attentional skills, to be thoughtful and fully aware. It teaches humans to be thankful for, and to celebrate, their full capabilities. It makes people, in other words, feel good about being fully human."[59] They "worry that the accoutrements of the digital age devalue literary language, pushing it to the margins of consciousness. In contrast, we see literary language as the epicenter of human activity for making sense and making meaning, the hallmark of human existence."[60] This is a romanticized articulation of reading's connection to our deepest selves.

Despite idealistic claims, deep reading is not pure. It is instrumentalized through its strong links with education; Wolf and Barzillai, for instance, advocate the explicit teaching of expert reading skills.[61] Academics provide students with strategies for doing deep reading as class preparation.[62] The instrumentalism of deep reading can go unacknowledged, so that deep reading masquerades as an absolute value rather than a means to an end. And, as I noted above, deep reading discourse can also be underwritten by prejudice and confusion about other media formats, including digital media. But this mode of thinking can also provide insights into the kind of experience provided by sustained, undistracted reading—insights that may be propounded by scholars and researchers but which are taken up by the media, such as the *New York Times*, and filter into the frames of understanding used by everyday readers. One insight relates to the value and pleasure of language. In their article on "The Evolution of Reading in the Age of Digitisation," Mangen and Adriaan van der Weel write that "the linguistic objectification enabled by reading/ writing helps us to think."[63] This observation moves beyond discussion of media formats to highlight how reading gives readers words to describe situations and feelings, and how the structure of language can draw attention to itself to create productive gaps between reading and experience—part of the aesthetic work that readers do. But the most resonant insight relates to the value of reflective reading experiences, which yield a special quality of attention and experience. This insight is also present in a third, less scientific, but equally powerful, discourse about private reading: reading as mindfulness.

Mindfulness, Meditation, and Reading

The website Book Riot is as frenetic as its name suggests. A pop-up invitation to subscribe to a newsletter splashes across seven personalized ads. Links to book-themed articles, quizzes, daily deals, giveaways, and horoscopes are accompanied by vibrant pictures and zippy graphics. The site's multiple, colorful calls for attention exemplify digital media at its most visually busy. Yet it was here that an article appeared in 2014 with a quiet title: "Reading as a Kind of Meditation."

"I recently got into meditation and I realized it's kind of like deep reading," wrote regular Book Riot romance columnist Jessica Tripler. "Just like meditation, being transported by a book quiets the constant stream of thoughts and connects me to something else." Recounting her experience reading Jennifer Weiner's *All Fall Down* (2014), a commercial women's fiction title about a suburban mother who becomes addicted to pain medication, Tripler reflected: "There were difficult scenes, but I felt open to the way they made me feel, and I trusted the writer to make them worthwhile. The outside distractions were still there, but they didn't get traction. Even when the story made me sad or scared, the reading experience itself felt good."[64] Tripler's evocation of an interior state of equilibrium and openness is an example of the third discourse of private reading that I wish to explore: reading as meditation, or, since meditation is one technique within a set of linked practices, reading as mindfulness.

Softer than neuroscientific deep reading and less sensual than eroticized reading, descriptions of mindful reading tap into broad social interest in mental health and well-being. Mindfulness has had increasing prominence across spheres of contemporary life in the twenty-first century, present everywhere from business to education and drawing on Buddhism and Western philosophical traditions.[65] The contemporary omnipresence of mindfulness has economic aspects: for example, mindfulness has been promoted in workplaces, often as part of a suite of well-being measures for employees. In this context, mindfulness obscures structural issues by individualizing wellness, and neutralizes negative feelings rather than channeling them into political action. For this reason, much ambivalence surrounds mindfulness discourse. And yet for many mindfulness is a tool or technique with genuine mental benefits. The enthusiasm for bringing mindfulness into various spheres of life has extended to reading. When people discuss reading as mindfulness or as meditation, they illuminate elements of what reading does and means for contemporary everyday readers by attempting to articulate its interior dimensions.

As with the eroticized and deep reading modes of understanding private reading, mindful reading has touchpoints with academia. A scholarly work by poet Bryan Walpert, for example, identifies key components of mindfulness that reading can activate: attention to the present moment, attention to sensory experience, an appreciation of the self as illusory, and an appreciation of connectedness.[66] Yet mindful reading is more common as a popular mode, and mindful reading advice proliferates across personal blogs, small business websites, and the book pages of newspapers.[67] An article on the website mindfulness.org introduces the concept of mindful reading as "a process of quiet reflection that requires mindful attentiveness, letting go of distracting thoughts and opinions to be fully in the moment with the text. It moves the reader into a calm awareness, allowing for a more profound experience and understanding," then offers three practical reading exercises to try: focusing on the breath before and during reading; savoring a resonant phrase; and reading aloud with others.[68] A *New York Times* article, "How to Be Mindful While Reading," from the newspaper's wellness section, advises that "reading can be a crucial opportunity for mindfulness—the ability to be in the present moment, aware while withholding judgement, both inside and outside of yourself."[69] On the site Medium, Josh Guilar, a blogger with the bio "Freelance writer, content marketer and SEO copywriter" who lists his interests as "Coffee | Conversation | Books," ruminates,

> I recently read War & Peace and I must say that getting lost in Tolstoy's novel was quite relaxing. War & Peace requires a fair amount of patience and attention, since Tolstoy was clearly in no rush when he wrote that tome. But it also requires, like many good books, for the reader to become so absorbed in what's happening that you forget the world around you. You forget everything and become absorbed in what's on the page, and it's this act of escapism, of being lost in a good book, that allows you to relax: if only for an hour or so each day.

This example is a model of mindful reading. Guilar goes on to emphasize that not all reading is like this, "just as all sitting is not meditative. Reading a business book that is trying to teach you something won't have the same effect as a novel. A novel is escapism, a business book or some other educational book is usually a person trying to solve a problem they have."[70] Guilar is thoughtful as to the different potential interior experiences offered by books of different genres, reserving mindfulness for recreational novel reading.

Similar nuance is evident on the blog "Simone and Her Books," where Simone offers a gentle and compassionate reflection on the links between reading and meditation. She notes that while reading isn't exactly the same as meditation, it has some of the same elements:

> you're not actively sitting down to meditate, but you're about to pick up a book and put all your energy to focus on the story. I don't know about you, but when a book is good and you're sucked into the story then it feels like everything else in the world falls away. [...] When you're in a book, you're **IN** it.

Simone then offers a caveat to this conceptualization of reading as meditation, writing that "reading might not work all the time. There are moments in our life when the invading thoughts or stress are too overpowering to withstand a bookish evening. **Make sure to always check in with yourself.** If reading isn't for you, then maybe meditation will work for you. If not, there's always a little Netflix"[71] (emphasis in original).

The six comments beneath Simone's blog post affirm and extend these thoughts, showing more ways in which reading, and other cultural activities, can be thought of as meditation. One commenter, for example, reflects that "I think any activity that puts you in 'the zone' is similar to meditation. When you read, your ego dissolves and you become one with the story. You are completely present, without discriminating thoughts getting in the way. If the book is good enough." The suggestion that the quality of the book matters, like Guilar's comment about genres, points to the interrelationship of the text and the reader, or even the author and the reader—this is not a completely independent experience, but one prompted and shaped by the book and its author.

The discourse of mindful reading emphasizes it as an internal experience. Yet meditative reading is also promoted and supported through a number of social structures—not least the publication of articles about mindful reading. As these articles affirm, those who read purposefully for mindfulness may reach out to others as part of this practice. One example is the suggestion from the mindfulness.org website noted above, to read aloud with others as a route to mindfulness.[72] In other cases, articulating and discussing reading as mindfulness may enhance its benefits. In the bibliomemoir *Tolstoy and the Purple Chair: My Year of Magical Reading* (2011) Nina Sankovitch charts a reading challenge she set for herself—to read a book a day for a year—to help her deal with the grief of losing her sister to cancer.[73] A reader's review on YouTube in 2021, ten years after the book's publication, uses Sankovitch's book to reflect on reading therapeutically, noting that for Sankovitch reading was not just "a way for her to put a pause on everything" but also "a crash course on all of the different elements that make up a life," in words "that she could wrap around herself like a warm blanket."[74] Another reader responded to this review, writing in a comment below the video, "How wonderful to see your review of this book! Way back in 2008/2009, I used to read Sankovitch's blog as she was going along … I think I might need to pick it up sometime. You're certainly right that it has a special kind of resonance right now during the pandemic." A 2008 blog, a 2011 published memoir, and a 2021 YouTube video—and their multiple reader-discussants—surround a private reading experience that was healing through being mindful.

One particularly striking social framework that supports mindful reading is bibliotherapy, a practice where specific books are recommended for their therapeutic benefits. As Leah Price has discussed, bibliotherapy in its currently understood sense began in the early 2000s with doctors "prescribing" self-help books for patients to read—a practice sometimes referred to as cognitive bibliotherapy. It has evolved to include creative bibliotherapy, which involves recommending literature and poetry that relate to particular challenges a reader might be facing.[75] The School of Life bibliotherapy service is perhaps the best known, having featured in the pages of the *Guardian*, the *New Yorker*, and a range of other media outlets. Through individual appointments and the associated website booksastherapy.com, the School of Life offers bibliotherapy as "an exercise in linking up some books with the needs of our souls."[76] The School of Life is a commercial service, but academic and public service organizations also support forms of bibliotherapy. For example, the Reading and Writing for Wellbeing group that I have described earlier in this book aimed to create personally enriching experiences of literature through the guided support of a group setting and through the selection of texts that supported discussion of people's lives.

As with deep reading, the context that frames contemporary reflections on reading as mindfulness is the increasing dominance of digital technology, especially interaction with screens. The *New York Times* article on mindful reading advises people to "consider reading in print. If much of your reading is on a screen—your phone, computer or tablet—then mindful reading from a tangible book could be a nice break from the pinging."[77] The centrality of digital technology in the reading as mindfulness discourse is both implicit and explicit. At the implicit level, all of the articles I've quoted were published digitally, as blogs, website articles, or ebooks, and I read them on a screen: these reflections are immersed in and speak from digital contexts, even as they invoke non-digital forms of reading. At the explicit level, reading fiction for mindfulness is offered as a practice to counterbalance scrolling; the distracted, overwhelming, numbing experience of reading snippets of information across multiple platforms. The digitization of contemporary life throws the affordances of print books and pre-digital modes of reading into relief as potential salve and savior.[78] These affordances include the focus and immersion, the special quality, of mindful reading, which in the post-digital era is framed as a counter to digital media even as it occurs among digital media.

Scrolling back to that clamorous Book Riot website for a moment, Tripler too recognizes mindful reading as a practice that works against the compulsions of digital media. She writes, "both meditation and deep reading encourage a combination of commitment and openness that the digital-social era can make harder to maintain." Tripler sees a need for a more mindful approach to reading that is explicitly set apart from her usual digital media practices, writing that

> because reading has become so social, I often pull myself from the text to look up a word, ask someone about something, or Tweet a passage of particular beauty or ugliness. The downside is that I find it more difficult lately to be transported by a book: to lose track of time, forget myself, and be totally immersed in the world the author has created.[79]

Yet unlike many other commentators, Tripler also sees positive aspects to digital reading, which she describes as both "a boon and a bane." Tripler not only reads in digital formats, but notes that she learned to meditate via an app; so digital technology works together with her self-care practices. In fact, they are mutually constitutive.

The discourse of reading as mindfulness or meditation shows an understanding of reading as a route to an interior experience that nurtures the self, even when socially mediated. Mindful reading is an opportunity for the reader to gain relief and distance from the immediate busyness of one's life. It isn't simple escapism. The epigraph to Tripler's article is a quote from David Mitchell's 2004 novel *Cloud Atlas*: "Books don't offer real escape, but they can stop a mind scratching itself raw." This is reading as respite with purpose; temporary withdrawal from the world as a route to healing and wellness.

When novelist Hilary Mantel died in 2022, journalist and screenwriter Michael Holden wrote a Twitter thread about her impact on him as a reader, a thread that was liked over a thousand times.[80] Holden's tweets described his experience being hospitalized for a psychological breakdown five years earlier, a time when he was thinking "this is it, you're finished—there will never be any escape from this, and these unbearable feelings will be with you for the rest of your life." He goes on: "Eventually I got out of bed and made my way to the ward's common room. There were only a half dozen books there, one of which was Wolf Hall. I didn't imagine I could concentrate but I needed to get away from what was happening inside my mind, so I started to read it." As he read,

> my mind kind of slowly snapped into a kind of flickering but reverent focus that took my attention away from itself—and allowed some kind of background repair to begin … I took the book to my room and read that page again and again. Each time coming a little more together, feeling it work on me like medicine, like touch.

Holden's thread includes specific quotes and photographs of pages as he describes in detail how the novel affected him. His beautiful and moving account puts into words an experience that happened inside his mind, as words and story absorbed his attention. It powerfully illustrates the value of mindful reading as a framework for understanding the value of fiction. Mindful reading frames reading as an occasion for sustained concentration, for focus, so as to encounter one's self and build one's capacity to withstand the stresses of life. Accounts of reading as mindfulness show how private reading can nourish the self.

Conclusion

There is an intimate core to what everyday recreational readers do, a distinctively private, restorative practice. These are peaceful moments of silently turning the pages of a book, or intimate moments when an audiobook narrator speaks directly into your ear. By definition, these private experiences are hard for researchers to access and understand. Studying popular media discourses that describe these private moments may seem a roundabout approach, but it captures one of the realities of contemporary recreational reading. Yes, private reading moments exist—and the ways these are experienced and understood by individuals are influenced by wider social narratives about what reading can do. There are powerful, long-lasting lineages of thought that shape individual reading experiences. These proliferate across accessible media sites, such as blogs and newspapers, and also interact with academic and intellectual understandings of reading: with the work of Barthes, Woolf, Sontag, or contemporary scholars of reading and the brain such as Wolf.

Contemporary modes of describing reading across media formats, from *New York Times* how-tos to blogs, include three dominant frames for understanding the value of private reading: as eroticized (sensual, satisfying, intimate), as deep (supporting development of the brain), and as mindful (promoting well-being and mental health). In each case, these frameworks help readers make sense of the value of their reading with particular reference to the contemporary dominance of digital technologies in everyday life. In this post-digital context, quiet, individual moments of focused attention on a book have a heightened resonance, becoming, as Price has written, symbolic: "the digital era," she writes, "seems to have invested these objects [books] with new glamour."[81] The book becomes a bulwark against change, a "bolt-hole" for readers battling "digital-era threats to the kind of self that reading had once engendered."[82] Contemporary discussions of private reading pulsate with visions of how reading can nourish this ideal self. The eroticized, deep, and mindful modes I've considered in this chapter are not the only ones available to readers as they make sense of the place reading holds in their lives. Yet they are dominant: each derives force from a normative claim about what private reading should be and pays scant regard to readers who might feel less passionate about or immersed in their reading The authority of these frameworks means that readers interact with them as they experience and articulate a whole range of private reading emotions and insights, including negative affects like boredom, dislike, and frustration.

Researchers may never know what readers experience during their private reading moments. No single framework explains it all; mystery remains. But research can acknowledge private reading, create and hold space for it, and honor the plural ways of talking about it by maintaining open-textured research methods that account for different private experiences. A networked study shows that private reading exists alongside and interspersed with all the other practices of contemporary readers. Intimate, private reading moments are surrounded by shared experiences: talking about books and reading, purchasing or acquiring books from a retailer or library, keeping an eye on prize shortlists or newspaper reviews, and all of the other aesthetic and moral practices of readers. Through these actions, some intimations of the value of private reading, for some readers, emerge. Understanding private reading through some of the most prevalent contemporary media discourses gives a hint of not only what reading is, but what reading can be. If reading is often imagined and sometimes experienced as a nurturing, restorative practice, this can not only benefit individual readers but can unfold into practices that can nourish communities, linking the private reading moment with the wider aesthetic and moral conduct of readers in the world.

CONCLUSION

What do readers do? There's a tempting, obvious answer. Readers read! But it's clear that the answer is not so straightforward. There is no single category of reader. Even when one narrows the scope, as I have, to contemporary recreational readers, there is an incredible variety of practices and affects associated with reading. The identity of "reader" is taken on and off, configured and re-configured across diverse contexts and as part of different networks. A teenager on TikTok showing off the Post-it notes in her favorite romance fiction is a reader. A commuter tuning into an audiobook is a reader. A harried grandparent at the beach trying over and over to read the first page of a book then giving up is a reader. What contemporary recreational readers have in common is the act of engaging, body and mind, with a text—but that's neither a simple thing nor the full story. Reading is connection, imagination, reflection, action.

In this book, I've presented an exploded view of contemporary recreational reading to show how readers act and interact. Readers are private and social. They are attached to print at the same time, often, as being au fait with digital platforms; they inhabit a post-digital world. Recreational readers relax and they perform tasks that constitute labor. They navigate different institutions and systems, including those of the state, the publishing industry, and techno-capitalism. Multiply the number of different recreational readers by their individual practices, and the question of what contemporary readers do starts to look unanswerable. Yet it can be answered, and in a way that doesn't fall back on stereotypes (readers are middle-aged women drinking wine at book club) or journalistic hype (readers are online warriors changing the publishing industry). Instead, what I've proposed in this book is a flexible, capacious descriptive model of contemporary recreational reading that is built from the ground up. I've drawn on the panoply of twenty-first-century reader practices to identify two main clusters of activity that illuminate what reading is and means today. The most significant things that contemporary readers fall into two overlapping domains: aesthetic and moral conduct. Readers engage in these forms of conduct as they make and break connections in networks, as they interact with others in the world, and as they pursue their own private cultural practice.

In developing this model of contemporary reading, I've emphasized the need for a conceptual toolkit supplied from two disciplinary traditions: literary studies, with its nuanced, self-reflexive attention to texts and reading methods, and the social sciences—principally book history but also cultural sociology—with their attention to materiality, to social structures, and to people outside the academy. From literary studies, and especially its reader response and phenomenological traditions, come concepts as rich as Louise Rosenblatt's "aesthetic reading," Judith Fetterley's "resistant reader," and Rita Felski's distillation of different motives for, and attachments to, reading. From book history and cultural sociology come profound insights into how reading interacts with people's lives, such as Elizabeth Long's work on the impact of book clubs for women, and Danielle Fuller and DeNel Rehberg Sedo's account of "citizen readers" who participate in civic reading events.[1]

In debt to and communality with these scholars, I have proposed harmonizing disciplinary approaches through an actor-network-theory-influenced model that approaches readers as actors, considers their relational situations, is attentive to power dynamics, and is curious about how texts, objects, people and organizations interact to produce practices of reading. This model also draws on other grounded traditions of research such as pragmatic sociology, which highlights actors' own meaning-making and judgments.[2] A network-based approach to reading starts from practice not theory, and incorporates qualitative research into the behavior and statements of a range of twenty-first-century readers. For researchers and teachers, a network-based study of contemporary recreational reading involves, as I proposed in Chapter 1, four steps. The first is to identify a particular reader or group of readers, and see what they are reading. The second is to read one of those books. The third is to investigate the networks that produced the book and its reception, and the final step is to consider the book, its readers, and its networks of production and reception in relation to one another.

Such an approach has been followed in significant contemporary reading studies scholarship, such as Megan Sweeney's work on women's reading in prisons.[3] It's an approach that tends to produce case studies, and in this book I have presented a number of mini versions of reader-centered networks. For example, in Chapter 3 I considered Azar Nafisi's *The Republic of Imagination*, a bibliomemoir by a professor of literature that takes Mark Twain's *The Adventures of Huckleberry Finn* as a touchstone for her life as an immigrant to America, and builds around it an understanding of family and friendship, protest and politics. In Chapter 4, I wrote of Charls, whose TikTok video about her relationship with Colleen Hoover's book, *It Ends with Us*, actively generated connections between herself and other readers, Hoover, Hoover's publisher, and media outlets that led to the cancellation of a proposed coloring book and the restatement of key values for this reading network. In Chapter 5, I introduced screenwriter Michael Holden, who tweeted about his powerful experience reading Hilary Mantel's *Wolf Hall*, an experience "of flickering but reverent focus" that contributed to his healing from mental illness. Like Charls's video, Holden's statement about reading radiated out along the networks of social media. One of my most detailed case studies, which appeared in nearly every chapter, was an in-person Reading and Writing for Wellbeing group that I facilitated at a local library in 2017; over the course of a few months, readers in this group responded to Seamus Heaney, to Susan Sontag, to the meeting space, to me, and to each other, testing out their ideas about the value of reading in their lives.

These are accounts of reading that start with readers, move to the books they read, and then take in digital platforms, marketing, academic institutional overlays, politics, and more. Each account could open out into a larger study. Rather than offering fully detailed case studies, however, in this book I have prioritized the provision of a useful model for understanding contemporary reading by working through the different conceptual facets that come into play: the networks of readers, the nature of the aesthetic and moral conduct that readers engage in, and how these come together in the private reading experience.

As I've shown in this book, reading, in the post-digital age, is a cultural practice with aesthetic and moral, social and private aspects. These dimensions, reflected upon and combined, yield an understanding of the richness of reading as a component of contemporary culture. What might this understanding indicate about the future of recreational reading? Book reading, as I noted in the introduction, has proved remarkably adaptable, versatile, and persistent. The practices identified in this book indicate some of the adaptations that might develop over the next decades, particularly within the context of Anglophone countries.

First, book reading will continue to benefit from its situation in multiple networks that include long-lasting institutions. As I demonstrated in Chapter 2, one of the key things contemporary recreational readers do is assume that identity, however partially or temporarily, by making associative links and forming groups. The longevity of reading is strengthened by the robust positions and identities that readers can adopt—as consumers (in bookstores), as learners (in the education system), as citizens (in libraries), as audiences (in events and the creative industries), and as content creators (on social media). The networks where readers' associative energies cluster enable them to assume different identities and pursue various activities. Bricks-and-mortar and online bookstores, for example, encourage readers to fashion themselves as the personalized consumers of late capitalism and take up a position in relation to multinational corporations and small local businesses. The education system (from primary school to university) and public libraries as state institutions promote readers as citizens, and readers may embrace or distance themselves from this identity. In other networks, readers are sociable discussants to varying degrees. At book-related events, readers are audience members (but not always passive), and on online sites, they are entertainers, critics, and lurkers.

Readers' different online and offline affiliative practices establish relations between themselves and others: fellow readers (in the same place or across the globe), organizations, publishers, authors, platforms, retailers. These relations have power dynamics that readers navigate, from the restrictions built into digital platforms, to the selection of book club titles, to the programming of writers festivals. In many of these relations, readers are a source of direct or indirect profit. Digital companies harvest data and extract value from readers' unpaid online labor. Publishing companies push readers toward the handful of big books each season that they hope will become bestsellers. As this book has shown, there is more at play in these networks than commerce, and plenty of scope for reader agency. What is true is that readers' actions and interactions further strengthen powerful networks of communication, culture, education, and commerce, networks that have durability and longevity. Book reading's entrenchment in diverse, sturdy networks assures its future, so that recreational book reading will be able to withstand competition from (or cooperation with) other media forms and cultural activities.

Within these networks, readers will continue to use book reading as part of their aesthetic and moral expression. The heart of this book, Chapters 3 and 4, focused on these dimensions of what readers do. In relation to the aesthetic conduct of readers, I showed how readers use books to fashion their self-image, including presenting this to others. Books become part of the stories that readers tell about their lives. Readers engage in expressions of taste, including articulating an alignment with bookishness as a general category; identifying favorite genres, authors, or books; and applying the style of a book or books to their own lives. Readers' aesthetic conduct takes a number of forms. Bibliomemoirs, books about reading, are high prestige legacy publishing products that offer extended examples of how readers use books aesthetically to understand the shape of a life. Image-heavy social media platforms prompt readers to display and comment on books in ways that are explicitly aesthetic and styled, in order to craft a presentation of the self. Finally, book club members express aesthetic judgments; I offered the specific example of the read-aloud community group I co-facilitated, where participants responded to short stories, poems, each other, and the context of the group as they articulated the value of these texts.

The aesthetic conduct of readers varies across online and offline sites, can be overt or subtle, and takes place in dynamic tension with commercial imperatives, from book marketing, to the algorithms that raise an Instagrammer's visibility, to the contrasting nonprofit aims of community libraries and university research. Amid all this variety, the drive to use reading for pleasure, for the sake of beauty, and to make aesthetic sense out of life and the world persists as a key component of what readers do. The aesthetic uses to which books are put may be even more significant in the future, as books gain greater purchase as nostalgic objects of a pre-digital era and, through the workings of the publishing industry, become ever more collectible and attractive through their cover designs and marketing. The symbolic potency, the aura, of books and reading has potential to grow further.

Readers will also continue to flex their moral capabilities in relation to books. One of the most striking ways in which readers are figured today is as online activists exerting their newly amplified voices to influence the industry, but this is just one part of the broad swathe of contemporary recreational readers' moral conduct. Moral conduct overlaps and interacts with the aesthetic conduct of readers. Readers use books to make sense of their lives, not only as stylistic models, but as prompts to negotiate and express views about right and wrong behavior. In Chapter 4, I presented three levels at which the moral conduct of readers plays out. First, reading itself is a morally weighted activity. There is a basic, positive moral status that fiction reading holds, as a liberal, open-minded, tolerant, empathetic practice. This is most clearly evident in the framing of book festivals as arenas for intellectual discourse and socially progressive programming. Second, readers respond morally to the books they read: their characters, plots, and themes. This is especially the case when readers read for empathy. Third, readers respond morally to book culture and the publishing industry, often using online sites to critique authors or publishers on ethical grounds. As digital technologies become ever more participatory, proactive readers will find more ways to communicate their moral judgments. And as the aesthetic status of books evolves, so too will the moral connotations of this status. Reading will entrench its reputation as a reflective, compassionate, and empathetic pastime, and this reputation is something that individual readers may embrace or interrogate.

The romance of reading, then, will persist, and this will remain central to the work some readers do in using reading as self-care, an intimate practice that shores up their sense of self within a highly connected, late capitalist world. The examples I elaborated in Chapters 3 and 4 took place in public or group settings, where reading can look like a noisy business. But there is also a quieter aspect that remains core to many people's understanding of what reading is. In Chapter 5, I looked at private, solitary reading as an intense site for readers' aesthetic and moral conduct. The ineffable and mysterious core of reading poses a challenge to research; the approach I modeled is to analyze media accounts that describe private reading. Prevailing frameworks in contemporary media that help readers make sense of their private practice include eroticized reading, deep reading, and reading as mindfulness. These modes are strongly normative and occlude more low-key forms of recreational reading; some private reading experiences are not like this, are instead dull, fragmented, or irritating. But these frameworks speak to the aspiration and the perceived capacity for reading to be an intimate experience that nourishes the reader.

Recreational reading is just one form of reading, and its romanticization as a special or elite practice in a cultural hierarchy can mean its benefits are overstated and its shortcomings glossed over. Reading has limits and gaps. It can produce narrow aesthetic models and smug self-satisfaction. Readers can ignore or misunderstand great books, or be prejudiced toward authors. Even well-intentioned book reading cannot save the world on its own—no matter how many anti-racist reading lists circulate on social media.[4] The limitations of reading are an inevitable part of its adaptive relationship with capitalism and the institutions of the state. In this book, I have chosen to step back from judging specific reader practices, in favor of maintaining an openness that allows the diversity of reading to emerge. But there are moments when I observe reader actions that seem to reduce book culture. One that gave me pause for thought was in 2023, when author Elizabeth Gilbert removed her forthcoming historical novel *The Snow Forest* from its publication schedule following readers' objections to its setting in Russia, given the current war in Ukraine. In a social media video explaining her decision, Gilbert acknowledged her Ukrainian readers' "anger, sorrow, disappointment, and pain," and stated "I do not want to add any harm to a group of people … who are continuing to experience grievous and extreme harm."[5] My own moral judgment is that making a book inaccessible on the basis of its setting alone unduly straitens culture; my aesthetic judgment is that I like Gilbert's writing and would have been interested to read the novel. Yet even here, I am most interested in the emotional interplay in the relationship between author and readers, an interplay that might not always produce the "right" result, but which builds a strong, diverse, multivocal network.

The very adaptability and interactivity of readers gives me hope. Reading is a practice that negotiates between multiple industries, institutions, and structures, that is flexibly private and social, that is easy to access (in print and digital formats, in level of skill required). Recreational fiction reading also has distinctive resonance, status, and credibility, satisfying people's desires to participate in culture through both online and offline practices. People can use book reading as a component of broader political action, or as a safe space to sustain a sense of self in systems that are dehumanizing. In the introduction to this book, I laid out my normative position, alongside my aim to describe. Without wanting to over-celebrate recreational reading, I do want to celebrate it: to advocate for readers, and for the benefits of reading.

The many strands of reader practice that I've pulled out throughout this book confirm my enthusiasm for reading as a versatile, creative practice for the present day and the future. It is good for readers to be able to find diverse ways to take pleasure in aesthetic works and express their own style—whether that is on social media, at an event, or in the way they decorate their lives. It is good for readers to be able to test, challenge, and communicate their moral views. And it is good for readers to experience moments of escape and interiority that sustain their energy and provide respite. All these forms of reading practice, and all the diverse books and authors that are incorporated into them, can be valued. As readers continually show through their actions, there are many right ways to be a reader.

NOTES

Introduction

1 "About Us," *Wirlomin Noongar Language and Stories*, accessed January 16, 2023, https://www.wirlomin.com.au/about-us/.

2 "IBISWorld—Industry Market Research, Reports, and Statistics," accessed January 16, 2023, https://www.ibisworld.com/global/market-size/global-book-publishing/.

3 Alison Flood, "Book Sales Defy Pandemic to Hit Eight-Year High," *The Guardian*, January 25, 2021, http://www.theguardian.com/books/2021/jan/25/bookshops-defy-pandemic-to-record-highest-sales-for-eight-years; Jim Milliot, "Print Book Sales Rose 8.2% in 2020," *PublishersWeekly.com*, accessed May 27, 2021, https://www.publishersweekly.com/pw/by-topic/industry-news/bookselling/article/85256-print-unit-sales-rose-8-2-in-2020.html; "Nielsen: Australian Book Sales up 7.8% in 2020," *Books + Publishing*, January 18, 2021, https://www.booksandpublishing.com.au/articles/2021/01/18/161393/nielsen-australian-book-sales-up-7-8-in-2020/.

4 Jim Milliot, "Print Book Sales Fell 6.5% in 2022," *PublishersWeekly.com*, accessed January 16, 2023, https://www.publishersweekly.com/pw/by-topic/industry-news/financial-reporting/article/91245-print-book-sales-fell-6-5-in-2022.html; "Making Sense of 2022—Nielsenbook-UK," accessed January 16, 2023, https://nielsenbook.co.uk/making-sense-of-2022/.

5 Elizabeth Long, *Book Clubs: Women and the Uses of Reading in Everyday Life* (Chicago: University of Chicago Press, 2003), 8.

6 Danielle Fuller and DeNel Rehberg Sedo, *Reading beyond the Book: The Social Practices of Contemporary Literary Culture* (New York and London: Routledge, 2013), 17; Danielle Fuller and DeNel Rehberg Sedo, *Reading Bestsellers* (Cambridge: Cambridge University Press, 2023).

7 "#booktok," *TikTok*, accessed June 13, 2023, https://www.tiktok.com/tag/booktok?lang=en.

8 Goodreads membership figure quoted in Ann-Marie Alcántara, "Reese Witherspoon's New App Adds to Growing Crowd of Virtual Book Clubs," *Wall Street Journal*, March 1, 2021, https://www.wsj.com/articles/reese-witherspoons-new-app-adds-to-growing-crowd-of-virtual-book-clubs-11614642579.

9 "Why Philippines Remains to Be Wattpad's Key Market," *AdSpark, Inc.* (blog), May 9, 2018, https://adspark.ph/phl-remains-wattpads-key-market/; "Press and Announcements | Wattpad HQ," *wattpad*, accessed September 20, 2021, https://company.wattpad.com/press.

10 For an elaboration of this argument, see Leah Price, *What We Talk About When We Talk About Books: The History and Future of Reading* (New York: Basic Books, 2019).

11 Kim Wilkins, Beth Driscoll, and Lisa Fletcher, *Genre Worlds: Popular Fiction and Twenty-First Century Book Culture* (Amherst: University of Massachusetts Press, 2022).

12 Fuller and Rehberg Sedo, *Reading Bestsellers*.

13 Christian Ulrik Andersen, Geoff Cox, and Giorgios Papadopoulos, "Postdigital Research," *APRJA* 3, no. 1 (2014).

14 Matthew Rubery, *Reader's Block: A History of Reading Differences* (Stanford: Stanford University Press, 2022).

15 Rita Felski, *Uses of Literature* (Hoboken: Wiley-Blackwell, 2008).

16 Anamik Saha and Sandra Van Lente, *Rethinking Diversity in Publishing* (London: Goldsmiths Press, 2020), https://research.gold.ac.uk/id/eprint/28692/1/Rethinking_diversity_in_publishing_full_booklet_v2.pdf; Fuller and Rehberg Sedo, *Reading Bestsellers*, 79.

17 "This Is How Much Global Literacy Has Changed over 200 Years," *World Economic Forum*, accessed January 16, 2023, https://www.weforum.org/agenda/2022/09/reading-writing-global-literacy-rate-changed/.

18 Max Roser and Esteban Ortiz-Ospina, "Literacy," *Our World in Data*, August 13, 2016, https://ourworldindata.org/literacy.

19 Wendy Griswold, Terry McDonnell, and Nathan Wright, "Reading and the Reading Class in the Twenty-First Century," *Annual Review of Sociology* 31, no. 1 (2005): 127–41, https://doi.org/10.1146/annurev.soc.31.041304.122312; 128.

20 Australia Council, "Reading the Reader: A Survey of Australian Reading Habits," May 26, 2017, https://australiacouncil.gov.au/advocacy-and-research/reading-the-reader/.

21 "The National Reading Survey 2021," *Australia Reads*, accessed April 14, 2023, https://australiareads.org.au/research/the-national-reading-survey-2021/.

22 Gallup Inc, "Americans Reading Fewer Books than in Past," *Gallup.com*, January 10, 2022, https://news.gallup.com/poll/388541/americans-reading-fewer-books-past.aspx.

23 Rachel Noorda and Kathi Inman Berens, "Immersive Media and Books 2020: New Insights About Book Pirates, Libraries and Discovery, Millennials, and Cross-Media Engagement: Before and during COVID," *Publishing Research Quarterly* 37, no. 2 (June 1, 2021): 227–40, https://doi.org/10.1007/s12109-021-09810-z.

24 Griswold, McDonnell, and Wright, "Reading and the Reading Class"; Wendy Griswold, *Regionalism and the Reading Class* (Chicago: University of Chicago Press, 2008), 167.

25 Noorda and Berens, "Immersive Media," 232.

26 Griswold, McDonnell, and Wright, "Reading and the Reading Class," 129.

27 Kinohi Nishikawa, "Merely Reading," *PMLA* 130, no. 3 (May 2015): 697–703, https://doi.org/10.1632/pmla.2015.130.3.697.

28 Nishikawa, "Merely Reading," 697.

29 Griswold, McDonnell, and Wright, "Reading and the Reading Class," 131.

30 Noorda and Berens, "Immersive Media," 231.

31 Beth Driscoll, *The New Literary Middlebrow: Tastemakers and Reading in the Twenty-First Century* (New York: Palgrave Macmillan, 2014).

32 See Beth Driscoll and Claire Squires, "The Epistemology of Ullapoolism: Making Mischief from within Contemporary Book Cultures," *Angelaki* 25, no. 5 (2020): 137-155.

33 Joyce Goggin, "Playbour, Farming and Leisure," *Ephemera: Theory & Politics in Organization* 11, no. 4 (2011): 357-368; Kathleen Kuehn and Thomas F. Corrigan, "Hope Labor: The Role of Employment Prospects in Online Social Production," *The Political Economy of Communication* 1, no. 1 (May 16, 2013): 9-25; Lisa Nakamura, "'Words with Friends': Socially Networked Reading on Goodreads," *PMLA* 128, no. 1 (January 1, 2013): 238–43, https://doi.org/10.1632/pmla.2013.128.1.238.

34 Ken Gelder, *Popular Fiction: The Logics and Practices of a Literary Field* (London and New York: Routledge, 2004).

35 Graham Allen, *Intertextuality* (Abingdon and New York: Routledge, 2011), 1.

36 Raymond Williams, *Keywords: A Vocabulary of Culture and Society* (Oxford: Oxford University Press, 2014), 49.

37 Williams, 49.

38 Joshua Rothman, "The Meaning of 'Culture,'" *The New Yorker*, December 26, 2014, http://www.newyorker.com/books/joshua-rothman/meaning-culture.

39 Judith Fetterley, *The Resisting Reader: A Feminist Approach to American Fiction* (Bloomington: Indiana University Press, 1978); Louise M. Rosenblatt, *The Reader, The Text, The Poem*; Felski, *Uses of Literature*.

40 Barbara Sicherman, *Well-Read Lives: How Books Inspired a Generation of American Women* (Chapel Hill: University of North Carolina Press, 2010); Elizabeth McHenry, *Forgotten Readers: Recovering the Lost History of African American Literary Societies* (Durham: Duke University Press, 2002); Susan K. Martin, "Tracking Reading in Nineteenth-Century Melbourne Diaries," *Australian Humanities Review*, no. 56 (2014): 27–54.

41 Megan Sweeney, *Reading Is My Window: Books and the Art of Reading in Women's Prisons* (Chapel Hill: University of North Carolina Press, 2010); Janice A. Radway, *Reading the Romance: Women, Patriarchy, and Popular Literature* (Chapel Hill: University of North Carolina Press, 1982).

42 Giselinde Kuipers, Thomas Franssen, and Sylvia Holla, "Clouded Judgments? Aesthetics, Morality and Everyday Life in Early 21st Century Culture," *European Journal of Cultural Studies* 22, no. 4 (2019): 383–98.

Chapter 1

1 The variability of reading practices has been pointed out by numerous scholars. To take just two examples, DeNel Rehberg Sedo writes, "there is no universal theory of how readers read" in "Reading Reception in the Digital Era," *Oxford Research Encyclopedia of Literature*, June 28, 2017, https://doi.org/10.1093/acrefore/9780190201098.013.285; and Bethan Benwell, James Procter, and Gemma Robinson write, "[T]here are many ways to read a book" in "Not Reading Brick Lane," *New Formations* 73, no. Winter (November 25, 2011): 90–116, https://doi.org/info:doi/10.3898/NEWF.73.06.2011, 90.

2 See, for example, the special issue of *Poetics Today* on modes of reading, which includes work from the disciplines of literary theory, media studies, aesthetics, anthropology, psychology, and linguistics. Tore Rye Andersen, Stefan Kjerkegaard, and Birgitte Stougaard Pedersen, "Introduction: Modes of Reading," *Poetics Today* 42, no. 2 (June 1, 2021): 131–47, https://doi.org/10.1215/03335372-8883164.

3 Ato Quayson, *Calibrations: Reading for the Social* (Minneapolis: University of Minnesota Press, 2003); Stephen Best and Sharon Marcus, "Surface Reading: An

Introduction," *Representations* 108, no. 1 (2009): 1–21; Ken Gelder, "Proximate Reading: Australian Literature in Transnational Reading Frameworks," *Journal of the Association for the Study of Australian Literature* (August 5, 2010), https://openjournals.library.sydney.edu.au/index.php/JASAL/article/view/9615; Heather Love, "Close but Not Deep: Literary Ethics and the Descriptive Turn," *New Literary History* 41, no. 2 (October 31, 2010): 371–91, https://doi.org/10.1353/nlh.2010.0007; Rita Felski, *The Limits of Critique* (Chicago: University of Chicago Press, 2015).

4   Nan Z. Da, "The Computational Case against Computational Literary Studies," *Critical Inquiry* 45, no. 3 (March 1, 2019): 601–39, https://doi.org/10.1086/702594; Lauren Klein, "Distant Reading after Moretti," *Arcade* (blog), 2018, https://arcade.stanford.edu/blogs/distant-reading-after-moretti.

5   Terry Lovell, *Consuming Fiction* (London and New York: Verso, 1987), 12.

6   While Matthew Arnold may have created the idea of the canon in *Culture and Anarchy* (New Haven: Yale University Press, 1994 [1869]), its cultural power was entrenched in the early part of the twentieth century. See Jim Collins, *Bring on the Books for Everybody: How Literary Culture Became Popular Culture* (Durham, Duke University Press, 2010).

7   Peter Widdowson, *Literature* (London and New York: Routledge, 1999), 56.

8   Q. D. Leavis, *Fiction and the Reading Public* (London: Chatto & Windus, 1932).

9   Claire Squires, *Marketing Literature: The Making of Contemporary Literature in Britain* (Basingstoke: Palgrave Macmillan, 2007), 41; Lovell, *Consuming Fiction*; Kate Flint, *The Woman Reader 1837–1914* (Oxford: Clarendon Press, 1993).

10   Stefan Collini, *Common Reading: Critics, Historians, Publics* (Oxford: Oxford University Press, 2008).

11   Merve Emre, *Paraliterary: The Making of Bad Readers in Postwar America* (Chicago: University of Chicago Press, 2017), 3.

12   See Rehberg Sedo, "Reading Reception in the Digital Era."

13   I. A. Richards, *Practical Criticism: A Study of Literary Judgment* (New York: Routledge, 2017 [1926]); Louise M. Rosenblatt, *Literature as Exploration* (New York: Modern Language Association of America, 1995 [1938]).

14   Wolfgang Iser, *The Implied Reader: Patterns of Communication in Prose Fiction from Bunyan to Beckett* (Baltimore: Johns Hopkins University Press, 1974); Stanley E. Fish, "Interpreting the 'Variorum,'" *Critical Inquiry* 2, no. 3 (April 1, 1976): 465–85, https://doi.org/10.1086/447852.

15   Judith Fetterley, *The Resisting Reader: A Feminist Approach to American Fiction* (Bloomington: Indiana University Press, 1978).

16   Roland Barthes, *Image, Music, Text*, trans. Stephen Heath (London: Fotana, 1977).

17   Michel de Certeau, *The Practice of Everyday Life*, trans. Steven Rendall (Berkeley: University of California Press, 2011[1984]).

18   Shafquat Towheed and W. R. Owens, *The History of Reading: International Perspectives, c. 1500–1990* (Basingstoke: Palgrave Macmillan, 2011), 3. See also Chapter 2, "Readers," in Ika Willis, *Reception* (Abingdon and New York: Routledge, 2017).

19   Felski, *Uses of Literature*, 16.

20   See Rehberg Sedo, "Reading Reception in the Digital Era."

21   Mary Louise Pratt, "Interpretive Strategies/Strategic Interpretations: On Anglo-American Reader Response Criticism," *Boundary 2* 11, no. 1/2 (1982): 201–31, https://doi.org/10.2307/303026, 201.

22   Pratt, "Interpretive Strategies/Strategic Interpretations," 202. See also Susan Rubin Suleiman, "Introduction: Varieties of Author-Oriented Criticism," in *The Reader in*

the Text: Essays on Audience and Interpretation, ed. Susan Rubin Suleiman and Inge Crosman (Princeton: Princeton University Press, 1980), 3–45.

23 For a self-reflexive account of the challenges I faced in teaching a Nora Roberts romance novella to a large class of literature undergraduate students, see Beth Driscoll, "Genre, Author, Text, Reader: Teaching Nora Roberts's Spellbound," *Journal of Popular Romance Studies* 4, no. 2 (October 24, 2014): n.p. https://www.jprstudies.org/2014/10/genre-author-text-reader-teaching-nora-robertss-spellboundby-beth-driscoll/.

24 John Guillory, "The Ethical Practice of Modernity: The Example of Reading," in *The Turn to Ethics*, ed. Marjorie B. Garber, Beatrice Hanssen, and Rebecca L. Walkowitz (New York: Routledge, 2000), 29–46; 31; John Guillory, *Professing Criticism: Essays on the Organization of Literary Study* (Chicago: University of Chicago Press, 2022), 333–4.

25 Guillory, *Professing Criticism*, 323.

26 There are numerous scholarly accounts of these disciplinary threats; for an example, see Paul L. Jay, *The Humanities "Crisis" and the Future of Literary Studies* (Basingstoke: Palgrave Macmillan, 2014).

27 Charlotte Wood, "Reading Isn't Shopping," *Sydney Review of Books*, August 14, 2018, https://sydneyreviewofbooks.com/reading-isnt-shopping/.

28 For an account of this process, see Janice A. Radway, *A Feeling for Books: The Book-of-the-Month Club, Literary Taste, and Middle-Class Desire* (Chapel Hill: University of North Carolina Press, 1997).

29 Deidre Lynch, *Loving Literature: A Cultural History* (Chicago: University of Chicago Press, 2015).

30 Guillory, *Professing Criticism*, 331–2.

31 Felski, *Uses of Literature*, 14.

32 Felski, *The Limits of Critique*, 184.

33 Guillory, *Professing Criticism*, 81.

34 Lynch, *Loving Literature*, 1, 2.

35 On this potential synergy, see also work on reading that comes from the field of cultural studies, e.g., John Frow, *The Practice of Value: Essays on Literature in Cultural Studies* (Crawley: UWA Publishing, 2013).

36 Marco Caracciolo, "Narrative Space and Readers' Responses to Stories: A Phenomenological Account," *Style* 47, no. 4 (2013): 425–44, 426.

37 Caracciolo, "Narrative Space," 427.

38 See, for example, Richard D. Altick, *The English Common Reader: A Social History of the Mass Reading Public, 1800–1900* (Columbus: Ohio State University Press, 1998); Guglielmo Cavallo and Roger Chartier, eds., *A History of Reading in the West*, trans. Lydia Cochrane (Amherst: University of Massachusetts Press, 1999); Martyn Lyons, "The History of Reading from Gutenberg to Gates," *The European Legacy* 4, no. 5 (October 1, 1999): 50–7, https://doi.org/10.1080/10848779908579994; Leah Price, "Reading: The State of the Discipline," *Book History* 7, no. 1 (October 15, 2004): 303–20, https://doi.org/10.1353/bh.2004.0023; Stephen Colclough, *Consuming Texts: Readers and Reading Communities, 1695–1870* (Basingstoke: Palgrave Macmillan, 2007); Rosalind Crone, Katie Halsey, and Shafquat Towheed, eds., *The History of Reading* (London: Routledge, 2010); Towheed and Owens, *The History of Reading*; Frank Felsenstein and James J. Connolly, *What Middletown Read: Print Culture in an American Small City* (Amherst: University of Massachusetts Press, 2015).

39 Simone Murray, "Reading Online: Updating the State of the Discipline," *Book History* 21, no. 1 (December 4, 2018): 370–96.

40 Robert Darnton, "What Is the History of Books?" *Daedalus* 111, no. 3 (1982): 65–83, 67.

41 Darnton, "What Is the History," 66, 74.

42 For examples of work based on oral history, see Martyn Lyons and Lucy Taksa, *Australian Readers Remember: An Oral History of Reading, 1890–1930* (Oxford: Oxford University Press, 1992); Lovro Škopljanac, "What American Readers Remember: A Case Study," *American Studies in Scandinavia* 55, no. 1 (May 10, 2023): 44–69, https://doi.org/10.22439/asca.v55i1.6857; Shelley Trower, "Forgetting Fiction: An Oral History of Reading: (Centred on Interviews in South London, 2014–15)," *Book History* 23, no. 1 (2020): 269–98, https://doi.org/10.1353/bh.2020.0007; for oral history and other evidential traces, see the "Read-It Project," accessed April 14, 2023, https://readit-project.eu.

43 Lydia Wevers, *Reading on the Farm: Victorian Fiction and the Colonial World* (Wellington: Victoria University Press, 2010); Susan K. Martin, "Tracking Reading in Nineteenth-Century Melbourne Diaries," *Australian Humanities Review*, no. 56 (2014): 27–54.

44 Martin, "Tracking Reading," 28.

45 Barbara Sicherman, *Well-Read Lives: How Books Inspired a Generation of American Women* (Chapel Hill: University of North Carolina Press, 2010).

46 Roger Chartier, "Laborers and Voyagers: From the Text to the Reader," trans. J. A. Gonzalez, *Diacritics* 22, no. 2 (1992): 49–61, https://doi.org/10.2307/465279, 53.

47 Alberto Manguel, *A History of Reading* (New York: Penguin, 2014 [1996]).

48 Gillian Silverman, "Neurodiversity and the Revision of Book History," *PMLA* 131, no. 2 (March 2016): 307–23, https://doi.org/10.1632/pmla.2016.131.2.307.

49 Laura Dietz, "Auditioning for Permanence: Reputation and Legitimacy of Electronically Distributed Novels," *Logos* 26, no. 4 (March 1, 2015): 22–36, https://doi.org/10.1163/1878-4712-11112088; Simon Rowberry, *Four Shades of Gray: The Amazon Kindle Platform* (Cambridge: MIT Press, 2022).

50 James F. English, "Everywhere and Nowhere: The Sociology of Literature after 'the Sociology of Literature,'" *New Literary History* 41, no. 2 (2010): v–xxiii, https://doi.org/10.1353/nlh.2010.0005, v-vi.

51 Radway, *Reading the Romance*; Radway, *A Feeling for Books*.

52 Fuller and Rehberg Sedo, *Reading beyond the Book*.

53 Sweeney, *Reading Is My Window*.

54 Long, *Book Clubs*; James Procter and Bethan Benwell, *Reading across Worlds: Transnational Book Groups and the Reception of Difference* (Basingstoke: Palgrave Macmillan, 2015), 1; Frances Devlin-Glass, "More than a Reader and Less than a Critic: Literary Authority and Women's Book-Discussion Groups," *Women's Studies International Forum* 24, no. 5 (September 1, 2001): 571–85, https://doi.org/10.1016/S0277-5395(01)00192-3; Sarah Twomey, "Reading 'Woman': Book Club Pedagogies and the Literary Imagination," *Journal of Adolescent & Adult Literacy* 50, no. 5 (2007): 398–407, https://doi.org/10.1598/JAAL.50.5.6; Jane Missner Barstow, "Reading in Groups: Women's Clubs and College Literature Classes," *Publishing Research Quarterly* 18, no. 4 (December 1, 2003): 3–17, https://doi.org/10.1007/s12109-003-0010-x; C. Clayton Childress and Noah E. Friedkin, "Cultural Reception and Production: The Social Construction of Meaning in Book Clubs," *American Sociological Review* 77, no. 1 (February 1, 2012): 45–68, https://doi.org/10.1177/0003122411428153.

55 Wendy Griswold, "A Methodological Framework for the Sociology of Culture," *Sociological Methodology* 17 (1987): 1–35, https://doi.org/10.2307/271027; 4.

56 María Angélica Thumala Olave, "Reading Matters: Towards a Cultural Sociology of Reading," *American Journal of Cultural Sociology* 6, no. 3 (October 1, 2018): 417–54,

https://doi.org/10.1057/s41290-017-0034-x, 418; Clayton Childress, *Under the Cover* (Princeton: Princeton University Press, 2017).

57 Pierre Bourdieu, *Distinction: A Social Critique of the Judgement of Taste*, trans. Richard Nice (Cambridge, MA: Harvard University Press, 1984).

58 Tony Bennett, Michael Emmison, and John Frow, *Accounting for Tastes: Australian Everyday Cultures* (Cambridge: Cambridge University Press, 1999), 2, 148, 168. Other examples of surveys of cultural taste include Tony Bennett et al., *Fields, Capitals, Habitus: Australian Culture, Inequalities and Social Divisions* (Abingdon and New York: Routledge, 2020); Tony Bennett et al., *Culture, Class, Distinction* (London: Routledge, 2008); Semi Purhonen and David Wright, "Methodological Issues in National-Comparative Research on Cultural Tastes: The Case of Cultural Capital in the UK and Finland," *Cultural Sociology* 7, no. 2 (June 1, 2013): 257–73; Giselinde Kuipers, "Television and Taste Hierarchy: The Case of Dutch Television Comedy," *Media, Culture & Society* 28, no. 3 (May 1, 2006): 359–78, https://doi. org/10.1177/0163443706062884.

59 Geert Vandermeersche and Ronald Soetaert, "Perspectives on Literary Reading and Book Culture," *CLCWEB-Comparative Literature and Culture* 15, no. 3 (2013), http:// hdl.handle.net/1854/LU-4132405, 9.

60 Driscoll and Squires, "The Epistemology of Ullapoolism."

61 Beth Driscoll and Claire Squires, *The Frankfurt Book Fair and Bestseller Business* (Cambridge: Cambridge University Press, 2020).

62 On the reasons for Anglo-American literary scholars' hesitancy regarding Bourdieu, see John Guillory, "Bourdieu's Refusal," *Modern Language Quarterly* 58, no. 4 (December 1, 1997): 367–98, https://doi.org/10.1215/00267929-58-4-367.

63 Bruno Latour and Steve Woolgar, *Laboratory Life: The Social Construction of Scientific Facts* (Beverly Hills: SAGE Publications, 1979); and Bruno Latour, *Science in Action: How to Follow Scientists and Engineers through Society* (Cambridge: Harvard University Press, 1987).

64 Hélène Buzelin, "Unexpected Allies," *The Translator* 11, no. 2 (November 1, 2005): 193–218, https://doi.org/10.1080/13556509.2005.10799198, 195.

65 Bruno Latour, "Why Has Critique Run out of Steam? From Matters of Fact to Matters of Concern," *Critical Inquiry* 30, no. 2 (January 1, 2004): 225–48, https://doi. org/10.1086/421123, 246.

66 Bruno Latour, *Reassembling the Social: An Introduction to Actor-Network-Theory* (Oxford: Oxford University Press, 2005), 15.

67 Latour, *Reassembling the Social*, 7.

68 Anselm Strauss and Juliet M. Corbin, *Grounded Theory in Practice* (Thousand Oaks: SAGE Publications, 1997).

69 Dorothy E. Smith, *The Everyday World as Problematic: A Feminist Sociology* (Toronto: University of Toronto Press, 1987), 90.

70 Luc Boltanski and Laurent Thévenot, "The Sociology of Critical Capacity," *European Journal of Social Theory* 2, no. 3 (1999): 359–77, https://doi. org/10.1177/136843199002003010, 359.

71 Elizabeth Outka, "Dead Men, Walking: Actors, Networks, and Actualized Metaphors in Mrs. Dalloway and Raymond," *Novel* 46, no. 2 (June 20, 2013): 253–74, https://doi. org/10.1215/00295132-2088130.

72 Outka, "Dead Men," 254.

73 Emmett Stinson and Beth Driscoll, "Difficult Literature on Goodreads: Reading Alexis Wright's The Swan Book," *Textual Practice* 36, no. 1 (2022): 94–115, https:// doi.org/10.1080/0950236X.2020.1786718.

74   Nathan K. Hensley, "Network: Andrew Lang and the Distributed Agencies of Literary Production," *Victorian Periodicals Review* 48, no. 3 (October 2, 2015): 359–82, https://doi.org/10.1353/vpr.2015.0045, 361, 467.

75   Latour, *Reassembling the Social*, 1, 11, 12.

76   Latour, *Reassembling the Social*, 28, 31–2.

77   Latour, *Reassembling the Social*, 23–4.

78   Hensley, "Network," 373.

79   Felski, *Uses of Literature*; Felski, *The Limits of Critique*; Felski, *Hooked*, see also Rita Felski, "Introduction," *New Literary History* 47, no. 2 (September 20, 2016): 215–29, https://doi.org/10.1353/nlh.2016.0010, 215.

80   Felski, *The Limits of Critique*, 184.

81   Amy Hungerford, *Making Literature Now* (Stanford: Stanford University Press, 2016).

82   Felski, *Hooked*, xii.

83   Latour, *Reassembling the Social*, 23.

84   Searching TikTok with this phrase yields a series of videos with a combined 37.4 million views. "Books I Would Sell My Soul to Read Again|TikTok Search," TikTok, accessed March 20, 2023, https://tiktok.com/discover/books-i-would-sell-my-soul-to-read-again?lang=en.

85   Latour, *Reassembling the Social*, 30.

86   For a thoughtful take on how literary studies scholars react to the diversity of students' reading practices, see Michael Warner, "Uncritical Reading," in *Polemic: Critical or Uncritical*, ed. Jane Gallop (New York: Routledge, 2004), 13–38.

87   Shai M. Dromi and Eva Illouz, "Recovering Morality: Pragmatic Sociology and Literary Studies," *New Literary History* 41, no. 2 (October 31, 2010): 351–69, https://doi.org/10.1353/nlh.2010.0004. 353, 359.

88   Dromi and Illouz, "Recovering Morality," 367.

89   See Guillory, *Professing Criticism*, 84.

90   See Bruce Robbins, "Fashion Conscious Phenomenon," *American Book Review* 38, no. 5 (2017): 5–6, https://doi.org/10.1353/abr.2017.0078.

91   Nakamura, "Words with Friends," 243–4.

92   Beth Driscoll and DeNel Rehberg Sedo, "Faraway, So Close: Seeing the Intimacy in Goodreads Reviews," *Qualitative Inquiry* 25, no. 3 (2019): 248–59.

93   Simon Susen, "Towards a Dialogue between Pierre Bourdieu's 'Critical Sociology' and Luc Boltanski's 'Pragmatic Sociology of Critique,'" in *The Spirit of Luc Boltanski: Essays on the 'Pragmatic Sociology of Critique'* (London: Anthem Press, 2014), 313–48, 334–5.

94   Pierre Bourdieu, *The Rules of Art: Genesis and Structure of the Literary Field*, trans. Susan Emanuel (Stanford: Stanford University Press, 1996), 232; Pierre Bourdieu, *The Logic of Practice*, trans. Richard Nice (Stanford: Stanford University Press, 1990), 53.

95   Driscoll, *New Literary Middlebrow*.

96   Cecilia Konchar Farr, *Reading Oprah: How Oprah's Book Club Changed the Way America Reads* (Albany: SUNY Press, 2005); Timothy Aubry, *Reading as Therapy: What Contemporary Fiction Does for Middle-Class Americans* (Iowa City: University of Iowa Press, 2011).

97   Aubry, *Reading as Therapy*, 41, 12.

98   Fuller and Rehberg Sedo, *Reading beyond the Book*, 17–18.

99   Hanna Kuusela, "On the Materiality of Contemporary Reading Formations: The Case of Jari Tervo's Layla," *New Formations* 78, no. 78 (July 1, 2013): 65–82, https://doi.org/10.3898/NeWf.78.03.2013.

100 Sara Tanderup Linkis, "Resonant Listening: Reading Voices and Places in Born-Audio Literary Narratives," *Canadian Review of Comparative Literature / Revue Canadienne de Littérature Comparée* 47, no. 4 (2020): 407–23, https://doi.org/10.1353/crc.2020.0037; Bronwen Thomas, "The #bookstagram: Distributed Reading in the Social Media Age," *Language Sciences*, 84 (March 1, 2021): 101358, https://doi.org/10.1016/j.langsci.2021.101358.

101 See Rebecca Lund and Janne Tienari, who write, "critical potential derives from the situated knowledge of those whose experience has been devalued or made invisible within dominant institutions and institutional representations" in "Passion, Care, and Eros in the Gendered Neoliberal University," *Organization* 26, no. 1 (January 1, 2019): 98–121, https://doi.org/10.1177/1350508418805283,101.

102 On reading with the grain, see Timothy Bewes, "Reading with the Grain: A New World in Literary Criticism," *Differences* 21, no. 3 (December 1, 2010): 1–33, https://doi.org/10.1215/10407391-2010-007; and Wilkins, Driscoll, and Fletcher, *Genre Worlds*.

103 Sweeney, *Reading Is My Window*, 145.

104 Procter and Benwell, *Reading across Worlds*.

105 Fuller and Rehberg Sedo, *Reading beyond the Book*, Methods Appendix.

106 Padmini Ray Murray and Claire Squires, "The Digital Publishing Communications Circuit," *Book 2.0* 3, no. 1 (June 1, 2013): 3–23, https://doi.org/10.1386/btwo.3.1.3_1; Claire Parnell, "Mapping the Entertainment Ecosystem of Wattpad: Platforms, Publishing and Adaptation," *Convergence* 27, no. 2 (November 10, 2020): 524–38, https://doi.org/10.1177/1354856520970141.

107 Lisa Mendelman and Anna Mukamal, "The Generative Dissensus of Reading the Feminist Novel, 1995–2020: A Computational Analysis of Interpretive Communities," *Journal of Cultural Analytics* 6, no. 3 (2021); Anatoliy Gruzd and DeNel Rehberg Sedo, "#1b1t: Investigating Reading Practices at the Turn of the Twenty-First Century," *Mémoires Du Livre / Studies in Book Culture* 3, no. 2 (2012), https://erudit.org/revue/memoires/2012/v3/n2/1009347ar.html.

108 Elizabeth A. Harris, "How TikTok Became a Best-Seller Machine," *The New York Times*, July 1, 2022, sec. Books, https://nytimes.com/2022/07/01/books/tiktok-books-booktok.html.

Chapter 2

1 Bernard Lahire's work on the double lives of writers works through the multiple identities that writers take on in different fields; the same may be said of readers. See Bernard Lahire, *The Plural Actor* trans. David Fernbach (Newark: Polity, 2011).

2 See, for example, Timothy B. Powell, William Weems, and Freeman Owle, "Native/American Digital Storytelling: Situating the Cherokee Oral Tradition within American Literary History," *Literature Compass* 4, no. 1 (2007): 1–23, https://doi.org/10.1111/j.1741-4113.2006.00376.x.

3 Kathleen M. Alley, Mukoma Wa Ngugi, and Wendy R. Williams, "Amanda Gorman's Poetry Shows Why Spoken Word Belongs in School," *The Conversation*, February 5, 2021, http://theconversation.com/amanda-gormans-poetry-shows-why-spoken-word-belongs-in-school-153838; Seth Perlow, "Perspective | What Made Amanda Gorman's Poem so Much Better than Other Inaugural Verse," *Washington Post*, January 23, 2021, https://www.washingtonpost.com/outlook/gorman-performance-vital-poetry/2021/01/22/010c35dc-5c2e-11eb-8bcf-3877871c819d_story.html.

4   For an example, see "Austea E. Kette on TikTok," TikTok, accessed March 29, 2023, https://www.tiktok.com/@austea.kette/video/7203024353066323205.

5   Other ways of acquiring books include winning them as prizes or stealing them, as noted by Julie Rak in "Genre in the Marketplace: The Scene of Bookselling in Canada," in *From Codex to Hypertext: Reading at the Turn of the Twenty-First Century*, ed. Anouk Lang (Amherst: University of Massachusetts Press, 2012), 159.

6   For work on the prestige and celebrity of authors, see Rebecca Braun and Emily Spiers, "Introduction: Re-Viewing Literary Celebrity," *Celebrity Studies* 7, no. 4 (2016): 449–56; Joe Moran, *Star Authors: Literary Celebrity in America* (London: Pluto Press, 2000).

7   Wood, "Reading Isn't Shopping."

8   See Kristen Doyle Highland, *The Spaces of Bookselling: Stores, Streets, and Pages*, (Cambridge: Cambridge University Press, 2023).

9   Laura J. Miller, *Reluctant Capitalists: Bookselling and the Culture of Consumption* (Chicago: University of Chicago Press, 2006), 5; see also the discussion in Childress, *Under the Cover*, 157–69.

10   For some examples in the Australian context, see Michael Heyward, "Flooding Australia with Imported Books Would Be an Assault on Our Literary Culture," *The Guardian*, May 10, 2016, sec. Books, https://www.theguardian.com/books/2016/may/10/flooding-australia-with-imported-books-would-be-an-assault-on-our-literary-culture; Shalailah Medhora, "Cheaper Books? What's the Cost?," triple j, December 21, 2016, https://www.abc.net.au/triplej/programs/hack/cheaper-books-but-at-what-price/8139436.

11   Ed Finn, "New Literary Cultures: Mapping the Digital Networks of Toni Morrison," in *From Codex to Hypertext: Reading at the Turn of the Twenty-First Century*, ed. Anouk Lang (Amherst: University of Massachusetts Press, 2012), 180.

12   Rak, "Genre in the Marketplace," 159.

13   Eben J. Muse, *Fantasies of the Bookstore* (Cambridge: Cambridge University Press, 2022).

14   Ann Patchett, "Ann Patchett on Running a Bookshop in Lockdown: 'We're a Part of Our Community as Never Before,'" *The Guardian*, April 10, 2020, sec. Books, https://www.theguardian.com/books/2020/apr/10/ann-patchett-nashville-bookshop-coronavirus-lockdown-publishing; "Birchbark Books & Native Arts / Minneapolis, Minnesota," Birchbark Books, accessed February 1, 2023, https://birchbarkbooks.com/; Louise Erdrich, *The Sentence* (New York, NY: Harper, 2021).

15   Jireh Deng, "'These Are My Stomping Grounds': The First Black-Owned Bookstore Opens in Octavia Butler's Home Town," *The Guardian*, March 23, 2023, sec. Books, https://www.theguardian.com/books/2023/mar/23/nikki-high-octavias-bookshelf-pasadena-california.

16   Jessica Pressman, *Bookishness: Loving Books in a Digital Age* (New York: Columbia University Press, 2020).

17   Rak, "Genre in the Marketplace," 160.

18   Miller, *Reluctant Capitalists*, 92.

19   David Wright, "Commodifying Respectability: Distinctions at Work in the Bookshop," *Journal of Consumer Culture* 5, no. 3 (November 1, 2005): 295–314, https://doi.org/10.1177/1469540505056792, 303.

20   Wright, "Commodifying Respectability," 304.

21   Wright, "Commodifying Respectability," 307.

22 Kwanghui Lim, "What Really Went Wrong for Borders and Angus & Robertson," *The Conversation*, March 24, 2011, http://theconversation.com/what-really-went-wrong-for-borders-and-angus-and-robertson-341.

23 Rosemary Neill, "Australian Books Sales Dominated by Big W, Says Meredith Drake," *The Australian*, November 20, 2015, https://www.theaustralian.com.au/arts/review/australian-books-sales-dominated-by-big-w-says-meredith-drake/news-story/89d69 9ac491737cbb438e70559d3d72e.

24 Childress, *Under the Cover*, 164.

25 Rak, "Genre in the Marketplace," 159, 165.

26 See more in Kenna MacTavish, "Crisis Book Browsing: Restructuring the Retail Shelf Life of Books," in *Bookshelves in the Age of the COVID-19 Pandemic*, ed. Corinna Norrick-Rühl and Shafquat Towheed, (Cham: Springer International Publishing, 2022), 49–68.

27 Ted Striphas, *The Late Age of Print: Everyday Book Culture from Consumerism to Control* (New York: Columbia University Press, 2009); Simone Murray, *The Digital Literary Sphere: Reading, Writing, and Selling Books in the Internet Era* (Baltimore: Johns Hopkins University Press, 2018).

28 Brent Smith and Greg Linden, "Two Decades of Recommender Systems at Amazon.Com," *IEEE Internet Computing*, June 2017, https://doi.org/10.1109/MIC.2017.72, 12.

29 See, for example, Finn, "New Literary Cultures."

30 Fuller and Rehberg Sedo, *Reading Bestsellers*.

31 Laura J. Miller, "The Best-Seller List as Marketing Tool and Historical Fiction," *Book History* 3 (2000): 286–304.

32 Beth Driscoll and DeNel Rehberg Sedo, "The Transnational Reception of Bestselling Books between Canada and Australia," *Global Media Communications* 16, no. 2 (2020): 243–58.

33 Samantha Rideout and DeNel Rehberg Sedo, "Novel Ideas: The Promotion of North American Book Club Books and the Creation of Their Readers," in *The Edinburgh History of Reading Vol 3: Common Readers*, ed. Jonathan Rose (Edinburgh: Edinburgh University Press, 2020), 280–98.

34 See Marc Verboord, "Market Logic and Cultural Consecration in French, German and American Bestseller Lists, 1970–2007," *Poetics* 39, no. 4 (August 2011): 290–315, https://doi.org/10.1016/j.poetic.2011.05.002; Childress, *Under the Cover*, 236.

35 Driscoll and Rehberg Sedo, "Transnational Reception."

36 Beth Driscoll, "Using Harry Potter to Teach Literacy: Different Approaches," *Cambridge Journal of Education* 43, no. 2 (2013): 259–71.

37 See, for example, Guang Chen et al., "A Comparison of Reading Comprehension across Paper, Computer Screens, and Tablets: Does Tablet Familiarity Matter?," *Journal of Computers in Education* 1, no. 2 (2014): 213–25; Virginia Clinton, "Reading from Paper Compared to Screens: A Systematic Review and Meta-Analysis," *Journal of Research in Reading* 42, no. 2 (2019): 288–325; Ferris Jabr, "The Reading Brain in the Digital Age: The Science of Paper versus Screens," *Scientific American* 11, no. 5 (2013); Sara J. Margolin et al., "E-Readers, Computer Screens, or Paper: Does Reading Comprehension Change across Media Platforms?" *Applied Cognitive Psychology* 27, no. 4 (2013): 512–19; Kaveri Subrahmanyam et al., "Learning from Paper, Learning from Screens: Impact of Screen Reading and Multitasking Conditions on Reading and Writing among College Students," *International Journal of Cyber Behavior, Psychology and Learning (IJCBPL)* 3, no. 4 (2013): 1–27.

38 "What's the Best Book of the Past 125 Years? We Asked Readers to Decide," *The New York Times*, December 29, 2021, sec. Books, https://www.nytimes.com/interactive/2021/12/28/books/best-book-winners.html.

39 Pierre Bourdieu and Jean Claude Passeron, *Reproduction in Education, Society and Culture*, trans. Richard Nice (London and Newbury Park: SAGE Publications, 1990).

40 Anna Poletti et al., "The Affects of Not Reading: Hating Characters, Being Bored, Feeling Stupid," *Arts and Humanities in Higher Education* 15, no. 2 (2016): 231–47.

41 Leonie Rutherford et al., "Do Digital Devices Enhance Teenagers' Recreational Reading Engagement? Issues for Library Policy from a Recent Study in Two Australian States," *Public Library Quarterly* 37, no. 3 (July 3, 2018): 318–40, https://doi.org/10.1080/01616846.2018.1511214; DeNel Rehberg Sedo, "'I Used to Read Anything That Caught My Eye, But … ': Cultural Authority and Intermediaries in a Virtual Young Adult Book Club," in *Reading Communities from Salons to Cyberspace* (Basingstoke: Palgrave Macmillan, 2011), 101–22, https://doi.org/10.1057/9780230308848_6.

42 Marilyn Johnson, "Oprah Winfrey: A Life in Books," *Life*, September 1997.

43 Naaman Zhou, "Canberra's Libraries Join Nationwide Trend of Scrapping Fines for Late Books," *The Guardian*, November 1, 2019, sec. Australia news, http://www.theguardian.com/australia-news/2019/nov/01/canberras-libraries-join-nationwide-trend-of-scrapping-fines-for-late-books.

44 See Jacqueline Pearson, *Women's Reading in Britain, 1750–1835: A Dangerous Recreation* (Cambridge: Cambridge University Press, 1999), 152.

45 For example Jan Fergus, *Provincial Readers in Eighteenth-Century England* (Oxford: Oxford University Press, 2007); Julieanne Lamond, "Communities of Readers: Australian Reading History and Library Loan Records," in *Republics of Letters: Literary Communities in Australia*, ed. Peter Kirkpatrick and Robert Dixon (Sydney: Sydney University Press, 2012), Isabelle Lehuu, "Reconstructing Reading Vogues in the Old South: Borrowings from the Charleston Library Society, 1811–1817," in *The History of Reading, Volume 1: International Perspectives, c.1500–1990*, ed. Shafquat Towheed and W. R. Owens (Basingstoke: Palgrave Macmillan, 2011), 64–83.

46 See for example Annabel Gutterman, "Here Are the 10 Most Borrowed Books of All Time at the New York Public Library," *Time*, January 13, 2020, https://time.com/5763611/new-york-public-library-top-checkouts/; "Australian Novels the Most Popular Choices amongst Readers," *Civica*, accessed March 14, 2023, https://www.civica.com/en-au/news-library/australian-novels-the-most-popular-choices-amongst-readers/.

47 See Daniel A. Gross, "The Surprisingly Big Business of Library E-Books," *The New Yorker*, September 2, 2021, https://www.newyorker.com/news/annals-of-communications/an-app-called-libby-and-the-surprisingly-big-business-of-library-e-books.

48 Long, *Book Clubs*, 52.

49 See for example Jenny Hartley, *Reading Groups* (Oxford: Oxford University Press, 2001), vii; Long, *Book Clubs*; Marilyn Poole, "The Women's Chapter: Women's Reading Groups in Victoria," *Feminist Media Studies* 3, no. 3 (November 1, 2003): 263–81, https://doi.org/10.1080/1468077032000166513; Sebastian Partogi, "Book Clubs Provide Intellectual, Emotional Common Ground," *The Jakarta Post*, July 27, 2019, https://www.thejakartapost.com/news/2019/07/27/book-clubs-provide-intellectual-emotional-common-ground.html.

50 Long, *Book Clubs*, 91, 122.

51 Danielle Fuller, DeNel Rehberg Sedo, and Claire Squires, "Marionettes and Puppeteers? The Relationship between Book Club Readers and Publishers,"

in *Reading Communities from Salons to Cyberspace*, ed. DeNel Rehberg Sedo (Basingstoke: Palgrave Macmillan, 2011), 181–99, https://doi.org/10.1057/9780230308848_10; Rideout and Rehberg Sedo, "Novel Ideas."

52 Driscoll, *New Literary Middlebrow*, 45.

53 Researchers who record, or participate in, book club discussions include Procter and Benwell, *Reading across Worlds*; Brigid Magner and Emily Potter, "Recognizing the Mallee: Reading Groups and the Making of Literary Knowledge in Regional Australia," *Mémoires Du Livre / Studies in Book Culture* 12, no. 1 (2021), https://doi.org/10.7202/1077807ar; David Peplow et al., *The Discourse of Reading Groups: Integrating Cognitive and Sociocultural Perspectives* (London and New York: Routledge, 2015).

54 Long, *Book Clubs*.

55 DeNel Rehberg Sedo, "Readers in Reading Groups: An Online Survey of Face-to-Face and Virtual Book Clubs," *Convergence: The International Journal of Research into New Media Technologies* 9, no. 1 (March 1, 2003): 66–90, https://doi.org/10.1177/135485650300900105.

56 Maxine Branagh-Miscampbell and Stevie Marsden, "'Eating, Sleeping, Breathing, Reading': The Zoella Book Club and the Young Woman Reader in the 21st Century," *Participations: Journal of Audience and Reception Studies* 16, no. 1 (2019): 64–79; Lauren Cameron, "Adapting Jane Eyre for the Celebrity Book Club," *Victorians Institute Journal* 48, no. 1 (December 17, 2021): 65–86, https://doi.org/10.5325/victinstj.48.2021.0065.

57 Fuller and Rehberg Sedo, *Reading beyond the Book*.

58 Beth Driscoll and Claire Squires, "Serious Fun: Gaming the Book Festival," *Mémoires Du Livre / Studies in Book Culture* 9, no. 2 (2018): 1–37.

59 Fuller and Rehberg Sedo, *Reading beyond the Book*, 4.

60 See Beth Driscoll, "Sentiment Analysis and the Literary Festival Audience," *Continuum* 29, no. 6 (November 2, 2015): 861–73, https://doi.org/10.1080/10304312.2015.1040729; Simone Murray and Millicent Weber, "'Live and Local'?: The Significance of Digital Media for Writers' Festivals," *Convergence* 23, no. 1 (February 1, 2017): 61–78, https://doi.org/10.1177/1354856516677531.

61 Beth Driscoll and Claire Squires, "Experiments with Book Festival People (Real and Imaginary)," *Mémoires Du Livre / Studies in Book Culture* 11, no. 2 (2020); Wenche Ommundsen, "Literary Festivals and Cultural Consumption," *Australian Literary Studies*, January 2009, https://search.informit.org/doi/abs/10.3316/IELAPA.200912218; Katya Johanson and Robin Freeman, "The Reader as Audience: The Appeal of the Writers' Festival to the Contemporary Audience," *Continuum* 26, no. 2 (April 1, 2012): 303–14, https://doi.org/10.1080/10304312.2011.590575.

62 In line with the University of Melbourne ethics approval (ID 1442334.1) granted for this research, I refer to interviewees by pseudonyms.

63 Claire G. Coleman, "The Risks of Question Time: Not So Black and White," *Westerly Magazine*, September 6, 2018, https://westerlymag.com.au/the-risks-of-question-time-not-so-black-and-white/.

64 Bronwen Thomas, *Literature and Social Media* (Abingdon and New York: Routledge, 2020), https://doi.org/10.4324/9781315207025, 41.

65 R. Lyle Skains, "The Shifting Author—Reader Dynamic: Online Novel Communities as a Bridge from Print to Digital Literature," *Convergence: The International Journal of Research into New Media Technologies* 16, no. 1 (February 1, 2010): 95–111, https://doi.org/10.1177/1354856509347713; Millicent Weber, "'Reading' the Public Domain: Narrating and Listening to Librivox Audiobooks," *Book History* 24, no. 1 (2021): 209–43.

66 Parnell, "Mapping the Entertainment Ecosystem"; Federico Pianzola, Simone Rebora, and Gerhard Lauer, "Wattpad as a Resource for Literary Studies. Quantitative and Qualitative Examples of the Importance of Digital Social Reading and Readers' Comments in the Margins," *PloS One* 15, no. 1 (2020): e0226708; Melanie Ramdarshan Bold, "The Return of the Social Author: Negotiating Authority and Influence on Wattpad," *Convergence* 24, no. 2 (April 1, 2018): 117–36, https://doi.org/10.1177/1354856516654459.

67 Hannah Pardey, "Middlebrow 2.0: The Digital Affect and the New Nigerian Novel," in *Imperial Middlebrow*, ed. Christoph Eland and Jana Gohrisch (Leiden: Brill, 2020), 218–39, https://doi.org/10.1163/9789004426566_013.

68 Parnell, "Mapping the Entertainment Ecosystem"; José van Dijck, *The Culture of Connectivity: A Critical History of Social Media* (Oxford: Oxford University Press, 2013).

69 Pianzola et al., "Wattpad as a Resource."

70 Beth Driscoll, "Book Blogs as Tastemakers," *Participations Journal of Audience and Reception Studies* 16, no. 1 (2019): 280–305.

71 Anne-Mette Bech Albrechtslund, "Amazon, Kindle, and Goodreads: Implications for Literary Consumption in the Digital Age," *Consumption Markets & Culture* 23, no. 6 (November 1, 2020): 553–68, https://doi.org/10.1080/10253866.2019.1640216.

72 See for example Simone Murray, "Secret Agents: Algorithmic Culture, Goodreads and Datafication of the Contemporary Book World," *European Journal of Cultural Studies*, December 5, 2019, 1367549419886026, https://doi.org/10.1177/1367549419886026; Joachim Vlieghe, Jaël Muls, and Kris Rutten, "Everybody Reads: Reader Engagement with Literature in Social Media Environments," *Poetics* 54 (February 2016): 25–37, https://doi.org/10.1016/j.poetic.2015.09.001.

73 Nakamura, "Words with Friends."

74 "About Goodreads," accessed July 4, 2019, https://www.goodreads.com/about/us; Ann-Marie Alcántara, "Reese Witherspoon's New App Adds to Growing Crowd of Virtual Book Clubs," *Wall Street Journal*, March 1, 2021, sec. C Suite, https://www.wsj.com/articles/reese-witherspoons-new-app-adds-to-growing-crowd-of-virtual-book-clubs-11614642579.

75 Mike Thelwall and Kayvan Kousha, "Goodreads: A Social Network Site for Book Readers," *Journal of the Association for Information Science and Technology* 68, no. 4 (2016): 972–83.

76 Melanie Walsh and Maria Antoniak, "The Goodreads 'Classics': A Computational Study of Readers, Amazon, and Crowdsourced Amateur Criticism," *Journal of Cultural Analytics* 6, no. 2 (April 20, 2021), https://doi.org/10.22148/001c.22221.

77 J. Trant, "Studying Social Tagging and Folksonomy: A Review and Framework," *Journal of Digital Information* 10, no. 1 (January 6, 2009), https://jodi-ojs-tdl.tdl.org/jodi/article/view/269.

78 Walsh and Antoniak, "The Goodreads 'Classics.'" On the overlap and differences between the academy and Goodreads reviewers, see also Karen Bourrier and Mike Thelwall, "The Social Lives of Books: Reading Victorian Literature on Goodreads," *Journal of Cultural Analytics* 5, no. 1 (February 20, 2020), https://doi.org/10.22148/001c.12049.

79 Driscoll and Rehberg Sedo, "Faraway, So Close."

80 Ann Steiner has discussed this dynamic in relation to Amazon reviews in "Private Criticism in the Public Space: Personal Writing on Literature in Readers' Reviews on Amazon," *Participations: Journal of Audience & Reception Studies* 5, no. 2 (November 2008).

Chapter 3

1   Immanuel Kant, *Critique of the Power of Judgment*, trans. Paul Guyer and Eric Matthews (Cambridge: Cambridge University Press, 2000), 75–8.
2   Kant, *Critique*, 17.
3   Christine Ross, *The Aesthetics of Disengagement: Contemporary Art and Depression* (Minneapolis: University of Minnesota Press, 2006), 97.
4   Antoine Hennion, "Pragmatics of Taste," in *The Blackwell Companion to the Sociology of Culture*, ed. Mark D. Jacobs and Nancy Weiss Hanrahan (Oxford: Blackwell Publishing Ltd, 2007), https://doi.org/10.1002/9780470996744.ch9, 131, 132, 134.
5   Louise M. Rosenblatt, *The Reader, the Text, the Poem: The Transactional Theory of the Literary Work* (Carbondale: Southern Illinois University Press, [1978] 1994), 31
6   Rosenblatt, *The Reader*, 22.
7   Rosenblatt, *The Reader*, 24, 25.
8   Rosenblatt, *The Reader*, 34.
9   Marielle Macé, "Ways of Reading, Modes of Being," trans. Marlon Jones, *New Literary History* 44, no. 2 (August 8, 2013): 213–29, https://doi.org/10.1353/nlh.2013.0017.
10 Angelique Chrisafis, "'Family Is the Place for Madness': Constance Debré on the Book That Has Shocked France," *The Guardian*, January 14, 2023, sec. Books, https://www.theguardian.com/books/2023/jan/14/family-is-the-place-for-madness-constance-debre-on-the-book-that-has-shocked-france.
11 Macé, "Ways of Reading," 213.
12 Rita Felski, *The Limits of Critique* (Chicago: University of Chicago Press, 2015), 175.
13 Jean-François Hamel, "Émanciper la lecture. Formes de vie et gestes critiques d'après Marielle Macé et Yves Citton," *Tangence*, no. 107 (2015): 89–107, https://doi.org/10.7202/1033952ar, Translation: Google Translate.
14 Hamel, "Émanciper la lecture."
15 Nan Z. Da, "Other People's Books," *New Literary History* 51, no. 3 (2020): 475–500, https://doi.org/10.1353/nlh.2020.0031.
16 Hamel, "Émanciper la lecture."
17 See Emre, *Paraliterary*.
18 See, for example, Danielle Fuller and DeNel Rehberg Sedo, "'Boring, Frustrating, Impossible': Tracing the Negative Affects of Reading from Interviews to Story Circles," *Participations: Journal of Audience and Reception Studies* 16, no. 1 (2019); Poletti et al., "The Affects of Not Reading."
19 Sianne Ngai, *Our Aesthetic Categories: Zany, Cute, Interesting* (Cambridge: Harvard University Press, 2015).
20 Kant, *Critique*, 39.
21 See, for example, Tony Bennett et al., *Fields, Capitals, Habitus: Australian Culture, Inequalities and Social Divisions* (London and New York: Routledge, 2020).
22 Pierre Bourdieu, *Distinction: A Social Critique of the Judgement of Taste* (Cambridge: Harvard University Press, 1984).
23 Driscoll, "Readers of Popular Fiction."
24 "Sales of Romance Novels Are Rising in Britain," *The Economist*, March 6, 2023, https://www.economist.com/britain/2023/03/06/sales-of-romance-novels-are-rising-in-britain?gclid=CjwKCAjwiOCgBhAgEiwAjv5whFoAaHThW1yfJvB4xKUS4vQRfEr8Ra0LfzZlTjtQW60gQEVyeigTuBoC_YcQAvD_BwE&gclsrc=aw.ds.
25 Felski, *Uses of Literature*, 105, 108.
26 Ian Woodward and Michael Emmison, "From Aesthetic Principles to Collective Sentiments: The Logics of Everyday Judgements of Taste," *Poetics* 29, no. 6

(December 1, 2001): 295–316, https://doi.org/10.1016/S0304-422X(00)00035-8, 296 and 315.

27 David Wright, *Understanding Cultural Taste: Sensation, Skill and Sensibility* (New York: Palgrave Macmillan, 2015), 5.

28 Hennion, "Pragmatics of Taste," 132.

29 Hennion, "Pragmatics of Taste," 135.

30 Hannah Wohl, "Community Sense: The Cohesive Power of Aesthetic Judgment," *Sociological Theory* 33, no. 4 (December 1, 2015): 299–326, https://doi.org/10.1177/0735275115617800.

31 Wohl, "Community Sense," 300

32 Hamel, "Émanciper la lecture."

33 Hamel, "Émanciper la lecture," para 5.

34 Felski, *The Limits of Critique*, 12.

35 Wright, *Understanding Cultural Taste*, 8.

36 Fuller and Rehberg Sedo, *Reading Bestsellers*; Marianne Martens, *Publishers, Readers, and Digital Engagement* (London: Palgrave Macmillan, 2016); Thomas, *Literature and Social Media*.

37 Wilkins, Driscoll, and Fletcher, *Genre Worlds*.

38 Jessica Pressman, "The Aesthetic of Bookishness in Twenty-First-Century Literature," *Michigan Quarterly Review* 48, no. 4 (2009) (n.p.; http://hdl.handle.net/2027/spo.act2080.0048.402); see also Jessica Pressman, *Bookishness: Loving Books in a Digital Age* (New York: Columbia University Press, 2020); and Nicola Rodger, "From Bookshelf Porn and Shelfies to #bookfacefriday: How Readers Use Pinterest to Promote Their Bookishness," *Participations: Journal of Audience and Reception Studies*, 2019, https://www.participations.org/Volume%2016/Issue%201/22.pdf.

39 N. Katherine Hayles, "Combining Close and Distant Reading: Jonathan Safran Foer's Tree of Codes and the Aesthetic of Bookishness," *PMLA* 128, no. 1 (January 1, 2013): 226–31, https://doi.org/10.1632/pmla.2013.128.1.226.

40 Wendy Lesser, *Why I Read: The Serious Pleasure of Books* (New York: Farrar Straus & Giroux, 2014); Anne Bogel, *I'd Rather Be Reading: The Delights and Dilemmas of the Reading Life* (Grand Rapids: Baker Books, 2018).

41 Pamela Paul, *My Life with Bob: Flawed Heroine Keeps Book of Books, Plot Ensues* (New York: Henry Holt and Co., 2017), 239.

42 Geoff Dyer, *Out of Sheer Rage: Wrestling with D. H. Lawrence* (New York: Picador, 2009 [1997]); Sam Jordison, "A Book for the Beach: Out of Sheer Rage by Geoff Dyer | Sam Jordison," *The Guardian*, July 18, 2014, sec. Books, https://www.theguardian.com/books/booksblog/2014/jul/18/book-beach-out-of-sheer-rage-geoff-dyer-sam-jordison; Rebecca Mead, *My Life in Middlemarch* (New York: Crown Publishers, 2014).

43 María Angélica Thumala Olave, "Reading Matters: Towards a Cultural Sociology of Reading," *American Journal of Cultural Sociology* 6, no. 3 (October 1, 2018): 417–54, https://doi.org/10.1057/s41290-017-0034-x, 445.

44 Pamela Paul, *My Life with Bob: Flawed Heroine Keeps Book of Books, Plot Ensues* (New York: Henry Holt and Co., 2017); Rick Gekoski, *Outside of a Dog: A Bibliomemoir* (London: Constable, 2011).

45 Cited in Lucy Scholes, "Close Readings: The Rise of the Bibliomemoir," *Financial Times*, February 23, 2018, https://www.ft.com/content/92812c26-17d4-11e8-9c33-02f893d608c2.

46 Scholes, "Close Readings."

47 Driscoll, "Readers of Popular Fiction."

48 Driscoll, *New Literary Middlebrow*.

49 On the Book-of-the-Month Club and radio programs, see Radway, *A Feeling for Books*; Joan Shelley Rubin, *The Making of Middlebrow Culture* (Chapel Hill: The University of North Carolina Press, 1992).

50 Andy Miller, *The Year of Reading Dangerously: How Fifty Great Books (and Two Not-So-Great Ones) Saved My Life* (New York: Harper Perennial, 2014), 2.

51 David Wright, "Literary Taste and List Culture in a Time of 'Endless Choice,'" in *From Codex to Hypertext : Reading at the Turn of the Twenty-First Century*, ed. Anouk Lang (Amherst: University of Massachusetts Press, 2012), 108–23; Alex Johnson, *A Book of Book Lists: A Bibliophile's Compendium* (London: British Library Publishing, 2017).

52 Susan Hill, *Howards End Is on the Landing: A Year of Reading from Home* (London: IPS—Profile Books, 2010).

53 Phyllis Rose, *The Shelf: From LEQ to LES: Adventures in Extreme Reading* (New York: Farrar, Straus and Giroux, 2014).

54 Miller, *The Year of Reading Dangerously*, 101.

55 See Driscoll, *New Literary Middlebrow*; Konchar Farr, *Reading Oprah*; Cecilia Konchar Farr and Jaime Harker, eds., *The Oprah Affect: Critical Essays on Oprah's Book Club* (Albany: SUNY Press, 2008).

56 Alberto Manguel, *A Reading Diary* (Toronto: Vintage Canada, [2004] 2005); Alberto Manguel, *The Library at Night* (New Haven: Yale University Press, [2005] 2009); Alberto Manguel, *A Reader on Reading* (New Haven: Yale University Press, 2011); Manguel, *A History of Reading*; Alberto Manguel, *Packing My Library: An Elegy and Ten Digressions* (New Haven: Yale University Press, 2018).

57 Mark Oppenheimer, "Alberto Manguel and the Library of Babel," *Tablet Magazine*, November 18, 2013, /sections/arts-letters/articles/alberto-manguel.

58 Alberto Manguel, "A 30,000-Volume Window on the World," *The New York Times*, May 15, 2008, sec. Home & Garden, https://www.nytimes.com/2008/05/15/garden/15library.html.

59 Walter Benjamin, *Illuminations*, ed. Hannah Arendt, trans. Harry Zohn (Boston: Mariner Books, Houghton Mifflin Harcourt, 2019).

60 Alberto Manguel, *Packing My Library: An Elegy and Ten Digressions* (New Haven: Yale University Press, 2018), loc 116.

61 Claire Armitstead, "Packing My Library by Alberto Manguel Review—a Bibliophile's Demons," *The Guardian*, April 14, 2018, sec. Books, https://www.theguardian.com/books/2018/apr/14/packing-my-library-alberto-manguel-review.

62 Manguel, *Packing My Library*, loc 69.

63 Manguel, *Packing My Library*, loc 105.

64 On this exclusionary potential, see also Tully Barnett, "'Reading Saved Me': Writing Autobiographically About Transformative Reading Experiences in Childhood," *Prose Studies* 35, no. 1 (2013): 84–96.

65 Barnett, "Reading Saved Me," 85.

66 Barnett, "Reading Saved Me," 94.

67 Alice Ozma, *The Reading Promise: My Father and the Books We Shared* (London: Hodder & Stoughton, 2011).

68 Scholes, "Close Readings"; Lucy Mangan, *Bookworm: A Memoir of Childhood Reading* (London: Square Peg, 2018).

69 Jane Sullivan, *Storytime* (Paddington: Ventura Press, 2019).

70 Sullivan, loc 162.

71 Sullivan, loc 2907, 4113, and 4008.

72 Sullivan, loc 3975, 3982.

73 Azar Nafisi, *The Republic of Imagination: A Life in Books*, Reprint edition (New York: Penguin Books, 2015).
74 Azar Nafisi, *Reading Lolita in Tehran* (New York: Random House, 2003).
75 See Millicent Weber, *Literary Festivals and Contemporary Book Culture* (London: Palgrave Macmillan, 2018).
76 Nafisi, *Republic*, 196.
77 Nafisi, *Republic*, 49.
78 Nafisi, *Republic*, 124.
79 Nafisi, *Republic*, 98.
80 Scholes, "Close Readings."
81 C. G. Drew, "How To Fabulously Get Started On #Bookstagram," *Paper Fury*, July 16, 2016, https://paperfury.com/how-to-started-bookstagram/.
82 "FairyLoot (@fairyloot) | Instagram," accessed April 17, 2023, https://www.instagram.com/p/CnuEw-ptA-i/; https://www.instagram.com/p/CnR_J9BNxSz/.
83 Corinna Norrick-Rühl, *Book Clubs and Book Commerce* (Cambridge: Cambridge University Press, 2020), https://doi.org/10.1017/9781108597258.
84 Madeline Halpert, "Viral TikTok Boosts Father's Thriller Book to Bestseller," *BBC News*, February 13, 2023, sec. US & Canada, https://www.bbc.com/news/world-us-canada-64577281.
85 Driscoll, "Book Blogs as Tastemakers."
86 See Fuller and Rehberg Sedo, *Reading Bestsellers*.
87 "Biggest Social Media Platforms 2022," *Statista*, accessed January 23, 2023, https://www.statista.com/statistics/272014/global-social-networks-ranked-by-number-of-users/; "Instagram: Age Distribution of Global Audiences 2022," *Statista*, accessed January 23, 2023, https://www.statista.com/statistics/325587/instagram-global-age-group/.
88 Maarit Jaakkola, "From Re-Viewers to Me-Viewers: The# Bookstagram Review Sphere on Instagram and the Uses of the Perceived Platform and Genre Affordances," *Interactions: Studies in Communication & Culture* 10, no. 1–2 (2019): 101.
89 Pavica Sheldon and Katherine Bryant, "Instagram: Motives for Its Use and Relationship to Narcissism and Contextual Age," *Computers in Human Behavior* 58 (May 1, 2016): 89–97, https://doi.org/10.1016/j.chb.2015.12.059.
90 Laura, "Bookstagram 101: How to Start a Bookstagram (Aka Book Instagram)," February 18, 2022, https://whatshotblog.com/how-to-start-a-bookstagram/.
91 Kenna MacTavish, *The Emerging Power of the Bookstagrammer: Reading #bookstagram as a Mediated Site of Twenty-First Century Book Culture*, in *Post-Digital Book Cultures*, ed. Alexandra Dane and Millicent Weber (Clayton: Monash University Publishing, 2021), 80–113.
92 Thomas, *Literature and Social Media*, 75.
93 Rodger, "From Bookshelf Porn and Shelfies."
94 Maarit Jaakkola, "From Re-Viewers to Me-Viewers: The# Bookstagram Review Sphere on Instagram and the Uses of the Perceived Platform and Genre Affordances," *Interactions: Studies in Communication & Culture* 10, no. 1–2 (2019), 105; Erving Goffman, *The Presentation of Self in Everyday Life* (New York: Anchor Books, 1959).
95 Jaakkola, "From Re-Viewers to Me-Viewers," 95.
96 Thomas, *Literature and Social Media*, 73.
97 MacTavish, "The Emerging Power of the Bookstagrammer."

98   Driscoll, *New Literary Middlebrow*; see also Branagh-Miscampbell and Marsden, "Eating, Sleeping, Breeathing, Reading."

99   Jaakkola, "From Re-Viewers to Me-Viewers," 101.

100 Berens, "E-Literature's# 1 Hit."

101 Jaakkola, "From Re-Viewers to Me-Viewers," 104

102 Fuller and Rehberg Sedo, *Reading Bestsellers*.

103 Jaakkola, "From Re-Viewers to Me-Viewers," 105.

104 Simone Murray, "Dark Academia: Bookishness, Readerly Self-Fashioning and the Digital Afterlife of Donna Tartt's The Secret History," *English Studies* 104, no. 2 (2023): 347–64, https://doi.org/10.1080/0013838X.2023.2170596.

105 Jaakkola, "From Re-Viewers to Me-Viewers," 95–6.

106 Mara White, "#Bookstagram: How Readers Changed The Way We Use Instagram," *HuffPost*, accessed May 6, 2018, https://www.huffingtonpost.com/entry/bookstagram-how-readers-changed-the-way-we-use-instagram_us_59f0aaa2e4b01ecaf1a3e867.

107 Thomas, *Literature and Social Media*, 75.

108 Holly Connolly, "Is Social Media Influencing Book Cover Design?" *The Guardian*, August 28, 2018, sec. Books, https://www.theguardian.com/books/2018/aug/28/is-social-media-influencing-book-cover-design.

109 Thomas, *Literature and Social Media*, 75.

110 Jaakkola, "From Re-Viewers to Me-Viewers," 102.

111 MacTavish, "The Emerging Power of the Bookstagrammer."

112 Barry Pierce, "In the Shallow World of BookTok, Being 'a Reader' Is More Important than Actually Reading," *British GQ*, February 1, 2023, https://www.gq-magazine.co.uk/culture/article/booktok-tiktok-books-community.

113 On identity work in book clubs, see Long, *Book Clubs* and Procter and Benwell, *Reading across Worlds*.

114 This model is also promoted by the UK's The Reader Organisation; see Jane Davis, "Enjoying and Enduring: Groups Reading Aloud for Wellbeing," *The Lancet* 373, no. 9665 (February 28, 2009): 714–15, https://doi.org/10.1016/S0140-6736(09)60426-8.

115 See Jenny Hartley, *Reading Groups* (Oxford: Oxford University Press, 2001), ix.

116 C. Clayton Childress and Noah E. Friedkin, "Cultural Reception and Production: The Social Construction of Meaning in Book Clubs," *American Sociological Review* 77, no. 1 (February 1, 2012), https://doi.org/10.1177/0003122411428153, 65.

117 Stinson and Driscoll, "Difficult Literature on Goodreads."

118 This quote was included in a presentation of qualitative findings from this project at the Australasian Association of Academic Primary Care Conference, August 2018.

119 Wohl, "Community Sense," 299.

120 Hennion, "Pragmatics of Taste," 135.

Chapter 4

1   The word "morality" comes from a Latin root, "ethics" from a Greek. Philosophers and other scholars distinguish between the two (often suggesting that morality relates more to society-wide expectations, and ethics to individual choices); however, in ordinary speech they are frequently used interchangeably.

2   Other books have explicitly addressed feminist concerns; see Rita Felski, *Beyond Feminist Aesthetics: Feminist Literature and Social Change* (Cambridge: Harvard University Press, 1989).

3   Driscoll and Rehberg Sedo, "Faraway, So Close"; Driscoll and Rehberg Sedo, "Transnational Reception."

4   "Amazon Review of The Weather Makers: How Man Is Changing the Climate and What It Means for Life on Earth," accessed February 9, 2023, https://www.amazon.ca/gp/aw/review/0002007517/R3MB81JQLPC7FS?ie=UTF8&ASIN=0871139359.

5   Miranda Jeanne Marie Iossifidis and Lisa Garforth, "Reimagining Climate Futures: Reading Annihilation," *Geoforum*, December 26, 2021, https://doi.org/10.1016/j.geoforum.2021.12.001.

6   Imogen Mathew, "Reviewing Race in the Digital Literary Sphere: A Case Study of Anita Heiss," *Australian Humanities Review* 60 (2016): 65–83. For an analysis of Heiss's literary career, see Fiannuala Morgan, *Aboriginal Writers and Popular Fiction: The Literature of Anita Heiss* (Cambridge: Cambridge University Press, 2021).

7   Pearson, *Women's Reading in Britain*; Lovell, *Consuming Fiction*.

8   Flic Everett, "Fifty Shades of Shame (or Why You Won't Find the Books I Read on My Shelves)," *The Guardian*, March 25, 2016, sec. Opinion, https://www.theguardian.com/commentisfree/2016/mar/25/fifty-shades-shame-books-dan-brown-christian-grey.

9   Driscoll, "Book Blogs as Tastemakers."

10   Wright, *Understanding Cultural Taste*, 2.

11   Fuller and Rehberg Sedo, *Reading beyond the Book*, 19.

12   Lovell, *Consuming Fiction*, 141.

13   Long, *Book Clubs*.

14   Elizabeth McHenry, *Forgotten Readers: Recovering the Lost History of African American Literary Societies* (Durham: Duke University Press, 2002).

15   McHenry, 188.

16   See Jaime Harker, *America the Middlebrow: Women's Novels, Progressivism, and the Middlebrow Authorship between the Wars* (Amherst: University of Massachusetts Press, 2007); Driscoll, *New Literary Middlebrow*: Tom Perrin, *The Aesthetics of Middlebrow Fiction: Popular US Novels, Modernism, and Form, 1945–75* (New York: Palgrave Macmillan, 2015).

17   Wendy Griswold, *Regionalism and the Reading Class* (Chicago: University of Chicago Press, 2008), 38–9.

18   Cited in Griswold, *Regionalism*, 38–9. Harvey J. Graff, *The Legacies of Literacy: Continuities and Contradictions in Western Culture and Society* (Bloomington: Indiana University Press, 1987).

19   Alberto Manguel, *Packing My Library: An Elegy and Ten Digressions* (New Haven: Yale University Press, 2018), 132.

20   Manguel, *Packing My Library*, 140.

21   Günter Leypoldt, "Spatial Reading: Evaluative Frameworks and the Making of Literary Authority," *American Journal of Cultural Sociology* 9, no. 2 (June 1, 2021): 150–76, https://doi.org/10.1057/s41290-020-00107-w.

22   Nicholas Dames, *The Physiology of the Novel: Reading, Neural Science, and the Form of Victorian Fiction* (Oxford and New York: Oxford University Press, 2007), 3.

23   Jason Tougaw, "The Physiology of the Novel: Reading, Neural Science, and the Form of Victorian Fiction, and Telegraphic Realism: Victorian Fiction and Other Information Systems (Review)," *WSQ: Women's Studies Quarterly* 37, no. 1 (June 3, 2009): 279–83, https://doi.org/10.1353/wsq.0.0151.

24 Ross Hunter, "Edinburgh Book Festival Director to Step Down Following 'Toxic' Workplace Allegations," *The National*, February 2, 2023, https://www.thenational. scot/news/23293980.edinburgh-book-festival-director-nick-barley-step/.

25 Beth Driscoll and Claire Squires, "Serious Fun: Gaming the Book Festival," *Mémoires Du Livre / Studies in Book Culture* 9, no. 2 (2018): 1–37.

26 Driscoll and Squires, "Serious Fun."

27 "The Toronto International Festival of Authors Is Reshaping the World through Stories | Shedoesthecity," accessed January 26, 2023, https://www.shedoesthecity. com/the-toronto-international-festival-of-authors-is-reshaping-the-world-through-stories/.

28 Driscoll, *The New Literary Middlebrow.*

29 Fuller and Rehberg Sedo, *Reading beyond the Book,* 19.

30 Millicent Weber, *Literary Festivals and Contemporary Book Culture* (London: Palgrave Macmillan, 2018), 39, citing Danielle Fuller, "Listening to the Readers of 'Canada Reads,'" in *The History of Reading*, ed. Shafquat Towheed, Rosalind Crone, and Katie Halsey (London and New York: Routledge, 2011), 411–26.

31 Kate Iselin, "Sex Workers Are Not Invisible. We're Just Being Ignored," *The Sydney Morning Herald*, July 26, 2016, sec. Lifestyle, https://www.smh.com.au/lifestyle/ sex-workers-are-not-invisible-were-just-being-ignored-20160726-gqe52k.html; Jennine Khalik, "Pulitzer Prize Winner Withdraws from Sydney Writers' Festival over Harassment Allegations," *ABC News*, May 5, 2018, https://www.abc.net. au/news/2018-05-05/junot-diaz-pulled-from-sydney-writers-festival-sexual-misconduct/9731000; Rod Nordland, "Lionel Shriver's Address on Cultural Appropriation Roils a Writers Festival," *The New York Times*, September 12, 2016, sec. Books, https://www.nytimes.com/2016/09/13/books/lionel-shriver-cultural-appropriation-brisbane-writers-festival.html.

32 Fuller and Rehberg Sedo, *Reading beyond the Book,* 244.

33 Fuller and Rehberg Sedo, *Reading beyond the Book,* 211.

34 Long, *Book Clubs.*

35 "Our Shared Shelf," *Goodreads*, accessed April 4, 2023, https://www.goodreads.com/ group/show/179584-our-shared-shelf.

36 "Suzzie's Review of Mercy," March 4, 2018, https://www.goodreads.com/review/ show/2312106766.

37 "Peeta Supremacy #peetamellark #humor #galeslander #darkhumour #fypシ …, " TikTok, accessed February 16, 2023, https://www.tiktok.com/@finnickspromise/ video/7161889195525410054?is_from_webapp=1&sender_device=pc&web_ id=7193160716789368321.

38 Dromi and Illouz, "Recovering Morality," 352.

39 Dromi and Illouz, "Recovering Morality," 353.

40 María Angélica Thumala Olave, "Reading Matters: Towards a Cultural Sociology of Reading," *American Journal of Cultural Sociology* 6, no. 3 (October 1, 2018): 417–54, https://doi.org/10.1057/s41290-017-0034-x, 430.

41 Marilynne Robinson and President Barack Obama, "President Obama & Marilynne Robinson: A Conversation—II," *The New York Review of Books*, November 19, 2015, https://www.nybooks.com/articles/2015/11/19/president-obama-marilynne-robinson-conversation-2/.

42 Veronica Sullivan, "'Speculative Fiction Is a Powerful Political Tool': From War of the Worlds to Terra Nullius," *The Guardian*, August 22, 2017, sec. Books, https://www. theguardian.com/books/australia-books-blog/2017/aug/22/speculative-fiction-is-a-powerful-political-tool-from-war-of-the-worlds-to-terra-nullius.

43   Maya Jaggi, "The Magician," *The Guardian*, December 17, 2005, sec. Stage, http://www.theguardian.com/books/2005/dec/17/booksforchildrenandteenagers.shopping.

44   Todd A. Czubek and Janey Greenwald, "Understanding Harry Potter: Parallels to the Deaf World," *The Journal of Deaf Studies and Deaf Education* 10, no. 4 (October 1, 2005): 442–50, https://doi.org/10.1093/deafed/eni041; Christine Leland et al., "Talking about Books: Exploring Critical Literacy: You Can Hear a Pin Drop," *Language Arts* 77, no. 1 (1999): 70–7; Wendy Morgan, *Critical Literacy in the Classroom: The Art of the Possible* (London: Psychology Press, 1997).

45   Martha Craven Nussbaum, *Poetic Justice: The Literary Imagination and Public Life* (Boston: Beacon Press, 1995).

46   Manguel, *Packing My Library*, 128, 129–30.

47   Azar Nafisi, *The Republic of Imagination: A Life in Books* (New York: Penguin Books, 2015), 196.

48   K. X. Díaz-Galván, F. Ostrosky-Shejet, and C. Romero-Rebollar, "Cognitive and Affective Empathy: The Role in Violent Behavior and Psychopathy," *Revista Médica Del Hospital General De México* 78, no. 1 (January 1, 2015): 27–35, https://doi.org/10.1016/j.hgmx.2015.03.006; Laurie Batchelder, Mark Brosnan, and Chris Ashwin, "The Development and Validation of the Empathy Components Questionnaire (ECQ)," *PLOS ONE* 12, no. 1 (January 11, 2017): e0169185, https://doi.org/10.1371/journal.pone.0169185.

49   Michael Burke et al., "Empathy at the Confluence of Neuroscience and Empirical Literary Studies," *Scientific Study of Literature* 6, no. 1 (December 14, 2016): 6–41, https://doi.org/10.1075/ssol.6.1.03bur; Maja Djikic, Keith Oatley, and Mihnea C. Moldoveanu, "Reading Other Minds: Effects of Literature on Empathy," *Scientific Study of Literature* 3, no. 1 (January 1, 2013): 28–47, https://doi.org/10.1075/ssol.3.1.06dji; Eva Maria (Emy) Koopman and Frank Hakemulder, "Effects of Literature on Empathy and Self-Reflection: A Theoretical-Empirical Framework," *Journal of Literary Theory* 9, no. 1 (2015): 79–111, https://doi.org/10.1515/jlt-2015-0005.

50   See David Dodell-Feder and Diana I. Tamir, "Fiction Reading Has a Small Positive Impact on Social Cognition: A Meta-Analysis," *Journal of Experimental Psychology: General* 147, no. 11 (2018): 1713–27, https://doi.org/10.1037/xge0000395; Anežka Kuzmičová et al., "Literature and Readers' Empathy: A Qualitative Text Manipulation Study," *Language and Literature* 26, no. 2 (May 1, 2017): 137–52, https://doi.org/10.1177/0963947017704729; Maria Eugenia Panero et al., "Does Reading a Single Passage of Literary Fiction Really Improve Theory of Mind? An Attempt at Replication," *Journal of Personality and Social Psychology* 111, no. 5 (2016): e46–54, https://doi.org/10.1037/pspa0000064; Dalya Samur, Mattie Tops, and Sander L. Koole, "Does a Single Session of Reading Literary Fiction Prime Enhanced Mentalising Performance? Four Replication Experiments of Kidd and Castano (2013)," *Cognition and Emotion* 32, no. 1 (January 2, 2018): 130–44, https://doi.org/10.1080/02699931.2017.1279591; Iris van Kuijk et al., "The Effect of Reading a Short Passage of Literary Fiction on Theory of Mind: A Replication of Kidd and Castano (2013)," *Collabra: Psychology* 4, no. 1 (February 27, 2018), https://doi.org/10.1525/collabra.117.

51   Andrew Bennett, *Readers and Reading* (New York: Longman, 1995), 4.

52   Felski, *Hooked*, 79.

53   Felski, *Uses of Literature*, 30–1.

54   Felski, *Uses of Literature*, 91–2.

55 Rita Felski and Susan Fraiman, "Introduction," *New Literary History* 43, no. 3 (2012), v–xii. doi:10.1353/nlh.2012.0029.

56 Suzanne Keen, *Empathy and the Novel* (Oxford: Oxford University Press, 2007).

57 Driscoll, *The New Literary Middlebrow.*

58 Radway, *A Feeling for Books,* 228

59 Radway, *A Feeling for Books,* 284.

60 Paul Bloom, *Against Empathy: The Case for Rational Compassion* (New York, NY: Ecco Press, 2016); Megan Boler, "The Risks of Empathy: Interrogating Multiculturalism's Gaze," *Cultural Studies* 11, no. 2 (May 1, 1997): 253–73, https://doi.org/10.1080/09502389700490141.

61 William Davies, *Nervous States: Democracy and the Decline of Reason* (New York: W. W. Norton & Company, 2019); Bloom, *Against Empathy.*

62 Bloom, *Against Empathy*, cited in Namwali Serpell, "The Banality of Empathy," *The New York Review of Books*, 2019, https://www.nybooks.com/daily/2019/03/02/the-banality-of-empathy/.

63 Sarah Sentilles, *Draw Your Weapons* (New York: Random House, 2017).

64 Timothy Aubry, "Afghanistan Meets the *Amazon*: Reading *The Kite Runner* in America," *PMLA* 124, no. 1 (January 1, 2009): 25–43, https://doi.org/10.1632/pmla.2009.124.1.25.

65 C. Clayton Childress and Noah E. Friedkin, "Cultural Reception and Production: The Social Construction of Meaning in Book Clubs," *American Sociological Review* 77, no. 1 (February 1, 2012): 45–68, https://doi.org/10.1177/0003122411428153.

66 Childress and Friedkin, "Cultural Reception and Production," 46.

67 Susan Sontag, "The Way We Live Now," *The New Yorker*, November 16, 1986, https://www.newyorker.com/magazine/1986/11/24/the-way-we-live-now.

68 Robert Clarke and Marguerite Nolan, "Book Clubs and Reconciliation: A Pilot Study on Book Clubs Reading the 'Fictions of Reconciliation,'" *Australian Humanities Review* 56 (2014): 121–40.

69 Clarke and Nolan, "Book Clubs and Reconciliation."

70 Fuller and Rehberg Sedo, *Reading beyond the Book*, 241

71 Procter and Benwell, *Reading across Worlds*, 178–213.

72 Sandra R. Phillips and Clare Archer-Lean, "Decolonising the Reading of Aboriginal and Torres Strait Islander Writing: Reflection as Transformative Practice," *Higher Education Research & Development* 38, no. 1 (January 2, 2019): 24–37, https://doi.org/10.1080/07294360.2018.1539956.

73 Phillips and Archer-Lean, "Decolonising," 27.

74 Maggie Nolan and Janeese Henaway, "Decolonizing Reading: The Murri Book Club," *Continuum* 31, no. 6 (November 2, 2017): 791–801, https://doi.org/10.1080/10304312.2017.1372365.

75 Having said that, when coloring books for adults emerged as a high selling trend in the publishing industry around 2014, there was much critical commentary about the infantilization of culture; see for example Adrienne Raphel, "Adult Coloring Books and the Rise of the 'Peter Pan' Market," *The New Yorker*, July 12, 2015, https://www.newyorker.com/business/currency/why-adults-are-buying-coloring-books-for-themselves.

76 Alexandra Alter, "How Colleen Hoover Rose to Rule the Best-Seller List," *The New York Times*, October 10, 2022, sec. Books, https://www.nytimes.com/2022/10/09/books/colleen-hoover.html.

77 "Charls on TikTok," TikTok, accessed March 6, 2023, https://www.tiktok.com/@charlsbookshelves/video/7187084391506562309.

78 Kelly Burke, "Colleen Hoover Apologises for 'Tone-Deaf' Colouring Book Based on Domestic Violence Novel," *The Guardian*, January 13, 2023, sec. Books, https://www.theguardian.com/books/2023/jan/13/colleen-hoover-apologises-for-tone-deaf-colouring-book-based-on-domestic-violence-novel; Chloe Cawood and Kelsi Karruli, "Colleen Hoover Slammed over Coloring Book about Domestic Violence," *Daily Mail Online*, January 13, 2023, sec. Femail, https://www.dailymail.co.uk/femail/article-11632163/Colleen-Hoover-plans-release-coloring-book-based-novel-domestic-violence.html.

79 Weber, *Literary Festivals*; Thelwall and Kousha, "Goodreads."

80 See Safiya Umoja Noble, *Algorithms of Oppression: How Search Engines Reinforce Racism* (New York: NYU Press, 2018); Brooke Erin Duffy, *(Not) Getting Paid to Do What You Love: Gender, Social Media, and Aspirational Work* (New Haven: Yale University Press, 2017).

81 See Julian Pinder, "Online Literary Communities: A Case Study of LibraryThing," in *From Codex to Hypertext: Reading at the Turn of the Twenty-First Century*, ed. Anouk Lang (Amherst: University of Massachusetts Press, 2012), 68–87; Adam Worrall, "'Like a Real Friendship': Translation, Coherence, and Convergence of Information Values in Library Thing and Goodreads," 2015, https://www.ideals.illinois.edu/handle/2142/73641.

82 Lila Shapiro, "Can You Revise a Book to Make It More Woke?," *Vulture*, February 18, 2018, http://www.vulture.com/2018/02/keira-drake-the-continent.html.

83 Everdeen Mason, "After a 'Painful' Public Shaming, This Book Was Rewritten," *Washington Post*, March 19, 2018, https://www.washingtonpost.com/graphics/2018/entertainment/books/keira-drake-the-continent-book-comparisons/.

84 Alexandra Alter, "She Pulled Her Debut Book When Critics Found It Racist. Now She Plans to Publish," *The New York Times*, April 29, 2019, sec. Books, https://www.nytimes.com/2019/04/29/books/amelie-wen-zhao-blood-heir.html; Christina Morales, "Scholastic Halts Distribution of Book by 'Captain Underpants' Author," *The New York Times*, March 28, 2021, sec. Books, https://www.nytimes.com/2021/03/28/books/dav-pilkey-ook-gluk-racism.html.

85 Randy Boyagoda, "The 'American Dirt' Controversy Is Painfully Intramural," *The Atlantic*, January 30, 2020, https://www.theatlantic.com/ideas/archive/2020/01/american-dirt-controversy/605725/.

86 Grace Lapointe, "What Happened to the Own Voices Label?" *Book Riot*, April 25, 2022, https://bookriot.com/what-happened-to-the-own-voices-label/.

87 Judith Fetterley, *The Resisting Reader: A Feminist Approach to American Fiction* (Bloomington: Indiana University Press, 1978), xxii.

88 Kathleen Hale, "'Am I Being Catfished?' An Author Confronts Her Number One Online Critic," *The Guardian*, October 18, 2014, sec. Books, http://www.theguardian.com/books/2014/oct/18/am-i-being-catfished-an-author-confronts-her-number-one-online-critic. Kathleen Hale, *Kathleen Hale Is a Crazy Stalker* (New York: Grove Press, 2019).

89 Driscoll, "Readers of Popular Fiction."

90 Driscoll, "Book Blogs as Tastemakers."

91 "Jeann (Happy Indulgence) 's Review of No One Else Can Have You (No One Else Can Have You #1)," October 12, 2013, https://www.goodreads.com/review/show/739677682.

92 Karen Boyle, *#MeToo, Weinstein and Feminism* (Cham: Palgrave Macmillan, 2019).

93 Marsha Lederman, "Margaret Atwood, Susan Swan Release Joint Statement on UBC Accountable," *The Globe and Mail*, March 29, 2018, https://www.theglobeandmail.com/canada/article-margaret-atwood-susan-swan-release-joint-statement-on-ubc-accountable/.

94   Margaret Atwood, "Am I a Bad Feminist?," *The Globe and Mail*, January 13, 2018, https://www.theglobeandmail.com/opinion/am-i-a-bad-feminist/article37591823/.

95   Zoe Whittall, "CanLit Has a Sexual-Harassment Problem," *The Walrus*, February 5, 2018, https://thewalrus.ca/canlit-has-a-sexual-harassment-problem/.

96   Atwood, "Am I a Bad Feminist?"

97   Jason Proctor, "Appeal of Steven Galloway Lawsuit Pits Author's Fight for Reputation against Accuser's Right to Speak Out," *CBC News*, February 13, 2022, https://www.cbc.ca/news/canada/british-columbia/galloway-sexual-assault-defamation-appeal-1.6342820.

98   Alexandra Alter, Jonah Engel Bromwich, and Damien Cave, "The Writer Zinzi Clemmons Accuses Junot Díaz of Forcibly Kissing Her," *The New York Times*, May 4, 2018, sec. Books, https://www.nytimes.com/2018/05/04/books/junot-diaz-accusations.html; Alison Flood, "Two Children's Authors Dropped by Agents amid Claims of Sexual Harassment," *The Guardian*, February 15, 2018, sec. Books, https://www.theguardian.com/books/2018/feb/15/two-childrens-authors-dropped-by-agents-amid-claims-of-sexual-harassment; Sam Levin, "Author Sherman Alexie Apologizes amid Anonymous Allegations," *The Guardian*, March 1, 2018, sec. Books, https://www.theguardian.com/world/2018/mar/01/sherman-alexie-author-apologizes-amid-sexual-misconduct-allegations; Ed Pilkington, "New York Review of Books Editor Ian Buruma Departs amid Outrage over Essay," *The Guardian*, September 19, 2018, sec. US news, https://www.theguardian.com/us-news/2018/sep/19/new-york-review-of-books-editor-ian-buruma-steps-down.

99   J.K. Rowling [@jk_rowling], "Dress However You Please. Call Yourself Whatever You like. Sleep with Any Consenting Adult Who'll Have You. Live Your Best Life in Peace and Security. But Force Women out of Their Jobs for Stating That Sex Is Real? #IStandWithMaya #ThisIsNotADrill," Tweet, *Twitter*, December 19, 2019, https://twitter.com/jk_rowling/status/1207646162813100033; J.K. Rowling [@jk_rowling], "'People Who Menstruate.' I'm Sure There Used to Be a Word for Those People. Someone Help Me out. Wumben? Wimpund? Woomud? Opinion: Creating a More Equal Post-COVID-19 World for People Who Menstruate Https://T.Co/CVpZxG7gaA," Tweet, *Twitter*, June 6, 2020, https://twitter.com/jk_rowling/status/1269382518362509313; J.K. Rowling [@jk_rowling], "If Sex Isn't Real, There's No Same-Sex Attraction. If Sex Isn't Real, the Lived Reality of Women Globally Is Erased. I Know and Love Trans People, but Erasing the Concept of Sex Removes the Ability of Many to Meaningfully Discuss Their Lives. It Isn't Hate to Speak the Truth" Tweet, *Twitter*, June 6, 2020, https://twitter.com/jk_rowling/status/1269389298664701952; J.K. Rowling [@jk_rowling], "Delighted to Announce That after a Surprise Visit to the Real World, Where She Reluctantly Admitted a Hulking Great Rapist Doesn't Become a Woman by Putting on a Wig, Our Illustrious Leader Has Made It Safely Home to You're All Just Bigots Territory. Https://T.Co/Ji12j9HTqE," Tweet, *Twitter*, January 28, 2023, https://twitter.com/jk_rowling/status/1619358295852208129.

100   Annabel Gutterman, "How Chimamanda Ngozi Adichie's Viral Essay Has Implications Far beyond the Literary World," *Time*, July 1, 2021, https://time.com/6076606/chimamanda-adichie-akwaeke-emezi-trans-rights-essay/.

101   Alison Flood, "War of Words Breaks out after YA Novelist's Fans Go after Critical Reader," *The Guardian*, November 15, 2019, sec. Books, https://www.theguardian.com/books/2019/nov/15/ya-novelist-fans-go-after-critical-reader-sarah-dessen-twitter.

102 Lisa Gitelman, "Not," in *Further Reading*, ed. Matthew Rubery and Leah Price (Oxford: Oxford University Press, 2020), 371–80.

103 Bethan Benwell, James Procter, and Gemma Robinson, "Not Reading Brick Lane," *New Formations* 73, no. Winter (November 25, 2011): 90–116, 93–4.

104 Amy Hungerford, *Making Literature Now* (Stanford: Stanford University Press, 2016).

105 Amy Hungerford, "On Not Reading," *The Chronicle of Higher Education*, September 11, 2016, https://www.chronicle.com/article/on-not-reading/.

106 Hungerford, "On Not Reading."

107 Louise Hill, "Affective Exchange: Amy Hungerford's 'Making Literature Now,'" *Los Angeles Review of Books*, accessed May 14, 2020, https://lareviewofbooks.org/article/affective-exchange-amy-hungerfords-making-literature-now/; Tom LeClair, "Making Literature Now—Amy Hungerford," *Full Stop* (blog), accessed November 23, 2020, http://www.full-stop.net/2016/10/20/reviews/tomleclair/making-literature-now-amy-hungerford/.

108 Edmund G. C. King, "Unpacking the 'Red Flag' Bookshelf: Negotiating Literary Value on Twitter," *English Studies* 103, no. 5 (June 15, 2022): 706–31, https://doi.org/10.1080/0013838X.2022.2087037, 710.

109 Benwell, Procter, and Robinson, "Not Reading Brick Lane," 95, 102.

110 Rachel Bowdler, [@RachelBowdler_], "@__tastedcherry Lauren Hough Https://T.Co/2lKG2sYpnp," Tweet, *Twitter*, April 14, 2021, https://twitter.com/RachelBowdler_/status/1382248635690270720.

111 Michelle Goldsmith, "Exploring the Author—Reader Relationship in Contemporary Speculative Fiction: The Influence of Author Persona on Readers in the Era of the Online 'Author Platform,'" *Logos* 27, no. 1 (June 7, 2016): 31–44, https://doi.org/10.1163/1878-4712-11112096.

112 Wilkins, Driscoll, and Fletcher, *Genre Worlds*.

113 Goldsmith, "Exploring the Author—Reader Relationship," 39, 42–3.

114 Rosemary Sorenson, "Twitter's Book Burning Mob Comes for Author John Marsden," *Daily Review: Film, Stage and Music Reviews, Interviews and More*, July 26, 2019, sec. News & Commentary, https://dailyreview.com.au/twitters-book-burning-mob-come-john-marsden/.

Chapter 5

1 For an account of the importance of preserving time for private reading in schools, see Margaret Mackey, "Private Readerly Experiences of Presence: Why They Matter," *Journal of Literacy Research* 54, no. 2 (June 1, 2022): 137–57, https://doi.org/10.1177/1086296X221098068.

2 Paul Saenger, *Space between Words: The Origins of Silent Reading* (Stanford: Stanford University Press, 1997); John Ford, "Speaking of Reading and Reading the Evidence: Allusions to Literacy in the Oral Tradition of the Middle English Verse Romances," in *The History of Reading Volume 1: International Perspectives c. 1500–1990*, ed. Shafquat Towheed and W.R. Owens (Basingstoke: Palgrave Macmillan, 2011), 26.

3 See Stephen Colclough, *Consuming Texts: Readers and Reading Communities, 1695–1870* (Basingstoke: Palgrave Macmillan, 2007).

4 R. W. McCutcheon, "Silent Reading in Antiquity and the Future History of the Book," *Book History* 18, no. 1 (2015): 1–32, https://doi.org/10.1353/bh.2015.0011, 1.

5   McCutcheon, "Silent Reading in Antiquity," 2.
6   Martin, "Tracking Reading," 28.
7   "The Reading Experience Database 1450–1945 (RED)," accessed April 6, 2023, http://www.open.ac.uk/Arts/RED/index.html.
8   Martin, "Tracking Reading," 28.
9   For discussion of sock puppet book reviewing, see Simone Murray, *The Digital Literary Sphere: Reading, Writing, and Selling Books in the Internet Era* (Baltimore: Johns Hopkins University Press, 2018), 133–6.
10 Driscoll and Rehberg Sedo, "Faraway, So Close."
11 Thumala Olave, "Reading Matters," 417, 418.
12 Felski, *Uses of Literature*, 8.
13 Felski, *Uses of Literature*, 67.
14 "Readings on Instagram: '"A Book Is like a Key That Fits into the Tumbler of the Soul. The Two Parts Have to Match in Order for Each to Unlock. Then—Click—a World Opens."—Brad Kessler #bookstagram #shelfie #readersofinstagram #reading #readingsbooks #readingsbookstore,'" Instagram, March 28, 2019, https://www.instagram.com/p/BvinYo8Al5s/.
15 For example, "A Quote by Maria Augusta von Trapp," accessed April 10, 2023, https://www.goodreads.com/quotes/37268-music-acts-like-a-magic-key-to-which-the-most.
16 Hannah Giorgis et al., "What We're Reading: Writers and Readers on the Books They Enjoyed in July," *The Guardian*, July 28, 2022, sec. Books, https://www.theguardian.com/books/2022/jul/28/what-were-reading-writers-and-readers-on-the-books-they-enjoyed-in-july.
17 David Astle, "That Aching Feeling after Finishing a Good Book? There's a Word for That," *The Sydney Morning Herald*, August 10, 2022, sec. Books, https://www.smh.com.au/culture/books/that-aching-feeling-after-finishing-a-good-book-there-s-a-word-for-that-20220808-p5b864.html.
18 Susan Sontag, *Against Interpretation and Other Essays* (London: Penguin, 2013).
19 Felski, *Uses of Literature*, 51.
20 Felski, *Uses of Literature*, 54–5.
21 Lynch, *Loving Literature*, 13.
22 Hermione Lee, *Virginia Woolf* (London: Vintage, 1997), 409.
23 Bougie London Literary Woman [@BougieLitWoman], "A Eureka Moment in Packing for My Weekend Away! I Shall Eschew All Clothing to Make More Room in My Trunk for Books, and Go Nude but for an Overcoat and a Sharp Brogue," Tweet, *Twitter*, December 7, 2018, https://twitter.com/BougieLitWoman/status/1071015133994999808.
24 Bougie London Literary Woman [@BougieLitWoman], "I'll Never Reveal My Most Cloistered Secret … How Many of My Books I've Purchased Purely on the Basis of Their Intoxicating Smell," Tweet, *Twitter*, November 19, 2018, https://twitter.com/BougieLitWoman/status/1064548354661732353.
25 Roland Barthes, *The Pleasure of the Text*, trans. Richard Miller (New York: Hill and Wang, 1975).
26 Barthes, *Pleasure of the Text*, 14.
27 Barthes, *Pleasure of the Text*, 38, 40.
28 Radway, *A Feeling for Books*, 14.
29 Barthes, *Pleasure of the Text*, 39.
30 "Readings on Instagram: '"Think of This—That the Writer Wrote Alone, and the Reader Read Alone, and They Were Alone with Each Other."—A.S. Byatt [ID in

Alt-Text] #readingsbooks #readingscarlton,'" Instagram, May 16, 2022, https://www.instagram.com/p/CdmptB3JdxK/.

31 Ceridwen Dovey, "Can Reading Make You Happier?," *The New Yorker*, June 9, 2015, https://www.newyorker.com/culture/cultural-comment/can-reading-make-you-happier.

32 Alain De Botton, *How Proust Can Change Your Life: Not a Novel* (New York: Pantheon Books, 1997).

33 Maria Popova, "Proust on Why We Read," *The Marginalian* (blog), October 20, 2016, https://www.themarginalian.org/2016/10/20/proust-on-reading/.

34 Felski, *Uses of Literature*, 23.

35 Felski, *Uses of Literature*, 33.

36 Excerpt from the eleventh episode of Carl Sagan's 1980s *Cosmos* series, titled "The Persistence of Memory"; clip available on YouTube https://youtu.be/MVu4duLOF6Y, accessed 9 January 2023.

37 Maria Popova, "A Book Is a Heart That Only Beats in the Chest of Another: Rebecca Solnit on the Solitary Intimacy of Reading and Writing," *The Marginalian* (blog), October 13, 2014, https://www.themarginalian.org/2014/10/13/rebecca-solnit-faraway-nearby-reading-writing/.

38 Popova, "A Book Is a Heart."

39 Audre Lorde, "Uses of the Erotic: The Erotic as Power," in *Sister Outsider* (New York: Ten Speed Press, 2007), 57.

40 Lorde, "Uses of the Erotic," 56–7.

41 Audre Lorde, "Poetry Is Not a Luxury," in *Sister Outsider* (New York: Ten Speed Press, 2007), 36–9, 38.

42 Lorde, "Uses of the Erotic," 58, 59.

43 Lorde, "Uses of the Erotic," 59.

44 Radway, *Reading the Romance*, 150–1.

45 Lauren Berlant, *The Female Complaint: The Unfinished Business of Sentimentality in American Culture* (Durham: Duke University Press, 2008).

46 Fuller and Rehberg Sedo, *Reading beyond the Book*, 213.

47 The quote continues: "One such character was born out of the question: 'What if the essence of the band Belle and Sebastian was incarnated into male human form, and what would it be like if that man was your boyfriend?' The answer is: awful, in short. He would do things like turn up an hour late to dinner with your parents because he was upset about seeing a dead bird, or claim to be learning Catalan. Bougie London Literary Woman, or Clarissa as she was originally called, was this character's best friend, a woman on whom he had an extremely obvious crush that made you, as his girlfriend, uncomfortable." Imogen West-Knights, "Why I Created the Parody Twitter Account Bougie London Literary Woman," *New Statesman*, January 31, 2019, https://www.newstatesman.com/culture/books/2019/01/why-i-created-parody-twitter-account-bougie-london-literary-woman.

48 Blaire Squiscoll, *The Frankfurt Kabuff* (Glasgow and Melbourne: Kabuff Books, 2019), 23; see also Beth Driscoll and Claire Squires, *The Frankfurt Kabuff Critical Edition* (Waterloo: Wilfrid Laurier University Press, 2023).

49 See, for example, Associated Press, "'Nazis out': Violence at Frankfurt Book Fair over Far-Right Presence," *International Business Times UK*, October 15, 2017, sec. Society, https://www.ibtimes.co.uk/nazis-out-violence-frankfurt-book-fair-over-far-right-presence-1643239.

50   "Simone Siew on TikTok," TikTok, accessed April 10, 2023, https://www.tiktok.
      com/@balloonbreath/video/7004941871340391685?_t=8Q2shxXKI7u&_r=1.
      My discussion appears in Beth Driscoll, "The Aesthetic Conduct of Sally
      Rooney's Readers," *Sydney Review of Books*, accessed April 10, 2023, https://
      sydneyreviewofbooks.com/review/rooney-beautiful-world-where-are-you/.

51   "Gala Dragot on TikTok," TikTok, accessed April 11, 2023, https://www.tiktok.
      com/@galadragot/video/7184071772520713477?lang=en; Erica Nardozzi, "Franz
      Kafka Becomes an Unlikely HEARTTHROB on TikTok," *Daily Mail*, February 11,
      2023, https://www.dailymail.co.uk/femail/article-11737477/Franz-Kafka-unlikely-
      HEARTTHROB-TikTok.html.

52   Tina Jordan, "How to Be a Better Reader," *The New York Times*, October 26, 2022,
      sec. Books, https://www.nytimes.com/explain/2022/how-to-be-a-better-reader.

53   Sven Birkerts, *The Gutenberg Elegies: The Fate of Reading in an Electronic Age*, 2nd
      edition (originally published 1994) (New York: Farrar, Straus and Giroux, 2006).

54   Birkerts, 146.

55   Anne Mangen, "The Digitization of Narrative Reading: Theoretical Considerations
      and Narrative Evidence," in *The Unbound Book*, ed. Joost Kircz and Adriaan van der
      Weel (Amsterdam: Amsterdam University Press, 2013), 91–106, 103.

56   Mangen, 101.

57   Philip B. Gough, "The New Literacy: Caveat Emptor," *Journal of Research in Reading*
      18, no. 2 (1995): 79–86, 81.

58   Maryanne Wolf and Mirit Barzillai, "The Importance of Deep Reading," in
      *Challenging the Whole Child: Reflections on Best Practices in Learning, Teaching and
      Leadership*, ed. Marge Scherer (Alexandria, VA: ASCD, 2009), 130–40, 131.

59   Robert P. Waxler and Maureen P. Hall, *Transforming Literacy: Changing Lives through
      Reading and Writing* (Bingley: Emerald Group Publishing Limited, 2011), 30.

60   Waxler and Hall, *Transforming Literacy*, 128.

61   Wolf and Barzillai, "The Importance of Deep Reading," 134.

62   One such strategy is "Gather, Sort, Shrink and Wrap" in Barry Casey, "A Method for
      Deep Reading," *Faculty Focus | Higher Ed Teaching & Learning* (blog), September 15,
      2017, https://www.facultyfocus.com/articles/effective-teaching-strategies/method-
      deep-reading/.

63   Anne Mangen and Adriaan van der Weel, "The Evolution of Reading in the Age of
      Digitisation: An Integrative Framework for Reading Research," *Literacy* 50, no. 3
      (September 1, 2016): 116–24, https://doi.org/10.1111/lit.12086,118.

64   Jessica Tripler, "Reading as a Kind of Meditation," *Book Riot*, June 19, 2014, https://
      bookriot.com/reading-kind-meditation/.

65   Bryan Walpert, *Poetry and Mindfulness: Interruption to a Journey* (Cham: Springer,
      2017), 31–2.

66   Walpert, *Poetry and Mindfulness*, 31–2.

67   See, for example, Jennifer Cornick, "A Novel Idea: Meditative Reading—The Best
      Fiction for Meditation," *Impact Hub Vienna* (blog), July 11, 2018, https://vienna.
      impacthub.net/2018/07/11/a-novel-idea-meditative-reading-the-best-fiction-for-
      meditation/; Sarah Ditum, "Mindful Deep Reading: The Health Benefits of Reading
      Novels," *Calm Moment*, accessed November 2, 2022, https://www.calmmoment.
      com/mindfulness/mindfulness-deep-reading/; Neil Seligman, "Reading as a
      Form of Meditation," *The Conscious Professional*, March 23, 2018, https://www.
      theconsciousprofessional.com/reading-form-meditation/.

68 Mirabai Bush, "Three Simple Mindfulness Practices You Can Use Every Day," *Mindful* (blog), November 21, 2018, https://www.mindful.org/three-simple-mindfulness-practices-you-can-use-every-day/

69 David Gelles, "How to Be Mindful While Reading," *The New York Times*, July 19, 2017, sec. Well, https://www.nytimes.com/2017/07/19/well/mind/how-to-be-mindful-while-reading.html.

70 Josh Guilar, "Reading Fiction as Meditation," *Medium* (blog), August 30, 2018, https://medium.com/@JoshGuilar/reading-fiction-as-meditation-9a6bb42d9f82

71 Simone, "Reading as Meditation," *Simone and Her Books* (blog), July 16, 2019, https://simoneandherbooks.com/2019/07/16/reading-as-meditation/.

72 Bush, "Three Simple Mindfulness Practices."

73 Nina Sankovitch, *Tolstoy and the Purple Chair* (New York: Harper, 2011). For more on reading as therapy, see Timothy Aubry, *Reading as Therapy: What Contemporary Fiction Does for Middle-Class Americans* (Iowa City: University of Iowa Press, 2011).

74 abookolive, *Tolstoy and the Purple Chair by Nina Sankovitch | Book Review*, 2021, https://www.youtube.com/watch?v=FPOb1YP4Eik.

75 See Moniek M. Kuijpers, "Bibliotherapy in the Age of Digitization," *First Monday* 23, no. 10 (September 30, 2018), https://doi.org/10.5210/fm.v23i10.9429; Leah Price, "Prescribed Print: Bibliotherapy after Web 2.0," *Post45*, accessed April 10, 2023, http://post45.org/2019/09/prescribed-print-bibliotherapy-after-web-2-0/.

76 "Books as Therapy," accessed June 26, 2023, http://booksastherapy.com/about.

77 Gelles, "How to Be Mindful."

78 Price, *What We Talk About*.

79 Tripler, "A Kind of Meditation."

80 Michael Holden [@thewrongwriter], "1. I Want to Share Something about Hilary Mantel Which I Hope Is about Her as a Writer but Also Perhaps an Illustration of the Power and Potential of Writing Itself …, " Tweet, *Twitter*, September 25, 2022, https://twitter.com/thewrongwriter/status/1574005683107807241.

81 Price, *What We Talk About*, 19–20.

82 Price, *What We Talk About*, 25, 22.

Conclusion

1 Felski, *Uses of Literature*; Fetterley, *The Resisting Reader*; Fuller and Rehberg Sedo, *Reading beyond the Book*; Long, *Book Clubs*; Rosenblatt, *Literature as Exploration*.

2 Boltanski and Thévenot, "Sociology of Critical Capacity," 359.

3 Sweeney, *Reading Is My Window*.

4 See discussion in Alexandra Dane, *White Literary Taste Production in Contemporary Book Culture* (Cambridge: Cambridge University Press, 2023).

5 "Elizabeth Gilbert on Instagram: 'Important Announcement about THE SNOW FOREST. Please Note That If You Were Charged for Your Pre-Order, You Will Be Fully Refunded. Thank You so Much,'" Instagram, June 12, 2023, https://www.instagram.com/reel/CtY2mMkAM67/.

BIBLIOGRAPHY

"A Quote by Maria Augusta von Trapp." Accessed April 10, 2023. https://www.goodreads.com/quotes/37268-music-acts-like-a-magic-key-to-which-the-most.

abookolive. *Tolstoy and the Purple Chair by Nina Sankovitch | Book Review*, 2021. https://www.youtube.com/watch?v=FPOb1YP4Eik.

"About Goodreads." Accessed February 22, 2023. https://www.goodreads.com/about/us.

AdSpark, Inc. "Why Philippines Remains to Be Wattpad's Key Market," May 9, 2018. https://adspark.ph/phl-remains-wattpads-key-market/.

Albrechtslund, Anne-Mette Bech. "Amazon, Kindle, and Goodreads: Implications for Literary Consumption in the Digital Age." *Consumption Markets & Culture* 23, no. 6 (November 1, 2020): 553–68. https://doi.org/10.1080/10253866.2019.1640216.

Alcántara, Ann-Marie. "Reese Witherspoon's New App Adds to Growing Crowd of Virtual Book Clubs." *Wall Street Journal*, March 1, 2021, sec. C Suite. https://www.wsj.com/articles/reese-witherspoons-new-app-adds-to-growing-crowd-of-virtual-book-clubs-11614642579.

Allen, Graham. *Intertextuality*. Abingdon, New York: Routledge, 2011.

Alley, Kathleen M., Mukoma Wa Ngugi, and Wendy R. Williams. "Amanda Gorman's Poetry Shows Why Spoken Word Belongs in School." *The Conversation*, February 5, 2021. http://theconversation.com/amanda-gormans-poetry-shows-why-spoken-word-belongs-in-school-153838.

Alter, Alexandra. "She Pulled Her Debut Book When Critics Found It Racist. Now She Plans to Publish." *The New York Times*, April 29, 2019, sec. Books. https://www.nytimes.com/2019/04/29/books/amelie-wen-zhao-blood-heir.html.

Alter, Alexandra. "How Colleen Hoover Rose to Rule the Best-Seller List." *The New York Times*, October 10, 2022, sec. Books. https://www.nytimes.com/2022/10/09/books/colleen-hoover.html.

Alter, Alexandra, Jonah Engel Bromwich, and Damien Cave. "The Writer Zinzi Clemmons Accuses Junot Díaz of Forcibly Kissing Her." *The New York Times*, May 4, 2018, sec. Books. https://www.nytimes.com/2018/05/04/books/junot-diaz-accusations.html.

Altick, Richard D. *The English Common Reader: A Social History of the Mass Reading Public, 1800–1900*. Columbus: Ohio State University Press, 1998.

"Amazon Review of The Weather Makers: How Man Is Changing the Climate and What It Means for Life on Earth." Accessed February 9, 2023. https://www.amazon.ca/gp/aw/review/0002007517/R3MB81JQLPC7FS?ie=UTF8&ASIN=0871139359.

Andersen, Christian Ulrik, Geoff Cox, and Giorgios Papadopoulos. "Postdigital Research." *APRJA* 3, no. 1 (2014).

Andersen, Tore Rye, Stefan Kjerkegaard, and Birgitte Stougaard Pedersen. "Introduction: Modes of Reading." *Poetics Today* 42, no. 2 (June 1, 2021): 131–47. https://doi.org/10.1215/03335372-8883164.

Armitstead, Claire. "Packing My Library by Alberto Manguel Review—a Bibliophile's Demons." *The Guardian*, April 14, 2018, sec. Books. https://www.theguardian.com/books/2018/apr/14/packing-my-library-alberto-manguel-review.

Arnold, Matthew. *Culture and Anarchy*. Revised edition. New Haven: Yale University Press, 1994.

Associated Press. "'Nazis Out': Violence at Frankfurt Book Fair over Far-Right Presence." *International Business Times UK*, October 15, 2017, sec. Society. https://www.ibtimes.co.uk/nazis-out-violence-frankfurt-book-fair-over-far-right-presence-1643239.

Astle, David. "That Aching Feeling after Finishing a Good Book? There's a Word for That." *The Sydney Morning Herald*, August 10, 2022, sec. Books. https://www.smh.com.au/culture/books/that-aching-feeling-after-finishing-a-good-book-there-s-a-word-for-that-20220808-p5b864.html.

Atwood, Margaret. "Am I a Bad Feminist?" *The Globe and Mail*, January 13, 2018. https://www.theglobeandmail.com/opinion/am-i-a-bad-feminist/article37591823/.

Aubry, Timothy. "Afghanistan Meets the Amazon: Reading The Kite Runner in America." *PMLA* 124, no. 1 (January 1, 2009): 25–43. https://doi.org/10.1632/pmla.2009.124.1.25.

Aubry, Timothy. *Reading as Therapy: What Contemporary Fiction Does for Middle-Class Americans*. Iowa City: University of Iowa Press, 2011.

Australia Council. "Reading the Reader: A Survey of Australian Reading Habits," May 26, 2017. https://australiacouncil.gov.au/advocacy-and-research/reading-the-reader/.

Australia Reads. "The National Reading Survey 2021." Accessed April 14, 2023. https://australiareads.org.au/research/the-national-reading-survey-2021/.

Barnett, Tully. "'Reading Saved Me': Writing Autobiographically About Transformative Reading Experiences in Childhood." *Prose Studies* 35, no. 1 (2013): 84–96.

Barstow, Jane Missner. *The Pleasure of the Text*. Translated by Richard Miller. New York: Hill and Wang, 1975.

Barstow, Jane Missner. "Reading in Groups: Women's Clubs and College Literature Classes." *Publishing Research Quarterly* 18, no. 4 (December 1, 2003): 3–17. https://doi.org/10.1007/s12109-003-0010-x.

Barthes, Roland. *Image, Music, Text*. Translated by Stephen Heath. London: Fotana, 1977.

Batchelder, Laurie, Mark Brosnan, and Chris Ashwin. "The Development and Validation of the Empathy Components Questionnaire (ECQ)." *PLOS ONE* 12, no. 1 (January 11, 2017): e0169185. https://doi.org/10.1371/journal.pone.0169185.

Benjamin, Walter. *Illuminations*. Edited by Hannah Arendt. Translated by Harry Zohn. Boston: Mariner Books, Houghton Mifflin Harcourt, 2019.

Bennett, Andrew. *Readers and Reading*. New York: Longman, 1995.

Bennett, Tony, David Carter, Modesto Gayo, Michelle Kelly, and Greg Noble. *Fields, Capitals, Habitus: Australian Culture, Inequalities and Social Divisions*. Abingdon; New York: Routledge, 2020.

Bennett, Tony, Michael Emmison, and John Frow. *Accounting for Tastes: Australian Everyday Cultures*. Cambridge: Cambridge University Press, 1999.

Bennett, Tony, Mike Savage, Elizabeth Bortolaia Silva, Alan Warde, Modesto Gayo-Cal, and David Wright. *Culture, Class, Distinction*. London: Routledge, 2008. https://doi.org/10.4324/9780203930571.

Benwell, Bethan, James Procter, and Gemma Robinson. "Not Reading Brick Lane." *New Formations* 73, no. Winter (November 25, 2011): 90–116. https://doi.org/info:doi/10.3898/NEWF.73.06.2011.

Berens, Kathi Inman. "E-Literature's# 1 Hit: Is Instagram Poetry E-Literature?" *Electronic Book Review*, 2019.

Berlant, Lauren. *The Female Complaint: The Unfinished Business of Sentimentality in American Culture*. Durham: Duke University Press, 2008.

Birchbark Books. "Birchbark Books & Native Arts/Minneapolis, Minnesota." Accessed February 1, 2023. https://birchbarkbooks.com/.

Birkerts, Sven. *The Gutenberg Elegies: The Fate of Reading in an Electronic Age*. New York: Farrar, Straus and Giroux, 2006.

Bloom, Paul. *Against Empathy: The Case for Rational Compassion*. New York: Ecco Press, 2016.

Bogel, Anne. *I'd Rather Be Reading: The Delights and Dilemmas of the Reading Life*. Grand Rapids: Baker Books, 2018.

Bold, Melanie Ramdarshan. "The Return of the Social Author Negotiating Authority and Influence on Wattpad." *Convergence: The International Journal of Research into New Media Technologies*, June 16, 2016, 1354856516654459. https://doi.org/10.1177/1354856516654459.

Boler, Megan. "The Risks of Empathy: Interrogating Multiculturalism's Gaze." *Cultural Studies* 11, no. 2 (May 1, 1997): 253–73. https://doi.org/10.1080/09502389700490141.

Boltanski, Luc, and Laurent Thévenot. "The Sociology of Critical Capacity." *European Journal of Social Theory* 2, no. 3 (1999): 359–77. https://doi.org/10.1177/136843199002003010.

"Books as Therapy." Accessed June 26, 2023. http://booksastherapy.com/about.

Botton, Alain De. *How Proust Can Change Your Life: Not a Novel*. New York: Pantheon Books, 1997.

Bougie London Literary Woman [@BougieLitWoman]. "I'll Never Reveal My Most Cloistered Secret … How Many of My Books I've Purchased Purely on the Basis of Their Intoxicating Smell." Tweet. *Twitter*, November 19, 2018. https://twitter.com/BougieLitWoman/status/1064548354661732353.

Bougie London Literary Woman [@BougieLitWoman]. "A Eureka Moment in Packing for My Weekend Away! I Shall Eschew All Clothing to Make More Room in My Trunk for Books, and Go Nude but for an Overcoat and a Sharp Brogue." Tweet. *Twitter*, December 7, 2018. https://twitter.com/BougieLitWoman/status/1071015133994999808.

Bourdieu, Pierre. *Distinction: A Social Critique of the Judgement of Taste*. Translated by Richard Nice. Cambridge, MA: Harvard University Press, 1984.

Bourdieu, Pierre. *The Logic of Practice*. Translated by Richard Nice. Stanford: Stanford University Press, 1990.

Bourdieu, Pierre. *The Rules of Art: Genesis and Structure of the Literary Field*. Translated by Susan Emanuel. Stanford: Stanford University Press, 1996.

Bourdieu, Pierre, and Jean Claude Passeron. *Reproduction in Education, Society and Culture*. Translated by Richard Nice. London and Newbury Park: SAGE Publications, 1990.

Bourrier, Karen, and Mike Thelwall. "The Social Lives of Books: Reading Victorian Literature on Goodreads." *Journal of Cultural Analytics* 5, no. 1 (February 20, 2020). https://doi.org/10.22148/001c.12049.

Boyagoda, Randy. "The 'American Dirt' Controversy Is Painfully Intramural." *The Atlantic*, January 30, 2020. https://www.theatlantic.com/ideas/archive/2020/01/american-dirt-controversy/605725/.

Boyle, Karen. *MeToo, Weinstein and Feminism*. Cham: Palgrave Macmillan, 2019.

Branagh-Miscampbell, Maxine, and Stevie Marsden. "'Eating, Sleeping, Breathing, Reading': The Zoella Book Club and the Young Woman Reader in the 21st Century." *Participations: Journal of Audience and Reception Studies* 16, no. 1 (2019): 64–79.

Braun, Rebecca, and Emily Spiers. "Introduction: Re-Viewing Literary Celebrity." *Celebrity Studies* 7, no. 4 (2016): 449–56.

Burke, Kelly. "Colleen Hoover Apologises for 'Tone-Deaf' Colouring Book Based on Domestic Violence Novel." *The Guardian*, January 13, 2023, sec. Books. https://www.theguardian.com/books/2023/jan/13/colleen-hoover-apologises-for-tone-deaf-colouring-book-based-on-domestic-violence-novel.

Burke, Michael, Anežka Kuzmičová, Anne Mangen, and Theresa Schilhab. "Empathy at the Confluence of Neuroscience and Empirical Literary Studies." *Scientific Study of Literature* 6, no. 1 (December 14, 2016): 6–41. https://doi.org/10.1075/ssol.6.1.03bur.

Bush, Mirabai. "Three Simple Mindfulness Practices You Can Use Every Day." *Mindful* (blog), November 21, 2018. https://www.mindful.org/three-simple-mindfulness-practices-you-can-use-every-day/.

Buzelin, Hélène. "Unexpected Allies." *The Translator* 11, no. 4 (November 1, 2005): 193–218. https://doi.org/10.1080/13556509.2005.10799198.

Cameron, Lauren. "Adapting Jane Eyre for the Celebrity Book Club." *Victorians Institute Journal* 48, no. 1 (December 17, 2021): 65–86. https://doi.org/10.5325/victinstj.48.2021.0065.

Caracciolo, Marco. "Narrative Space and Readers' Responses to Stories: A Phenomenological Account." *Style* 47, no. 4 (2013): 425–44.

Casey, Barry. "A Method for Deep Reading." *Faculty Focus | Higher Ed Teaching & Learning* (blog), September 15, 2017. https://www.facultyfocus.com/articles/effective-teaching-strategies/method-deep-reading/.

Cavallo, Guglielmo, and Roger Chartier, eds. *A History of Reading in the West*. Translated by Lydia Cochrane. Amherst: University of Massachusetts Press, 1999.

Cawood, Chloe, and Kelsi Karruli. "Colleen Hoover Slammed over Coloring Book about Domestic Violence." *Daily Mail Online*, January 13, 2023, sec. Femail. https://www.dailymail.co.uk/femail/article-11632163/Colleen-Hoover-plans-release-coloring-book-based-novel-domestic-violence.html.

Certeau, Michel de. *The Practice of Everyday Life*. Translated by Steven Rendall. Berkeley: University of California Press, 2011.

Chen, Guang, Wei Cheng, Ting-Wen Chang, Xiaoxia Zheng, and Ronghuai Huang. "A Comparison of Reading Comprehension across Paper, Computer Screens, and Tablets: Does Tablet Familiarity Matter?" *Journal of Computers in Education* 1, no. 2 (2014): 213–25.

Childress, Clayton. *Under the Cover: The Creation, Production and Reception of a Novel*. Princeton: Princeton University Press, 2017.

Childress, C. Clayton, and Noah E. Friedkin. "Cultural Reception and Production: The Social Construction of Meaning in Book Clubs." *American Sociological Review* 77, no. 1 (February 1, 2012): 45–68. https://doi.org/10.1177/0003122411428153.

Chrisafis, Angelique. "'Family Is the Place for Madness': Constance Debré on the Book That Has Shocked France." *The Guardian*, January 14, 2023, sec. Books. https://www.theguardian.com/books/2023/jan/14/family-is-the-place-for-madness-constance-debre-on-the-book-that-has-shocked-france.

Civica. "Australian Novels the Most Popular Choices amongst Readers." Accessed March 14, 2023. https://www.civica.com/en-au/news-library/australian-novels-the-most-popular-choices-amongst-readers/.

Clarke, Robert, and Marguerite Nolan. "Book Clubs and Reconciliation: A Pilot Study on Book Clubs Reading the 'Fictions of Reconciliation.'" *Australian Humanities Review* 56 (2014): 121–40.

Clinton, Virginia. "Reading from Paper Compared to Screens: A Systematic Review and Meta-Analysis." *Journal of Research in Reading* 42, no. 2 (2019): 288–325.

Colclough, Stephen. *Consuming Texts: Readers and Reading Communities, 1695–1870.* Basingstoke: Palgrave Macmillan, 2007.

Coleman, Claire G. "The Risks of Question Time: Not So Black and White." *Westerly Magazine*, September 6, 2018. https://westerlymag.com.au/the-risks-of-question-time-not-so-black-and-white/.

Collini, Stefan. *Common Reading: Critics, Historians, Publics.* Oxford: Oxford University Press, 2008.

Collins, Jim. *Bring on the Books for Everybody: How Literary Culture Became Popular Culture.* Durham: Duke University Press, 2010.

Cornick, Jennifer. "A Novel Idea: Meditative Reading—The Best Fiction for Meditation." *Impact Hub Vienna* (blog), July 11, 2018. https://vienna.impacthub.net/2018/07/11/a-novel-idea-meditative-reading-the-best-fiction-for-meditation/.

Crone, Rosalind, Katie Halsey, and Shafquat Towheed, eds. *The History of Reading.* London: Routledge, 2010. http://www.routledge.com/books/details/9780415484213/.

Czubek, Todd A., and Janey Greenwald. "Understanding Harry Potter: Parallels to the Deaf World." *The Journal of Deaf Studies and Deaf Education* 10, no. 4 (October 1, 2005): 442–50. https://doi.org/10.1093/deafed/eni041.

Da, Nan Z. "The Computational Case against Computational Literary Studies." *Critical Inquiry* 45, no. 3 (March 1, 2019): 601–39. https://doi.org/10.1086/702594.

Da, Nan Z. "Other People's Books." *New Literary History* 51, no. 3 (2020): 475–500. https://doi.org/10.1353/nlh.2020.0031.

Dames, Nicholas. *The Physiology of the Novel: Reading, Neural Science, and the Form of Victorian Fiction.* Oxford, New York: Oxford University Press, 2007.

Dane, Alexandra. *White Literary Taste Production in Contemporary Book Culture.* Cambridge: Cambridge University Press, 2023.

Darnton, Robert. "What Is the History of Books?" *Daedalus* 111, no. 3 (1982): 65–83.

Davies, William. *Nervous States: Democracy and the Decline of Reason.* 1st edition. New York: W. W. Norton & Company, 2019.

Davis, Jane. "Enjoying and Enduring: Groups Reading Aloud for Wellbeing." *The Lancet* 373, no. 9665 (February 28, 2009): 714–15. https://doi.org/10.1016/S0140-6736(09)60426-8.

Deng, Jireh. "'These Are My Stomping Grounds': The First Black-Owned Bookstore Opens in Octavia Butler's Home Town." *The Guardian*, March 23, 2023, sec. Books. https://www.theguardian.com/books/2023/mar/23/nikki-high-octavias-bookshelf-pasadena-california.

Devlin-Glass, Frances. "More than a Reader and Less than a Critic: Literary Authority and Women's Book-Discussion Groups." *Women's Studies International Forum* 24, no. 5 (September 1, 2001): 571–85. https://doi.org/10.1016/S0277-5395(01)00192-3.

Díaz-Galván, K. X., F. Ostrosky-Shejet, and C. Romero-Rebollar. "Cognitive and Affective Empathy: The Role in Violent Behavior and Psychopathy." *Revista Médica Del Hospital General De México* 78, no. 1 (January 1, 2015): 27–35. https://doi.org/10.1016/j.hgmx.2015.03.006.

Dietz, Laura. "Auditioning for Permanence: Reputation and Legitimacy of Electronically Distributed Novels." *Logos* 26, no. 4 (March 1, 2015): 22–36. https://doi.org/10.1163/1878-4712-11112088.

Dijck, José van. *The Culture of Connectivity: A Critical History of Social Media.* Oxford: Oxford University Press, 2013.

Ditum, Sarah. "Mindful Deep Reading: The Health Benefits of Reading Novels." *Calm Moment.* Accessed November 2, 2022. https://www.calmmoment.com/mindfulness/mindfulness-deep-reading/.

Djikic, Maja, Keith Oatley, and Mihnea C. Moldoveanu. "Reading Other Minds: Effects of Literature on Empathy." *Scientific Study of Literature* 3, no. 1 (January 1, 2013): 28–47. https://doi.org/10.1075/ssol.3.1.06dji.

Dodell-Feder, David, and Diana I. Tamir. "Fiction Reading Has a Small Positive Impact on Social Cognition: A Meta-Analysis." *Journal of Experimental Psychology: General* 147, no. 11 (2018): 1713–27. https://doi.org/10.1037/xge0000395.

Dovey, Ceridwen. "Can Reading Make You Happier?" *The New Yorker*, June 9, 2015. https://www.newyorker.com/culture/cultural-comment/can-reading-make-you-happier.

Drew, C. G. "How to Fabulously Get Started on Bookstagram." Paper Fury, July 16, 2016. https://paperfury.com/how-to-started-bookstagram/.

Driscoll, Beth. "Using Harry Potter to Teach Literacy: Different Approaches." *Cambridge Journal of Education* 43, no. 2 (2013): 259–71.

Driscoll, Beth. *The New Literary Middlebrow: Tastemakers and Reading in the Twenty-First Century*. Basingstoke: Palgrave Macmillan, 2014.

Driscoll, Beth. "Genre, Author, Text, Reader: Teaching Nora Roberts's Spellbound." *Journal of Popular Romance Studies* 4, no. 2 (October 24, 2014): n.p.

Driscoll, Beth. "Sentiment Analysis and the Literary Festival Audience." *Continuum* 29, no. 6 (November 2, 2015): 861–73. https://doi.org/10.1080/10304312.2015.1040729.

Driscoll, Beth. "Readers of Popular Fiction and Emotion Online." In *New Directions in Popular Fiction*, edited by Ken Gelder, 425–49. London: Palgrave Macmillan, 2016. https://doi.org/10.1057/978-1-137-52346-4_21.

Driscoll, Beth. "Book Blogs as Tastemakers." *Participations: Journal of Audience and Reception Studies* 16, no. 1 (2019): 280–305.

Driscoll, Beth. "The Aesthetic Conduct of Sally Rooney's Readers." *Sydney Review of Books*. May 2, 2022. https://sydneyreviewofbooks.com/review/rooney-beautiful-world-where-are-you/.

Driscoll, Beth, and Claire Squires. "Serious Fun: Gaming the Book Festival." *Mémoires Du Livre/Studies in Book Culture* 9, no. 2 (2018): 1–37.

Driscoll, Beth, and Claire Squires. "Experiments with Book Festival People (Real and Imaginary)." *Memoires Du Livre/Studies in Book Culture* 11, no. 2 (2020).

Driscoll, Beth, and Claire Squires. "The Epistemology of Ullapoolism: Making Mischief from within Contemporary Book Cultures." *Angelaki* 25, no. 5 (2020): 137–55.

Driscoll, Beth, and Claire Squires. *The Frankfurt Book Fair and Bestseller Business*. Cambridge: Cambridge University Press, 2020.

Driscoll, Beth, and Claire Squires. *The Frankfurt Kabuff Critical Edition*. Waterloo: Wilfrid Laurier University Press, 2023.

Driscoll, Beth, and DeNel Rehberg Sedo. "Faraway, So Close: Seeing the Intimacy in Goodreads Reviews." *Qualitative Inquiry* 25, no. 3 (September 26, 2018): 248–59. https://doi.org/10.1177/1077800418801375.

Driscoll, Beth, and DeNel Rehberg Sedo. "The Transnational Reception of Bestselling Books Between Canada and Australia." *Global Media Communications* 16, no. 2 (2020): 243–58.

Dromi, Shai M., and Eva Illouz. "Recovering Morality: Pragmatic Sociology and Literary Studies." *New Literary History* 41, no. 2 (October 31, 2010): 351–69. https://doi.org/10.1353/nlh.2010.0004.

Duffy, Brooke Erin. *(Not) Getting Paid to Do What You Love: Gender, Social Media, and Aspirational Work*. New Haven: Yale University Press, 2017.

Dyer, Geoff. *Out of Sheer Rage: Wrestling with D. H. Lawrence*. New York: Picador, 2009.

Emre, Merve. *Paraliterary: The Making of Bad Readers in Postwar America*. Chicago: University of Chicago Press, 2017.

English, James F. "Everywhere and Nowhere: The Sociology of Literature After 'The Sociology of Literature.'" *New Literary History* 41, no. 2 (2010): v–xxiii. https://doi.org/10.1353/nlh.2010.0005.

Erdrich, Louise. *The Sentence*. New York: Harper, 2021.

Everett, Flic. "Fifty Shades of Shame (or Why You Won't Find the Books I Read on My Shelves)." *The Guardian*, March 25, 2016, sec. Opinion. https://www.theguardian.com/commentisfree/2016/mar/25/fifty-shades-shame-books-dan-brown-christian-grey.

"FairyLoot (@fairyloot) | Instagram." Accessed April 17, 2023. https://www.instagram.com/p/CnuEw-ptA-i/.

"FairyLoot (@fairyloot) | Instagram." Accessed April 17, 2023. https://www.instagram.com/p/CnR_J9BNxSz/.

Farr, Cecilia Konchar. *Reading Oprah: How Oprah's Book Club Changed the Way America Reads*. Albany: SUNY Press, 2005.

Farr, Cecilia Konchar, and Jaime Harker, eds. *The Oprah Affect: Critical Essays on Oprah's Book Club*. Albany: SUNY Press, 2008.

Felsenstein, Frank, and James J. Connolly. *What Middletown Read: Print Culture in an American Small City*. Amherst: University of Massachusetts Press, 2015.

Felski, Rita. *Beyond Feminist Aesthetics: Feminist Literature and Social Change*. Cambridge: Harvard University Press, 1989.

Felski, Rita. *Uses of Literature*. Hoboken: Wiley-Blackwell, 2008.

Felski, Rita. *The Limits of Critique*. Chicago: University of Chicago Press, 2015.

Felski, Rita. "Introduction." *New Literary History* 47, no. 2 (September 20, 2016): 215–29. https://doi.org/10.1353/nlh.2016.0010.

Felski, Rita. *Hooked: Art and Attachment*. Chicago: University of Chicago Press, 2020.

Felski, Rita, and Susan Fraiman. "Introduction: In the Mood." *New Literary History* 43, no. 3 (2012).

Fergus, Jan. *Provincial Readers in Eighteenth-Century England*. Oxford; New York: Oxford University Press, 2007.

Fetterley, Judith. *The Resisting Reader: A Feminist Approach to American Fiction*. Bloomington: Indiana University Press, 1978.

Finn, Ed. "New Literary Cultures: Mapping the Digital Networks of Toni Morrison." In *From Codex to Hypertext: Reading at the Turn of the Twenty-First Century*, edited by Anouk Lang, 177–202. Amherst: University of Massachusetts Press, 2012.

Fish, Stanley E. "Interpreting the 'Variorum.'" *Critical Inquiry* 2, no. 3 (April 1, 1976): 465–85. https://doi.org/10.1086/447852.

Flint, Kate. *The Woman Reader Rehberg Sedo. "'Boring, Frustrating 1837–1914*. Oxford: Clarendon Press, 1993.

Flood, Alison. "Two Children's Authors Dropped by Agents amid Claims of Sexual Harassment." *The Guardian*, February 15, 2018, sec. Books. https://www.theguardian.com/books/2018/feb/15/two-childrens-authors-dropped-by-agents-amid-claims-of-sexual-harassment.

Flood, Alison. "War of Words Breaks out after YA Novelist's Fans Go after Critical Reader." *The Guardian*, November 15, 2019, sec. Books. https://www.theguardian.com/books/2019/nov/15/ya-novelist-fans-go-after-critical-reader-sarah-dessen-twitter.

Flood, Alison. "Book Sales Defy Pandemic to Hit Eight-Year High." The Guardian, January 25, 2021. http://www.theguardian.com/books/2021/jan/25/bookshops-defy-pandemic-to-record-highest-sales-for-eight-years.

Ford, John. "Speaking of Reading and Reading the Evidence: Allusions to Literacy in the Oral Tradition of the Middle English Verse Romances." In *The History of Reading Volume 1: International Perspectives c. 1500–1990*, edited by Shafquat Towheed and W.R. Owens, 15–31. Basingstoke: Palgrave Macmillan, 2011.

Frow, John. *The Practice of Value: Essays on Literature in Cultural Studies*. Crawley: UWA Publishing, 2013.

Fuller, Danielle. "Listening to the Readers of 'Canada Reads'. The History of Reading." In *The History of Reading*, edited by Shafquat Towheed, Rosalind Crone, and Katie Halsey, 411–26. London and New York: Routledge, 2011.

Fuller, Danielle, and DeNel Rehberg Sedo. *Reading beyond the Book: The Social Practices of Contemporary Literary Culture*. New York: Routledge, 2013.

Fuller, Danielle, and DeNel Rehberg Sedo. "'Boring, Frustrating, Impossible': Tracing the Negative Affects of Reading from Interviews to Story Circles." *Participations: Journal of Audience and Reception Studies* 16, no. 1 (2019): 34.

Fuller, Danielle, and DeNel Rehberg Sedo. *Reading Bestsellers*. Cambridge: Cambridge University Press, 2023.

Fuller, Danielle, DeNel Rehberg Sedo, and Claire Squires. "Marionettes and Puppeteers? The Relationship between Book Club Readers and Publishers." In *Reading Communities from Salons to Cyberspace*, edited by DeNel Rehberg Sedo, 181–99. Basingstoke: Palgrave Macmillan, 2011. https://doi.org/10.1057/9780230308848_10.

Gallup Inc. "Americans Reading Fewer Books Than in Past." Gallup.com, January 10, 2022. https://news.gallup.com/poll/388541/americans-reading-fewer-books-past.aspx.

Gelder, Ken. *Popular Fiction: The Logics and Practices of a Literary Field*. London and New York: Routledge, 2004.

Gelder, Ken. "Proximate Reading: Australian Literature in Transnational Reading Frameworks." *Journal of the Association for the Study of Australian Literature*, August 5, 2010. https://openjournals.library.sydney.edu.au/index.php/JASAL/article/view/9615.

Gelles, David. "How to Be Mindful While Reading." *The New York Times*, July 19, 2017, sec. Well. https://www.nytimes.com/2017/07/19/well/mind/how-to-be-mindful-while-reading.html.

Giorgis, Hannah, Adam Roberts, David Edgerton, Guardian readers, and Joshua Chizoma. "What We're Reading: Writers and Readers on the Books They Enjoyed in July." *The Guardian*, July 28, 2022, sec. Books. https://www.theguardian.com/books/2022/jul/28/what-were-reading-writers-and-readers-on-the-books-they-enjoyed-in-july.

Gitelman, Lisa. "Not." In *Further Reading*, edited by Matthew Rubery, and Leah Price, 371–80. Oxford: Oxford University Press, 2020.

"Global Book Publishing. Industry Market Research Reports, Trends, Statistics, Data, Forecasts." Accessed September 20, 2018. https://www.ibisworld.com/industry-trends/global-industry-reports/manufacturing/book-publishing.html.

Goffman, Erving. *The Presentation of Self in Everyday Life*. New York: Anchor Books, 1959.

Goggin, Joyce. "Playbour, Farming and Leisure." *Ephemera: Theory & Politics in Organization* 11, no. 4 (2011).

Goldsmith, Michelle. "Exploring the Author–Reader Relationship in Contemporary Speculative Fiction: The Influence of Author Persona on Readers in the Era of the Online 'Author Platform.'" *Logos* 27, no. 1 (June 7, 2016): 31–44. https://doi.org/10.1163/1878-4712-11112096.

Goodreads. "Our Shared Shelf." Accessed April 4, 2023. https://www.goodreads.com/group/show/179584-our-shared-shelf.

Gough, Philip B. "The New Literacy: Caveat Emptor." *Journal of Research in Reading* 18, no. 2 (1995): 79–86.

Graff, Harvey J. *The Legacies of Literacy: Continuities and Contradictions in Western Culture and Society*. Bloomington: Indiana University Press, 1987.

Griswold, Wendy. "A Methodological Framework for the Sociology of Culture." *Sociological Methodology* 17 (1987): 1–35. https://doi.org/10.2307/271027.

Griswold, Wendy. *Regionalism and the Reading Class*. Chicago: University of Chicago Press, 2008.

Griswold, Wendy, Terry McDonnell, and Nathan Wright. "Reading and the Reading Class in the Twenty-First Century." *Annual Review of Sociology* 31, no. 1 (2005): 127–41. https://doi.org/10.1146/annurev.soc.31.041304.122312.

Gross, Daniel A. "The Surprisingly Big Business of Library E-Books." *The New Yorker*, September 2, 2021. https://www.newyorker.com/news/annals-of-communications/an-app-called-libby-and-the-surprisingly-big-business-of-library-e-books.

Gruzd, Anatoliy, and DeNel Rehberg Sedo. "1b1t: Investigating Reading Practices at the Turn of the Twenty-First Century." *Mémoires Du Livre/Studies in Book Culture* 3, no. 2 (2012). https://www.erudit.org/revue/memoires/2012/v3/n2/1009347ar.html.

Guilar, Josh. "Reading Fiction as Meditation." *Medium* (blog), August 30, 2018. https://medium.com/@JoshGuilar/reading-fiction-as-meditation-9a6bb42d9f82.

Guillory, John. "Bourdieu's Refusal." *Modern Language Quarterly* 58, no. 4 (December 1, 1997): 367–98. https://doi.org/10.1215/00267929-58-4-367.

Guillory, John. "The Ethical Practice of Modernity: The Example of Reading." In *The Turn to Ethics*, edited by Marjorie B. Garber, Beatrice Hanssen, and Rebecca L. Walkowitz, 29–46. New York: Routledge, 2000.

Guillory, John. *Professing Criticism: Essays on the Organization of Literary Study*. Chicago: University of Chicago Press, 2022.

Gutterman, Annabel. "Here Are the 10 Most Borrowed Books of All Time at the New York Public Library." *Time*, January 13, 2020. https://time.com/5763611/new-york-public-library-top-checkouts/.

Gutterman, Annabel. "How Chimamanda Ngozi Adichie's Viral Essay Has Implications Far beyond the Literary World." *Time*, July 1, 2021. https://time.com/6076606/chimamanda-adichie-akwaeke-emezi-trans-rights-essay/.

Hale, Kathleen. "'Am I Being Catfished?' An Author Confronts Her Number One Online Critic." *The Guardian*, October 18, 2014, sec. Books. http://www.theguardian.com/books/2014/oct/18/am-i-being-catfished-an-author-confronts-her-number-one-online-critic.

Hale, Kathleen. *Kathleen Hale Is a Crazy Stalker*. New York: Grove Press, 2019.

Halpert, Madeline. "Viral TikTok Boosts Father's Thriller Book to Bestseller." *BBC News*, February 13, 2023, sec. US & Canada. https://www.bbc.com/news/world-us-canada-64577281.

Hamel, Jean-François. "Émanciper la Lecture. Formes de Vie et Gestes Critiques d'après Marielle Macé et Yves Citton." *Tangence*, no. 107 (2015): 89–107. https://doi.org/10.7202/1033952ar.

Harker, Jaime. *America the Middlebrow: Women's Novels, Progressivism, and the Middlebrow Authorship between the Wars*. Amherst: University of Massachusetts Press, 2007. https://muse.jhu.edu/book/4336.

Harris, Elizabeth A. "How TikTok Became a Best-Seller Machine." *The New York Times*, July 1, 2022, sec. Books. https://www.nytimes.com/2022/07/01/books/tiktok-books-booktok.html.

Hartley, Jenny. *Reading Groups*. Oxford: Oxford University Press, 2001.

Hennion, Antoine. "Pragmatics of Taste." In *The Blackwell Companion to the Sociology of Culture*, edited by Mark D. Jacobs and Nancy Weiss Hanrahan, 131–44. Oxford, UK: Blackwell Publishing Ltd, 2007. https://doi.org/10.1002/9780470996744.ch9.

Heyward, Michael. "Flooding Australia with Imported Books Would Be an Assault on Our Literary Culture." *The Guardian*, May 10, 2016, sec. Books. https://www.theguardian.com/books/2016/may/10/flooding-australia-with-imported-books-would-be-an-assault-on-our-literary-culture.

Highland, Kristen Doyle. *The Spaces of Bookselling: Stores, Streets, and Pages*. Cambridge: Cambridge University Press, 2023.

Hill, Louise. "Affective Exchange: Amy Hungerford's 'Making Literature Now.'" *Los Angeles Review of Books*. December 14, 2016. https://lareviewofbooks.org/article/affective-exchange-amy-hungerfords-making-literature-now/.

Hill, Susan. *Howards End Is on the Landing: A Year of Reading from Home*. London: IPS—Profile Books, 2010.

Hungerford, Amy. *Making Literature Now*. Stanford: Stanford University Press, 2016.

Hungerford, Amy. "On Not Reading." *The Chronicle of Higher Education*, September 11, 2016. https://www.chronicle.com/article/on-not-reading/.

Hunter, Ross. "Edinburgh Book Festival Director to Step Down Following 'Toxic' Workplace Allegations." *The National*, February 2, 2023. https://www.thenational.scot/news/23293980.edinburgh-book-festival-director-nick-barley-step/.

"IBISWorld—Industry Market Research, Reports, and Statistics." Accessed April 14, 2023. https://www.ibisworld.com/default.aspx.

Instagram. "Readings on Instagram: "A Book Is like a Key That Fits into the Tumbler of the Soul. The Two Parts Have to Match in Order for Each to Unlock. Then—Click—a World Opens."—Brad Kessler #bookstagram #shelfie #readersofinstagram #reading #readingsbooks #readingsbookstore,'" March 28, 2019. https://www.instagram.com/p/BvinYo8Al5s/.

Instagram. "Readings on Instagram: "Think of This—That the Writer Wrote Alone, and the Reader Read Alone, and They Were Alone with Each Other."—A.S. Byatt [ID in Alt-Text] #readingsbooks #readingscarlton,'" May 16, 2022. https://www.instagram.com/p/CdmptB3JdxK/.

Instagram. "Elizabeth Gilbert on Instagram: 'Important Announcement about THE SNOW FOREST. Please Note That If You Were Charged for Your Pre-Order, You Will Be Fully Refunded. Thank You so Much.'" June 12, 2023. https://www.instagram.com/reel/CtY2mMkAM67/.

Iossifidis, Miranda Jeanne Marie, and Lisa Garforth. "Reimagining Climate Futures: Reading Annihilation." *Geoforum*, December 26, 2021. https://doi.org/10.1016/j.geoforum.2021.12.001.

Iselin, Kate. "Sex Workers Are Not Invisible. We're Just Being Ignored." *The Sydney Morning Herald*, July 26, 2016, sec. Lifestyle. https://www.smh.com.au/lifestyle/sex-workers-are-not-invisible-were-just-being-ignored-20160726-gqe52k.html.

Iser, Wolfgang. *The Implied Reader: Patterns of Communication in Prose Fiction from Bunyan to Beckett*. Baltimore: Johns Hopkins University Press, 1974.

Jaakkola, Maarit. "From Re-Viewers to Me-Viewers: The# Bookstagram Review Sphere on Instagram and the Uses of the Perceived Platform and Genre Affordances." *Interactions: Studies in Communication & Culture* 10, no. 1–2 (2019): 91–110.

Jabr, Ferris. "The Reading Brain in the Digital Age: The Science of Paper versus Screens." *Scientific American* 11, no. 5 (2013).

Jaggi, Maya. "The Magician." *The Guardian*, December 17, 2005, sec. Stage. http://www.theguardian.com/books/2005/dec/17/booksforchildrenandteenagers.shopping.

Jay, Paul L. *The Humanities "Crisis" and the Future of Literary Studies*. Basingstoke: Palgrave Macmillan, 2014.

"Jeann (Happy Indulgence) 's Review of No One Else Can Have You (No One Else Can Have You #1)," October 12, 2013. https://www.goodreads.com/review/show/739677682.

J.K. Rowling [@jk_rowling]. "Dress However You Please. Call Yourself Whatever You like. Sleep with Any Consenting Adult Who'll Have You. Live Your Best Life in Peace and Security. But Force Women out of Their Jobs for Stating That Sex Is Real? #IStandWithMaya #ThisIsNotADrill." Tweet. *Twitter*, December 19, 2019. https://twitter.com/jk_rowling/status/1207646162813100033.

J.K. Rowling [@jk_rowling]. "If Sex Isn't Real, There's No Same-Sex Attraction. If Sex Isn't Real, the Lived Reality of Women Globally Is Erased. I Know and Love Trans People, but Erasing the Concept of Sex Removes the Ability of Many to Meaningfully Discuss Their Lives. It Isn't Hate to Speak the Truth." Tweet. *Twitter*, June 6, 2020. https://twitter.com/jk_rowling/status/1269389298664701952.

J.K. Rowling [@jk_rowling]. "'People Who Menstruate.' I'm Sure There Used to Be a Word for Those People. Someone Help Me Out. Wumben? Wimpund? Woomud? Opinion: Creating a More Equal Post-COVID-19 World for People Who Menstruate Https://T. Co/CVpZxG7gaA." Tweet. *Twitter*, June 6, 2020. https://twitter.com/jk_rowling/status/1269382518362509313.

J.K. Rowling [@jk_rowling]. "Delighted to Announce That after a Surprise Visit to the Real World, Where She Reluctantly Admitted a Hulking Great Rapist Doesn't Become a Woman by Putting on a Wig, Our Illustrious Leader Has Made It Safely Home to You're All Just Bigots Territory. Https://T.Co/Ji12j9HTqE." Tweet. *Twitter*, January 28, 2023. https://twitter.com/jk_rowling/status/1619358295852208129.

Johanson, Katya, and Robin Freeman. "The Reader as Audience: The Appeal of the Writers' Festival to the Contemporary Audience." *Continuum* 26, no. 2 (April 1, 2012): 303–14. https://doi.org/10.1080/10304312.2011.590575.

Johnson, Alex. *A Book of Book Lists: A Bibliophile's Compendium*. London: British Library Publishing, 2017.

Johnson, Marilyn. "Oprah Winfrey: A Life in Books." *Life*, September 1997.

Jordan, Tina. "How to Be a Better Reader." *The New York Times*, October 26, 2022, sec. Books. https://www.nytimes.com/explain/2022/how-to-be-a-better-reader.

Kant, Immanuel. *Critique of the Power of Judgment*. Edited and translated by Paul Guyer, and translated by Eric Matthews. Cambridge: Cambridge University Press, 2000.

Keen, Suzanne. *Empathy and the Novel*. Oxford: Oxford University Press, 2007.

Khalik, Jennine. "Pulitzer Prize Winner Withdraws from Sydney Writers' Festival over Harassment Allegations." *ABC News*, May 5, 2018. https://www.abc.net.au/news/2018-05-05/junot-diaz-pulled-from-sydney-writers-festival-sexual-misconduct/9731000.

King, Edmund G. C. "Unpacking the 'Red Flag' Bookshelf: Negotiating Literary Value on Twitter." *English Studies* 103, no. 5 (June 15, 2022): 706–31. https://doi.org/10.1080/0013838X.2022.2087037.

Klein, Lauren. "Distant Reading After Moretti." *Arcade* (blog), 2018. https://arcade.stanford.edu/blogs/distant-reading-after-moretti.

Koopman, Eva Maria (Emy), and Frank Hakemulder. "Effects of Literature on Empathy and Self-Reflection: A Theoretical-Empirical Framework." *Journal of Literary Theory* 9, no. 1 (2015): 79–111. https://doi.org/10.1515/jlt-2015-0005.

Kuehn, Kathleen, and Thomas F. Corrigan. "Hope Labor: The Role of Employment Prospects in Online Social Production." *The Political Economy of Communication* 1, no. 1 (May 16, 2013). http://www.polecom.org/index.php/polecom/article/view/9.

Kuijk, Iris van, Peter Verkoeijen, Katinka Dijkstra, and Rolf A. Zwaan. "The Effect of Reading a Short Passage of Literary Fiction on Theory of Mind: A Replication of Kidd and Castano (2013)." *Collabra: Psychology* 4, no. 1 (February 27, 2018). https://doi.org/10.1525/collabra.117.

Kuijpers, Moniek M. "Bibliotherapy in the Age of Digitization." *First Monday* 23, no. 10 (September 30, 2018). https://doi.org/10.5210/fm.v23i10.9429.

Kuipers, Giselinde. "Television and Taste Hierarchy: The Case of Dutch Television Comedy." *Media, Culture & Society* 28, no. 3 (May 1, 2006): 359–78. https://doi.org/10.1177/0163443706062884.

Kuipers, Giselinde, Thomas Franssen, and Sylvia Holla. "Clouded Judgments? Aesthetics, Morality and Everyday Life in Early 21st Century Culture." *European Journal of Cultural Studies* 22, no. 4 (2019): 383–98.

Kuusela, Hanna. "On the Materiality of Contemporary Reading Formations: The Case of Jari Tervo's Layla." *New Formations* 78, no. 78 (July 1, 2013): 65–82. https://doi.org/10.3898/NeWf.78.03.2013.

Kuzmičová, Anežka, Anne Mangen, Hildegunn Støle, and Anne Charlotte Begnum. "Literature and Readers' Empathy: A Qualitative Text Manipulation Study." *Language and Literature* 26, no. 2 (May 1, 2017): 137–52. https://doi.org/10.1177/0963947017704729.

Lahire, Bernard. *The Plural Actor*. Translated by David Fernbach. Newark: Polity, 2011.

Lamond, Julieanne. "Communities of Readers: Australian Reading History and Library Loan Records." In *Republics of Letters: Literary Communities in Australia*, edited by Peter Kirkpatrick and Robert Dixon. Sydney: Sydney University Press, 2012.

Lapointe, Grace. "What Happened to the Own Voices Label?" *Book Riot*, April 25, 2022. https://bookriot.com/what-happened-to-the-own-voices-label/.

Latour, Bruno. *Science in Action: How to Follow Scientists and Engineers through Society*. Cambridge: Harvard University Press, 1987.

Latour, Bruno. "Why Has Critique Run Out of Steam? From Matters of Fact to Matters of Concern." *Critical Inquiry* 30, no. 2 (January 1, 2004): 225–48. https://doi.org/10.1086/421123.

Latour, Bruno. *Reassembling the Social: An Introduction to Actor-Network-Theory*. Clarendon Lectures in Management Studies. Oxford: Oxford University Press, 2005.

Latour, Bruno, and Steve Woolgar. *Laboratory Life: The Social Construction of Scientific Facts*. Beverly Hills: SAGE Publications, 1979.

Laura. "Bookstagram 101: How to Start a Bookstagram (Aka Book Instagram)," February 18, 2022. https://whatshotblog.com/how-to-start-a-bookstagram/.

Leavis, Q. D. *Fiction and the Reading Public*. London: Chatto & Windus, 1932.

LeClair, Tom. "Making Literature Now—Amy Hungerford." *Full Stop* (blog). Accessed November 23, 2020. http://www.full-stop.net/2016/10/20/reviews/tomleclair/making-literature-now-amy-hungerford/.

Lederman, Marsha. "Margaret Atwood, Susan Swan Release Joint Statement on UBC Accountable." *The Globe and Mail*, March 29, 2018. https://www.theglobeandmail.com/canada/article-margaret-atwood-susan-swan-release-joint-statement-on-ubc-accountable/.

Lee, Hermione. *Virginia Woolf*. London: Vintage, 1997.

Lehuu, Isabelle. "Reconstructing Reading Vogues in the Old South: Borrowings from the Charleston Library Society, 1811–1817." In *The History of Reading, Volume 1: International Perspectives, c.1500–1990*, edited by Shafquat Towheed, and W. R. Owens, 64–83. Basingstoke: Palgrave Macmillan, 2011.

Leland, Christine, Jerome Harste, Anne Ociepka, Mitzi Lewison, and Vivian Vasquez. "Talking about Books: Exploring Critical Literacy: You Can Hear a Pin Drop." *Language Arts* 77, no. 1 (1999): 70–7.

Lesser, Wendy. *Why I Read: The Serious Pleasure of Books*. New York: Farrar Straus & Giroux, 2014.

Levin, Sam. "Author Sherman Alexie Apologizes amid Anonymous Allegations." *The Guardian*, March 1, 2018, sec. Books. https://www.theguardian.com/world/2018/mar/01/sherman-alexie-author-apologizes-amid-sexual-misconduct-allegations.

Leypoldt, Günter. "Spatial Reading: Evaluative Frameworks and the Making of Literary Authority." *American Journal of Cultural Sociology* 9, no. 2 (June 1, 2021): 150–76. https://doi.org/10.1057/s41290-020-00107-w.

Lim, Kwanghui. "What Really Went Wrong for Borders and Angus & Robertson." *The Conversation*, March 24, 2011. http://theconversation.com/what-really-went-wrong-for-borders-and-angus-and-robertson-341.

Linkis, Sara Tanderup. "Resonant Listening: Reading Voices and Places in Born-Audio Literary Narratives." *Canadian Review of Comparative Literature/Revue Canadienne de Littérature Comparée* 47, no. 4 (2020): 407–23. https://doi.org/10.1353/crc.2020.0037.

Long, Elizabeth. *Book Clubs: Women and the Uses of Reading in Everyday Life*. Chicago: University of Chicago Press, 2003.

Lorde, Audre. "Poetry Is Not a Luxury." In *Sister Outsider* by Audre Lorde, 36–9. New York: Ten Speed Press, 2007.

Lorde, Audre. "Uses of the Erotic: The Erotic as Power." In *Sister Outsider* by Audre Lorde, 53–9. New York: Ten Speed Press, 2007.

Love, Heather. "Close but Not Deep: Literary Ethics and the Descriptive Turn." *New Literary History* 41, no. 2 (October 31, 2010): 371–91. https://doi.org/10.1353/nlh.2010.0007.

Lovell, Terry. *Consuming Fiction*. London, New York: Verso, 1987.

Lund, Rebecca, and Janne Tienari. "Passion, Care, and Eros in the Gendered Neoliberal University." *Organization* 26, no. 1 (January 1, 2019): 98–121. https://doi.org/10.1177/1350508418805283.

Lynch, Deidre. *Loving Literature: A Cultural History*. Chicago: University of Chicago Press, 2015.

Lyons, Martyn. "The History of Reading from Gutenberg to Gates." *The European Legacy* 4, no. 5 (October 1, 1999): 50–7. https://doi.org/10.1080/10848779908579994.

Macé, Marielle. "Ways of Reading, Modes of Being." Translated by Marlon Jones. *New Literary History* 44, no. 2 (August 8, 2013): 213–29. https://doi.org/10.1353/nlh.2013.0017.

Mackey, Margaret. "Private Readerly Experiences of Presence: Why They Matter." *Journal of Literacy Research* 54, no. 2 (June 1, 2022): 137–57. https://doi.org/10.1177/1086296X221098068.

MacTavish, Kenna. "The Emerging Power of the Bookstagrammer: Reading #bookstagram as a Mediated Site of Twenty-First Century Book Culture." In *Post-Digital Book Cultures*, edited by Alexandra Dane and Millicent Weber, 80–113. Clayton: Monash University Publishing, 2021.

MacTavish, Kenna. "Crisis Book Browsing: Restructuring the Retail Shelf Life of Books." In *Bookshelves in the Age of the COVID-19 Pandemic*, edited by Corinna Norrick-Rühl and Shafquat Towheed, 49–68. Cham: Springer International Publishing, 2022. https://doi.org/10.1007/978-3-031-05292-7_3.

Magner, Brigid, and Emily Potter. "Recognizing the Mallee: Reading Groups and the Making of Literary Knowledge in Regional Australia." *Mémoires Du Livre/Studies in Book Culture* 12, no. 1 (2021). https://doi.org/10.7202/1077807ar.

"Making Sense of 2022—Nielsenbook-UK." Accessed January 16, 2023. https://nielsenbook.co.uk/making-sense-of-2022/.

Mangan, Lucy. *Bookworm: A Memoir of Childhood Reading*. London: Square Peg, 2018.

Mangen, Anne. "The Digitization of Narrative Reading: Theoretical Considerations and Narrative Evidence." In *The Unbound Book*, edited by Joost Kircz and Adriaan van der Weel, 91–106. Amsterdam: Amsterdam University Press, 2013.

Mangen, Anne, and Adriaan van der Weel. "The Evolution of Reading in the Age of Digitisation: An Integrative Framework for Reading Research." *Literacy* 50, no. 3 (September 1, 2016): 116–24. https://doi.org/10.1111/lit.12086.

Manguel, Alberto. "A 30,000-Volume Window on the World." *The New York Times*, May 15, 2008, sec. Home & Garden. https://www.nytimes.com/2008/05/15/garden/15library.html.

Manguel, Alberto. *A Reading Diary*. Toronto: Vintage Canada, 2005.

Manguel, Alberto. *The Library at Night*. New Haven: Yale University Press, 2009.

Manguel, Alberto. *A Reader on Reading*. New Haven: Yale University Press, 2011.

Manguel, Alberto. *A History of Reading*. New York: Penguin, 2014 [1996].

Manguel, Alberto. *Packing My Library: An Elegy and Ten Digressions*. New Haven: Yale University Press, 2018.

Margolin, Sara J., Casey Driscoll, Michael J. Toland, and Jennifer Little Kegler. "E-Readers, Computer Screens, or Paper: Does Reading Comprehension Change across Media Platforms?" *Applied Cognitive Psychology* 27, no. 4 (2013): 512–19.

Martens, Marianne. *Publishers, Readers, and Digital Engagement*. London: Palgrave Macmillan, 2016.

Martin, Susan K. "Tracking Reading in Nineteenth-Century Melbourne Diaries." *Australian Humanities Review*, no. 56 (2014): 27–54.

Mason, Everdeen. "After a 'Painful' Public Shaming, This Book Was Rewritten." *Washington Post*, March 19, 2018. https://www.washingtonpost.com/graphics/2018/entertainment/books/keira-drake-the-continent-book-comparisons/.

Mathew, Imogen. "Reviewing Race in the Digital Literary Sphere: A Case Study of Anita Heiss." *Australian Humanities Review* 60 (2016): 65–83.

McCutcheon, R. W. "Silent Reading in Antiquity and the Future History of the Book." *Book History* 18, no. 1 (2015): 1–32. https://doi.org/10.1353/bh.2015.0011.

McHenry, Elizabeth. *Forgotten Readers: Recovering the Lost History of African American Literary Societies*. Durham: Duke University Press, 2002.

Medhora, Shalailah. "Cheaper Books? What's the Cost?" triple j, December 21, 2016. https://www.abc.net.au/triplej/programs/hack/cheaper-books-but-at-what-price/8139436.

Mendelman, Lisa, and Anna Mukamal. "The Generative Dissensus of Reading the Feminist Novel, 1995–2020: A Computational Analysis of Interpretive Communities." *Journal of Cultural Analytics* 6, no. 3 (2021).

Michael Holden [@thewrongwriter]. "1. I Want to Share Something about Hilary Mantel Which I Hope Is about Her as a Writer but Also Perhaps an Illustration of the Power and Potential of Writing Itself …." Tweet. *Twitter*, September 25, 2022. https://twitter.com/thewrongwriter/status/1574005683107807241.

Miller, Andy. *The Year of Reading Dangerously: How Fifty Great Books (and Two Not-So-Great Ones) Saved My Life*. New York: Harper Perennial, 2014.

Miller, Laura J. "The Best-Seller List as Marketing Tool and Historical Fiction." *Book History* 3 (2000): 286–304.

Miller, Laura J. *Reluctant Capitalists: Bookselling and the Culture of Consumption*. Chicago: University of Chicago Press, 2006.

Miller, Henry. *The Books in My Life*. New York: New Directions, 1952.

Milliot, Jim. "Print Book Sales Rose 8.2% in 2020." *Publishers Weekly*. Accessed May 27, 2021. https://www.publishersweekly.com/pw/by-topic/industry-news/bookselling/article/85256-print-unit-sales-rose-8-2-in-2020.html.

Milliot, Jim. "Print Book Sales Fell 6.5% in 2022." PublishersWeekly.com. Accessed January 16, 2023. https://www.publishersweekly.com/pw/by-topic/industry-news/financial-reporting/article/91245-print-book-sales-fell-6-5-in-2022.html.

Morales, Christina. "Scholastic Halts Distribution of Book by 'Captain Underpants' Author." *The New York Times*, March 28, 2021, sec. Books. https://www.nytimes.com/2021/03/28/books/dav-pilkey-ook-gluk-racism.html.

Moran, Joe. *Star Authors: Literary Celebrity in America*. London: Pluto Press, 2000.

Morgan, Fiannuala. *Aboriginal Writers and Popular Fiction: The Literature of Anita Heiss*. Cambridge: Cambridge University Press, 2021.

Morgan, Wendy. *Critical Literacy in the Classroom: The Art of the Possible*. London: Psychology Press, 1997.

Murray, Simone. *The Digital Literary Sphere: Reading, Writing, and Selling Books in the Internet Era*. Baltimore: Johns Hopkins University Press, 2018.

Murray, Simone. "Reading Online: Updating the State of the Discipline." *Book History* 21, no. 1 (December 4, 2018): 370–96.

Murray, Simone. "Secret Agents: Algorithmic Culture, Goodreads and Datafication of the Contemporary Book World." *European Journal of Cultural Studies*, December 5, 2019, 1367549419886026. https://doi.org/10.1177/1367549419886026.

Murray, Simone. "Dark Academia: Bookishness, Readerly Self-Fashioning and the Digital Afterlife of Donna Tartt's The Secret History." *English Studies* 104, no. 2 (2023): 346–364. https://doi.org/10.1080/0013838X.2023.2170596.

Murray, Simone, and Millicent Weber. "'Live and Local'?: The Significance of Digital Media for Writers' Festivals." *Convergence* 23, no. 1 (February 1, 2017): 61–78. https://doi.org/10.1177/1354856516677531.

Muse, Eben J. *Fantasies of the Bookstore*. Cambridge: Cambridge University Press, 2022. https://doi.org/10.1017/9781108646000.

Nafisi, Azar. *Reading Lolita in Tehran*. New York: Random House, 2003.

Nafisi, Azar. *The Republic of Imagination: A Life in Books*. New York: Penguin Books, 2015.

Nakamura, Lisa. "'Words with Friends': Socially Networked Reading on Goodreads." *PMLA* 128, no. 1 (January 1, 2013): 238–43. https://doi.org/10.1632/pmla.2013.128.1.238.

Nardozzi, Erica. "Franz Kafka Becomes an Unlikely HEARTTHROB on TikTok." *Daily Mail*, February 11, 2023. https://www.dailymail.co.uk/femail/article-11737477/Franz-Kafka-unlikely-HEARTTHROB-TikTok.html.

Neill, Rosemary. "Australian Books Sales Dominated by Big W, Says Meredith Drake." *The Australian*, November 20, 2015. https://www.theaustralian.com.au/arts/review/australian-books-sales-dominated-by-big-w-says-meredith-drake/news-story/89d699ac491737cbb438e70559d3d72e.

Ngai, Sianne. *Our Aesthetic Categories: Zany, Cute, Interesting*. Cambridge: Harvard University Press, 2015.

Nishikawa, Kinohi. "Merely Reading." *PMLA* 130, no. 3 (May 2015): 697–703. https://doi.org/10.1632/pmla.2015.130.3.697.

Nolan, Maggie, and Janeese Henaway. "Decolonizing Reading: The Murri Book Club." *Continuum* 31, no. 6 (November 2, 2017): 791–801. https://doi.org/10.1080/10304312.2017.1372365.

Noorda, Rachel, and Kathi Inman Berens. "Immersive Media and Books 2020: New Insights about Book Pirates, Libraries and Discovery, Millennials, and Cross-Media Engagement: Before and During COVID." *Publishing Research Quarterly* 37, no. 2 (June 1, 2021): 227–40. https://doi.org/10.1007/s12109-021-09810-z.

Nordland, Rod. "Lionel Shriver's Address on Cultural Appropriation Roils a Writers Festival." *The New York Times*, September 12, 2016, sec. Books. https://www.nytimes.com/2016/09/13/books/lionel-shriver-cultural-appropriation-brisbane-writers-festival.html.

Norrick-Rühl, Corinna. *Book Clubs and Book Commerce*. Cambridge: Cambridge University Press, 2020. https://doi.org/10.1017/9781108597258.

Nussbaum, Martha Craven. *Poetic Justice: The Literary Imagination and Public Life*. Boston: Beacon Press, 1995.

Ommundsen, Wenche. "Literary Festivals and Cultural Consumption." *Australian Literary Studies*, January 2009. https://search.informit.org/doi/abs/10.3316/IELAPA.200912218.

Oppenheimer, Mark. "Alberto Manguel and the Library of Babel." *Tablet Magazine*, November 18, 2013. https://www.tabletmag.com/sections/arts-letters/articles/alberto-manguel.

Outka, Elizabeth. "Dead Men, Walking: Actors, Networks, and Actualized Metaphors in Mrs. Dalloway and Raymond." *Novel* 46, no. 2 (June 20, 2013): 253–74. https://doi.org/10.1215/00295132-2088130.

Ozma, Alice. *The Reading Promise: My Father and the Books We Shared.* London: Hodder & Stoughton, 2011.

Panero, Maria Eugenia, Deena Skolnick Weisberg, Jessica Black, Thalia R. Goldstein, Jennifer L. Barnes, Hiram Brownell, and Ellen Winner. "Does Reading a Single Passage of Literary Fiction Really Improve Theory of Mind? An Attempt at Replication." *Journal of Personality and Social Psychology* 111, no. 5 (2016): e46–54. https://doi.org/10.1037/pspa0000064.

Pardey, Hannah. "Middlebrow 2.0: The Digital Affect and the New Nigerian Novel." In *Imperial Middlebrow*, edited by Christoph Eland and Jana Gohrisch, 218–39. Leiden: Brill, 2020. https://doi.org/10.1163/9789004426566_013.

Parnell, Claire. "Mapping the Entertainment Ecosystem of Wattpad: Platforms, Publishing and Adaptation." *Convergence* 27, no. 2 (November 10, 2020): 524–38. https://doi.org/10.1177/1354856520970141.

Partogi, Sebastian. "Book Clubs Provide Intellectual, Emotional Common Ground." *The Jakarta Post*, July 27, 2019. https://www.thejakartapost.com/news/2019/07/27/book-clubs-provide-intellectual-emotional-common-ground.html.

Patchett, Ann. "Ann Patchett on Running a Bookshop in Lockdown: 'We're a Part of Our Community as Never before.'" *The Guardian*, April 10, 2020, sec. Books. https://www.theguardian.com/books/2020/apr/10/ann-patchett-nashville-bookshop-coronavirus-lockdown-publishing.

Pearson, Jacqueline. *Women's Reading in Britain, 1750–1835: A Dangerous Recreation.* Cambridge: Cambridge University Press, 1999.

Peplow, David, Joan Swann, Paola Trimarco, and Sara Whiteley. *The Discourse of Reading Groups: Integrating Cognitive and Sociocultural Perspectives.* London and New York: Routledge, 2015.

Perlow, Seth. "Perspective | What Made Amanda Gorman's Poem so Much Better than Other Inaugural Verse." *Washington Post*, January 23, 2021. https://www.washingtonpost.com/outlook/gorman-performance-vital-poetry/2021/01/22/010c35dc-5c2e-11eb-8bcf-3877871c819d_story.html.

Perrin, Tom. *The Aesthetics of Middlebrow Fiction: Popular US Novels, Modernism, and Form, 1945–75.* New York: Palgrave Macmillan, 2015.

Phillips, Sandra R., and Clare Archer-Lean. "Decolonising the Reading of Aboriginal and Torres Strait Islander Writing: Reflection as Transformative Practice." *Higher Education Research & Development* 38, no. 1 (January 2, 2019): 24–37. https://doi.org/10.1080/07294360.2018.1539956.

Pianzola, Federico, Simone Rebora, and Gerhard Lauer. "Wattpad as a Resource for Literary Studies. Quantitative and Qualitative Examples of the Importance of Digital Social Reading and Readers' Comments in the Margins." *PloS One* 15, no. 1 (2020): e0226708.

Pilkington, Ed. "New York Review of Books Editor Ian Buruma Departs amid Outrage over Essay." *The Guardian*, September 19, 2018, sec. US news. https://www.theguardian.com/us-news/2018/sep/19/new-york-review-of-books-editor-ian-buruma-steps-down.

Pinder, Julian. "Online Literary Communities: A Case Study of LibraryThing." In *From Codex to Hypertext: Reading at the Turn of the Twenty-First Century*, edited by Anouk Lang, 68–87. Amherst: University of Massachusetts Press, 2012.

Poletti, Anna, Judith Seaboyer, Rosanne Kennedy, Tully Barnett, and Kate Douglas. "The Affects of Not Reading: Hating Characters, Being Bored, Feeling Stupid." *Arts and Humanities in Higher Education* 15, no. 2 (2016): 231–47.

Poole, Marilyn. "The Women's Chapter: Women's Reading Groups in Victoria." *Feminist Media Studies* 3, no. 3 (November 1, 2003): 263–81. https://doi.org/10.1080/14680770 32000166513.

Popova, Maria. "A Book Is a Heart That Only Beats in the Chest of Another: Rebecca Solnit on the Solitary Intimacy of Reading and Writing." *The Marginalian* (blog), October 13, 2014. https://www.themarginalian.org/2014/10/13/rebecca-solnit-faraway-nearby-reading-writing/.

Popova, Maria. "Proust on Why We Read." *The Marginalian* (blog), October 20, 2016. https://www.themarginalian.org/2016/10/20/proust-on-reading/.

Powell, Timothy B., William Weems, and Freeman Owle. "Native/American Digital Storytelling: Situating the Cherokee Oral Tradition within American Literary History." *Literature Compass* 4, no. 1 (2007): 1–23.

Pratt, Mary Louise. "Interpretive Strategies/Strategic Interpretations: On Anglo-American Reader Response Criticism." *Boundary 2* 11, no. 1/2 (1982): 201–31. https://doi.org/10.2307/303026.

Pressman, Jessica. *Bookishness: Loving Books in a Digital Age*. New York: Columbia University Press, 2020.

Pressman, Jessica. "The Aesthetic of Bookishness in Twenty-First-Century Literature." *Michigan Quarterly Review* 48, no. 4 (2009). http://hdl.handle.net/2027/spo.act2080.0048.402.

Price, Leah. "Reading: The State of the Discipline." *Book History* 7, no. 1 (October 15, 2004): 303–20. https://doi.org/10.1353/bh.2004.0023.

Price, Leah. *What We Talk About When We Talk about Books: The History and Future of Reading*. New York: Basic Books, 2019.

Price, Leah. "Prescribed Print: Bibliotherapy after Web 2.0." *Post45*. Accessed January 27, 2020. http://post45.org/2019/09/prescribed-print-bibliotherapy-after-web-2-0/.

Procter, James, and Bethan Benwell. *Reading across Worlds: Transnational Book Groups and the Reception of Difference*. Basingstoke: Palgrave Macmillan, 2015.

Proctor, Jason. "Appeal of Steven Galloway Lawsuit Pits Author's Fight for Reputation against Accuser's Right to Speak Out." *CBC News*, February 13, 2022. https://www.cbc.ca/news/canada/british-columbia/galloway-sexual-assault-defamation-appeal-1.6342820.

Prose, Francine. "Elizabeth Gilbert Is Pulling a Novel Set in Russia from Publication. That's Unsettling." *The Guardian*, June 15, 2023, sec. Opinion. https://www.theguardian.com/commentisfree/2023/jun/15/elizabeth-gilbert-the-snow-forest-russia.

Purhonen, Semi, and David Wright. "Methodological Issues in National-Comparative Research on Cultural Tastes: The Case of Cultural Capital in the UK and Finland." *Cultural Sociology* 7, no. 2 (June 1, 2013): 257–73. https://doi.org/10.1177/1749975512473462.

Quayson, Ato. *Calibrations: Reading for the Social*. Public Worlds, v. 12. Minneapolis: University of Minnesota Press, 2003.

Rachel Bowdler, [@RachelBowdler_]. "@__tastedcherry Lauren Hough Https://T.Co/2lKG2sYpnp." Tweet. *Twitter*, April 14, 2021. https://twitter.com/RachelBowdler_/status/1382248635690270720.

Radway, Janice A. *Reading the Romance: Women, Patriarchy, and Popular Literature*. Chapel Hill: University of North Carolina Press, 1982.

Radway, Janice A. *A Feeling for Books: The Book-of-the-Month Club, Literary Taste, and Middle-Class Desire*. Chapel Hill: University of North Carolina Press, 1997.

Rak, Julie. "Genre in the Marketplace: The Scene of Bookselling in Canada." In *From Codex to Hypertext: Reading at the Turn of the Twenty-First Century*, edited by Anouk Lang, 159–74. Amherst: University of Massachusetts Press, 2012.

Raphel, Adrienne. "Adult Coloring Books and the Rise of the 'Peter Pan' Market." *The New Yorker*, July 12, 2015. https://www.newyorker.com/business/currency/why-adults-are-buying-coloring-books-for-themselves.

Ray Murray, Padmini, and Claire Squires. "The Digital Publishing Communications Circuit." *Book 2.0* 3, no. 1 (June 1, 2013): 3–23. https://doi.org/10.1386/btwo.3.1.3_1.

Read-it project. "Read-It Project." Accessed April 14, 2023. https://readit-project.eu.

Rehberg Sedo, DeNel. "Readers in Reading Groups an Online Survey of Face-to-Face and Virtual Book Clubs." *Convergence: The International Journal of Research into New Media Technologies* 9, no. 1 (March 1, 2003): 66–90. https://doi.org/10.1177/135485650300900105.

Rehberg Sedo, DeNel. "'I Used to Read Anything That Caught My Eye, But …': Cultural Authority and Intermediaries in a Virtual Young Adult Book Club." In *Reading Communities from Salons to Cyberspace*, edited by DeNel Rehberg Sedo, 101–22. Basingstoke: Palgrave Macmillan, 2011. https://doi.org/10.1057/9780230308848_6.

Rehberg Sedo, DeNel. "Reading Reception in the Digital Era." *Oxford Research Encyclopedia of Literature*, June 28, 2017. https://doi.org/10.1093/acrefore/9780190201098.013.285.

Richards, I. A. *Practical Criticism: A Study of Literary Judgment*. New York: Routledge, 2017. https://doi.org/10.4324/9781315127194.

Rideout, Samantha, and DeNel Rehberg Sedo. "Novel Ideas: The Promotion of North American Book Club Books and the Creation of Their Readers." In *The Edinburgh History of Reading Vol 3: Common Readers*, edited by Jonathan Rose, 280–98. Edinburgh: Edinburgh University Press, 2020.

Robbins, Bruce. "Fashion Conscious Phenomenon." *American Book Review* 38, no. 5 (2017): 5–6. https://doi.org/10.1353/abr.2017.0078.

Robinson, Marilynne, and President Barack Obama. "President Obama & Marilynne Robinson: A Conversation—II." *The New York Review of Books*, November 19, 2015. https://www.nybooks.com/articles/2015/11/19/president-obama-marilynne-robinson-conversation-2/.

Rodger, Nicola. "From Bookshelf Porn and Shelfies to #bookfacefriday: How Readers Use Pinterest to Promote Their Bookishness." *Participations: Journal of Audience and Reception Studies*, 2019.

Rose, Phyllis. *The Shelf: From LEQ to LES: Adventures in Extreme Reading*. New York: Farrar, Straus and Giroux, 2014.

Rosenblatt, Louise M. *Literature as Exploration*. New York and London: D. Appleton-Century Company, 1938.

Rosenblatt, Louise M. *The Reader, the Text, the Poem: The Transactional Theory of the Literary Work*. Carbondale: Southern Illinois University Press, 1978.

Roser, Max, and Esteban Ortiz-Ospina. "Literacy." *Our World in Data*, August 13, 2016. https://ourworldindata.org/literacy.

Ross, Christine. *The Aesthetics of Disengagement: Contemporary Art and Depression*. Minneapolis: University of Minnesota Press, 2006.

Rothman, Joshua. "The Meaning of 'Culture.'" *The New Yorker*, December 26, 2014. http://www.newyorker.com/books/joshua-rothman/meaning-culture.

Rowberry, Simon. *Four Shades of Gray: The Amazon Kindle Platform*. Cambridge: MIT Press, 2022.

Rubery, Matthew. *Reader's Block: A History of Reading Differences*. Stanford: Stanford University Press, 2022.

Rutherford, Leonie, Andrew Singleton, Leonee Ariel Derr, and Margaret Kristin Merga. "Do Digital Devices Enhance Teenagers' Recreational Reading Engagement? Issues for Library Policy from a Recent Study in Two Australian States." *Public Library Quarterly* 37, no. 3 (July 3, 2018): 318–40. https://doi.org/10.1080/01616846.2018.15 11214.

Saenger, Paul. *Space Between Words: The Origins of Silent Reading*. Stanford: Stanford University Press, 1997.

Saha, Anamik, and Sandra Van Lente. *Rethinking Diversity in Publishing*. London: Goldsmiths Press, 2020. https://research.gold.ac.uk/id/eprint/28692/1/Rethinking_ diversity_in_publishing_full_booklet_v2.pdf.

Samur, Dalya, Mattie Tops, and Sander L. Koole. "Does a Single Session of Reading Literary Fiction Prime Enhanced Mentalising Performance? Four Replication Experiments of Kidd and Castano (2013)." *Cognition and Emotion* 32, no. 1 (January 2, 2018): 130–44. https://doi.org/10.1080/02699931.2017.1279591.

Sankovitch, Nina. *Tolstoy and the Purple Chair: My Year of Magical Reading*. New York: Harper, 2011.

Scutts, Joanna. "Read Me Like a Book: 7 Must-Read Memoirs for Book Lovers." *Signature Reads* (blog), January 13, 2014. http://www.signature-reads.com/2014/01/read-me-like-a-book-7-must-read-memoirs-for-book-lovers/.

Seligman, Neil. "Reading as a Form of Meditation." *The Conscious Professional*, March 23, 2018. https://www.theconsciousprofessional.com/reading-form-meditation/.

Sentilles, Sarah. *Draw Your Weapons*. New York: Random House, 2017.

Serpell, Namwali. "The Banality of Empathy." *The New York Review of Books*, 2019. https://www.nybooks.com/daily/2019/03/02/the-banality-of-empathy/.

Shapiro, Lila. "Can You Revise a Book to Make It More Woke?" *Vulture*, February 18, 2018. http://www.vulture.com/2018/02/keira-drake-the-continent.html.

Sheldon, Pavica, and Katherine Bryant. "Instagram: Motives for Its Use and Relationship to Narcissism and Contextual Age." *Computers in Human Behavior* 58 (May 1, 2016): 89–97. https://doi.org/10.1016/j.chb.2015.12.059.

Sicherman, Barbara. *Well-Read Lives: How Books Inspired a Generation of American Women*. Chapel Hill: University of North Carolina Press, 2010.

Silverman, Gillian. "Neurodiversity and the Revision of Book History." *PMLA* 131, no. 2 (March 2016): 307–23. https://doi.org/10.1632/pmla.2016.131.2.307.

Simone. "Reading as Meditation." *Simone and Her Books* (blog), July 16, 2019. https://simoneandherbooks.com/2019/07/16/reading-as-meditation/.

Skains, R. Lyle. "The Shifting Author—Reader Dynamic Online Novel Communities as a Bridge from Print to Digital Literature." *Convergence: The International Journal of Research into New Media Technologies* 16, no. 1 (February 1, 2010): 95–111. https://doi.org/10.1177/1354856509347713.

Škopljanac, Lovro. "What American Readers Remember: A Case Study." *American Studies in Scandinavia* 55, no. 1 (May 10, 2023): 44–69. https://doi.org/10.22439/asca.v55i1.6857.

Smith, Brent, and Greg Linden. "Two Decades of Recommender Systems at Amazon. Com." *IEEE Internet Computing*, June 2017. https://doi.org/10.1109/MIC.2017.72.

Smith, Dorothy E. *The Everyday World as Problematic: A Feminist Sociology*. Toronto: University of Toronto Press, 1987.

Sontag, Susan. "The Way We Live Now." *The New Yorker*, November 16, 1986. https://www.newyorker.com/magazine/1986/11/24/the-way-we-live-now.

Sontag, Susan. *Against Interpretation and Other Essays*. London: Penguin, 2013.

Sorenson, Rosemary. "Twitter's Book Burning Mob Comes for Author John Marsden." *Daily Review: Film, Stage and Music Reviews, Interviews and More*, July 26, 2019, sec. News & Commentary. https://dailyreview.com.au/twitters-book-burning-mob-come-john-marsden/.

Squires, Claire. *Marketing Literature: The Making of Contemporary Literature in Britain*. Basingstoke: Palgrave Macmillan, 2007.

Squiscoll, Blaire. *The Frankfurt Kabuff*. Glasgow and Melbourne: Kabuff Books, 2019.

Statista. "Biggest Social Media Platforms 2022." Accessed January 23, 2023. https://www.statista.com/statistics/272014/global-social-networks-ranked-by-number-of-users/.

Statista. "Instagram: Age Distribution of Global Audiences 2022." Accessed January 23, 2023. https://www.statista.com/statistics/325587/instagram-global-age-group/.

Steiner, Ann. "Private Criticism in the Public Space: Personal Writing on Literature in Readers' Reviews on Amazon." *Participations: Journal of Audience & Reception Studies* 5, no. 2 (November 2008). http://www.participations.org/Volume%205/Issue%20 2/5_02_steiner.htm.

Stinson, Emmett, and Beth Driscoll. "Difficult Literature on Goodreads: Reading Alexis Wright's The Swan Book." *Textual Practice* 36, no. 1 (2022): 94–115. https://doi.org/10.1080/0950236X.2020.1786718.

Strauss, Anselm, and Juliet M. Corbin. *Grounded Theory in Practice*. Thousand Oaks: SAGE Publications, 1997.

Striphas, Ted. *The Late Age of Print: Everyday Book Culture from Consumerism to Control*. New York: Columbia University Press, 2009.

Subrahmanyam, Kaveri, Minas Michikyan, Christine Clemmons, Rogelio Carrillo, Yalda T. Uhls, and Patricia M. Greenfield. "Learning from Paper, Learning from Screens: Impact of Screen Reading and Multitasking Conditions on Reading and Writing among College Students." *International Journal of Cyber Behavior, Psychology and Learning (IJCBPL)* 3, no. 4 (2013): 1–27.

Suleiman, Susan Rubin. "Introduction: Varieties of Author-Oriented Criticism." In *The Reader in the Text: Essays on Audience and Interpretation*, edited by Susan Rubin Suleiman and Inge Crosman, 3–45. Princeton: Princeton University Press, 1980.

Sullivan, Jane. *Storytime*. Paddington: Ventura Press, 2019.

Sullivan, Veronica. "'Speculative Fiction Is a Powerful Political Tool': From War of the Worlds to Terra Nullius." *The Guardian*, August 22, 2017, sec. Books. https://www.theguardian.com/books/australia-books-blog/2017/aug/22/speculative-fiction-is-a-powerful-political-tool-from-war-of-the-worlds-to-terra-nullius.

Susen, Simon. "Towards a Dialogue between Pierre Bourdieu's 'Critical Sociology' and Luc Boltanski's 'Pragmatic Sociology of Critique.'" In *The Spirit of Luc Boltanski: Essays on the "Pragmatic Sociology of Critique,"* 313–48. London: Anthem Press, 2014.

"Suzzie's Review of Mercy," March 4, 2018. https://www.goodreads.com/review/show/2312106766.

Sweeney, Megan. *Reading Is My Window: Books and the Art of Reading in Women's Prisons*. Chapel Hill: University of North Carolina Press, 2010.

Taksa, Lucy, and Martyn Lyons. *Australian Readers Remember: An Oral History of Reading, 1890–1930*. Melbourne: Oxford University Press, 1992. https://researchers.mq.edu.au/en/publications/australian-readers-remember-an-oral-history-of-reading-1890-1930.

The Economist. "Sales of Romance Novels Are Rising in Britain," March 6, 2023. https://www.economist.com/britain/2023/03/06/sales-of-romance-novels-are-rising-in-britai n?gclid=CjwKCAjwiOCgBhAgEiwAjv5whFoAaHThW1yfJvB4xKUS4vQRfEr8Ra0Lfz ZlTjtQW60gQEVyeigTuBoC_YcQAvD_BwE&gclsrc=aw.ds.

The New York Times. "What's the Best Book of the Past 125 Years? We Asked Readers to Decide." *The New York Times*, December 29, 2021, sec. Books. https://www.nytimes.com/interactive/2021/12/28/books/best-book-winners.html.

"The Reading Experience Database 1450–1945 (RED)." Accessed April 6, 2023. http://www.open.ac.uk/Arts/RED/index.html.

"The Toronto International Festival of Authors Is Reshaping the World through Stories | Shedoesthecity." Accessed January 26, 2023. https://www.shedoesthecity.com/the-toronto-international-festival-of-authors-is-reshaping-the-world-through-stories/.

Thelwall, Mike, and Kayvan Kousha. "Goodreads: A Social Network Site for Book Readers." *Journal of the Association for Information Science and Technology* 68, no. 4 (2016): 972–83.

Thomas, Bronwen. *Literature and Social Media*. Abingdon, New York: Routledge, 2020. https://doi.org/10.4324/9781315207025.

Thomas, Bronwen. "The #bookstagram: Distributed Reading in the Social Media Age." *Language Sciences*, 84 (March 1, 2021): 101358. https://doi.org/10.1016/j.langsci.2021.101358.

Thumala Olave, María Angélica. "Reading Matters: Towards a Cultural Sociology of Reading." *American Journal of Cultural Sociology* 6, no. 3 (October 1, 2018): 417–54. https://doi.org/10.1057/s41290-017-0034-x.

TikTok. "Peeta Supremacy #peetamellark #humor #galeslander #darkhumour #fyp シ … " Accessed February 16, 2023. https://www.tiktok.com/@finnickspromise/video/7161889195525410054?is_from_webapp=1&sender_device=pc&web_id=7193160716789368321.

TikTok. "Charl on TikTok." Accessed March 6, 2023. https://www.tiktok.com/@charlsbookshelves/video/7187084391506562309.

TikTok. "Austea E. Kette on TikTok." Accessed March 29, 2023. https://www.tiktok.com/@austea.kette/video/7203024353066323205.

TikTok. "Simone Siew on TikTok." Accessed April 10, 2023. https://www.tiktok.com/@balloonbreath/video/7004941871340391685?_t=8Q2shxXKI7u&_r=1.

TikTok. "Gala Dragot on TikTok." Accessed April 11, 2023. https://www.tiktok.com/@galadragot/video/7184071772520713477?lang=en.

TikTok. "#booktok." Accessed June 13, 2023. https://www.tiktok.com/tag/booktok?lang=en.

Tougaw, Jason. "The Physiology of the Novel: Reading, Neural Science, and the Form of Victorian Fiction, and Telegraphic Realism: Victorian Fiction and Other Information Systems (Review)." *WSQ: Women's Studies Quarterly* 37, no. 1 (June 3, 2009): 279–83. https://doi.org/10.1353/wsq.0.0151.

Towheed, Shafquat, and W. R. Owens. *The History of Reading: International Perspectives, c. 1500–1990*. Basingstoke: Palgrave Macmillan, 2011.

Trant, Jennifer. "Studying Social Tagging and Folksonomy: A Review and Framework." *Journal of Digital Information* 10, no. 1 (January 6, 2009). https://jodi-ojs-tdl.tdl.org/jodi/article/view/269.

Tripler, Jessica. "Reading as a Kind of Meditation." *Book Riot*, June 19, 2014. https://bookriot.com/reading-kind-meditation/.

Trower, Shelley. "Forgetting Fiction: An Oral History of Reading: (Centred on Interviews in South London, 2014–15)." *Book History* 23, no. 1 (2020): 269–98. https://doi.org/10.1353/bh.2020.0007.

Twomey, Sarah. "Reading 'Woman': Book Club Pedagogies and the Literary Imagination." *Journal of Adolescent & Adult Literacy* 50, no. 5 (2007): 398–407. https://doi.org/10.1598/JAAL.50.5.6.

Vandermeersche, Geert, and Ronald Soetaert. "Perspectives on Literary Reading and Book Culture." *CLCWEB-Comparative Literature and Culture* 15, no. 3 (2013). http://hdl.handle.net/1854/LU-4132405.

Verboord, Marc. "Market Logic and Cultural Consecration in French, German and American Bestseller Lists, 1970–2007." *Poetics* 39, no. 4 (August 1, 2011): 290–315. https://doi.org/10.1016/j.poetic.2011.05.002. verklaertenacht1899. *Carl Sagan "What an Astonishing Thing a Book Is,"* 2020. https://www.youtube.com/watch?v=MVu4duLOF6Y.

Vlieghe, Joachim, Jaël Muls, and Kris Rutten. "Everybody Reads: Reader Engagement with Literature in Social Media Environments." *Poetics* 54 (February 2016): 25–37. https://doi.org/10.1016/j.poetic.2015.09.001.

Walpert, Bryan. *Poetry and Mindfulness: Interruption to a Journey*. Cham: Springer, 2017.

Walsh, Melanie, and Maria Antoniak. "The Goodreads 'Classics': A Computational Study of Readers, Amazon, and Crowdsourced Amateur Criticism." *Journal of Cultural Analytics* 6, no. 2 (April 20, 2021). https://doi.org/10.22148/001c.22221.

Warner, Michael. "Uncritical Reading." In *Polemic: Critical or Uncritical*, edited by Jane Gallop, 13–38. New York: Routledge, 2004.

Wattpad. "Press and Announcements | Wattpad HQ." Accessed September 20, 2021. https://company.wattpad.com/press.

Waxler, Robert P., and Maureen P. Hall. *Transforming Literacy: Changing Lives through Reading and Writing*. Bingley: Emerald Group Publishing Limited, 2011.

Weber, Millicent. *Literary Festivals and Contemporary Book Culture*. London: Palgrave Macmillan, 2018.

Weber, Millicent. "'Reading' the Public Domain: Narrating and Listening to Librivox Audiobooks." *Book History* 24, no. 1 (2021): 209–43.

West-Knights, Imogen. "Why I Created the Parody Twitter Account Bougie London Literary Woman." *New Statesman*, January 31, 2019. https://www.newstatesman.com/culture/books/2019/01/why-i-created-parody-twitter-account-bougie-london-literary-woman.

Wevers, Lydia. *Reading on the Farm: Victorian Fiction and the Colonial World*. Wellington: Victoria University Press, 2010.

Whittall, Zoe. "CanLit Has a Sexual-Harassment Problem." *The Walrus*, February 5, 2018. https://thewalrus.ca/canlit-has-a-sexual-harassment-problem/.

Widdowson, Peter. *Literature*. London, New York: Routledge, 1999.

Wilkins, Kim, Beth Driscoll, and Lisa Fletcher. *Genre Worlds: Popular Fiction and Twenty-First Century Book Culture*. Amherst: University of Massachusetts Press, 2022.

Williams, Raymond. *Keywords: A Vocabulary of Culture and Society*. Oxford: Oxford University Press, 2014 [1976].

Willis, Ika. *Reception*. Abingdon and New York: Routledge, 2017.

Wirlomin Noongar Language and Stories. "About Us." Accessed January 16, 2023. https://www.wirlomin.com.au/about-us/.

Wohl, Hannah. "Community Sense: The Cohesive Power of Aesthetic Judgment." *Sociological Theory* 33, no. 4 (2015): 299–326. https://doi.org/10.1177/0735275115617800.

Wolf, Maryanne, and Mirit Barzillai. "The Importance of Deep Reading." In *Challenging the Whole Child: Reflections on Best Practices in Learning, Teaching and Leadership*, edited by Marge Scherer, 130–40. Alexandria, VA: ASCD, 2009.

Wood, Charlotte. "Reading Isn't Shopping." *Sydney Review of Books*, August 14, 2018. https://sydneyreviewofbooks.com/reading-isnt-shopping/.

World Economic Forum. "This Is How Much Global Literacy Has Changed over 200 Years." Accessed January 16, 2023. https://www.weforum.org/agenda/2022/09/reading-writing-global-literacy-rate-changed/.

Worrall, Adam. "'Like a Real Friendship': Translation, Coherence, and Convergence of Information Values in LibraryThing and Goodreads," 2015. https://www.ideals.illinois.edu/handle/2142/73641.

Wright, David. "Commodifying Respectability: Distinctions at Work in the Bookshop." *Journal of Consumer Culture* 5, no. 3 (November 1, 2005): 295–314. https://doi.org/10.1177/1469540505056792.

Wright, David. *Understanding Cultural Taste: Sensation, Skill and Sensibility*. New York: Palgrave Macmillan, 2015.

Zhou, Naaman. "Canberra's Libraries Join Nationwide Trend of Scrapping Fines for Late Books." *The Guardian*, November 1, 2019, sec. Australia news. http://www.theguardian.com/australia-news/2019/nov/01/canberras-libraries-join-nationwide-trend-of-scrapping-fines-for-late-books.

INDEX

Pew Research Centre study (2014) 5
The Philippines 1–2
Picoult, Jodi
   Mercy 96–7
   My Sister's Keeper 89
Pierce, Barry 80
Pilkey, Dav, *The Adventures of Ook and Gluk: Kung-Fu Cavemen from the Future* 106
Pinterest 53, 76–7
play labor/playbour 6
Popova, Maria
   "Proust on Why We Read" 122
   Brain Pickings (now *The Marginalian*) 122
popular fiction 15, 72, 91, 99
post-critical approach 14, 18–19, 28–9, 31
post-digital culture 3, 11, 25, 27, 35, 38, 63, 134, 136–7, 139
power relations 30–1, 36, 44, 46–7, 49–50, 65, 82, 105, 109, 113
Practical Criticism movement 15–16. *See also* New Criticism movement
practical reading exercises 131–2
pragmatism 58
   pragmatic sociology 9, 24–6, 29–30, 101, 138
   pragmatic thinking about aesthetics 58
Pressman, Jessica, bookishness 38, 63
principled identity 112
print books 2–5, 11, 24, 35, 38, 40–1, 86, 116, 134
printing press, development in Europe 116
private readers/reading 11, 115–20, 122, 127–8, 131, 133, 135–7
   contemporary 116, 118
   eroticization of 119–21
   Gough on 128–9
   mediated intimacy of reading 122–4
   principal modes of 118
Procter, James 33, 110–11
   Reading Across Worlds 102
professional reading/readers 6, 15, 17–18, 20, 36, 72, 111. *See also* non-professional readers
Project Gutenburg 53
protectionism 37
Proust, Marcel 122

Raddish online platform 53
Radway, Janice 9, 18, 121, 125

A Feeling for Books 22
   on personalism 100
   Reading the Romance 22
   variable literacies 5
Rak, Julie 38, 40
   on bookstores 37
reader-discussants 36, 46–8, 52–4, 56, 139
reader-response criticism 15–16, 20, 58
reader's criticism 109–10
Reading and Writing for Wellbeing group 47, 57, 82, 85, 101, 134, 139
reading class 3–4, 6
Reading Experience Database 117
Reading for Reconciliation bookclub 103
reading group 33, 55, 81–3. *See also* book clubs
   expressing aesthetic judgments 84–6
   participant feedback 85
Readings bookstore 37, 119, 122
recreational reading/readers 4, 6, 9, 11, 14–15, 17–18, 20–1, 23, 32, 43, 111, 132, 135, 139, 141–2
   adult 43
   contemporary 6–9, 13–14, 26, 28–9, 107, 135, 137–9, 141
red flag bookshelf 111
Reese's Book Club 2
Rehberg Sedo, DeNel 7, 30, 32–3, 42, 48, 55, 78, 90–1, 94–5, 102, 117, 125, 138, 145 n.1
   Reading Beyond the Book 22
   reading industry 2, 31
   on Whiteness 3
relatability 17, 102
resonant reading 31
Richards, I. A. 16
Richmond library 81–2
Robinson, Gemma 110–11
romance genre 1, 3, 18, 35, 37, 59–61, 63, 87, 91, 105, 115, 119, 121, 137
Rooney, Sally, *Beautiful World, Where Are You* 126–7
Rose, Phyllis, *The Shelf: From LEQ to LES* 65
Rosenblatt, Louise 9, 16, 58
   aesthetic reading 59, 138
Rothman, Joshua 8
Rowling, J. K., criticism of 109. *See also* Galbraith, Robert
Rubery, Matthew, *Reader's Block: A History of Reading Difference* 3
Rushdie, Salman, *The Satanic Verses* 111

United Nations Convention on the Rights of the Child 92
United Nations Declaration of Human Rights 92
The United States 2, 14–15, 32, 35, 42, 55, 92
urban fiction 5, 32

van der Weel, Adriaan, "The Evolution of Reading in the Age of Digitisation" 130
Vandermeer, Jeff, *Annihilation* 90
von Trapp, Maria Augusta, *Sound of Music* 119

Wallace, Foster, *Infinite Jest* 111
Walmart 37, 39
Waterstones bookstore 37–8
Watson, Emma 95
Wattpad 2, 53–4
    Stars program (2019) 2
Web 2.0 23, 106
Weber, Millicent 94
Weiner, Jennifer, *All Fall Down* 131
#WeNeedDiverseBooks campaign 105
West-Knights, Imogen 125–6
Wheeler Centre for Books, Writing and Ideas 2
White, T. H. 64
Whiteness (White readers/authors) 3, 5, 11, 49–50, 82, 94, 100, 104, 106–107
Whittall, Zoe 108

wiggle room 24–5
Wilkins, Kim 63
Winfrey, Oprah 32, 45
Witherspoon, Reese 2, 48, 96
Wohl, Hannah 62, 85
Wolf, Maryanne 129–30, 136
    The Story and Science of the Reading Brain 129
    Reader, Come Home: The Reading Brain in a Digital World 129
women's reading 9, 91–2, 125, 138
Wood, Charlotte 17–18
Woodward, Ian 61
Woolf, Virginia 120–2, 136
    Dovey on 122
    Mrs Dalloway 26
word frequency analysis 106
Wright, Alexis, *The Swan Book* 26
Wright, David 38, 63, 91
    Understanding Cultural Taste 61
Wright, Nathan 4–5
writers festival 17, 49, 51, 71, 93–5, 104–6, 114, 140

You've Got Mail (film) 37, 39
young adult fiction 44, 54, 60, 73, 77, 87, 89, 105–7
YouTube 36, 48, 53, 73, 78, 80, 105, 133
    BookTube/BookTuber 80

Zhao, Amelia Wen, *Blood Heir* 106
Zoella (YouTuber) 48